ALSO BY CYNTHIA CROSSEN

Tainted Truth:
The Manipulation of Fact in America

The
Rich
and
How They Got
That Way

The
Rich
and
How They Got
That Way

How the Wealthiest
People of All Time—
from Genghis Khan
to Bill Gates—
Made Their Fortunes

Cynthia Crossen

CROWN
BUSINESS
NEW YORK

Copyright © 2000 by Dow Jones and Company, Inc.

Published by Crown Publishers, New York, New York.
Member of the Crown Publishing Group.

Random House, Inc. New York, Toronto, London, Sydney, Auckland
www.randomhouse.com

CROWN is a trademark and the Crown colophon is a registered trademark
of Random House, Inc.

Printed in the United States of America on acid-free paper

Design by Leon Bolognese & Associates, Inc.

Library of Congress Cataloging-in-Publication Data

Crossen, Cynthia.
    The rich and how they got that way : how the wealthiest people of all time—
from Genghis Khan to Bill Gates—made their fortunes / Cynthia Crossen.
        p.   cm.
    Includes bibliographical references and index.
    ISBN 0-8129-3267-6
    1. Millionaires—United States—Biography.   2. Wealth—United States—
      Biography.   3. Capitalists and financiers—United States—Biography.
    I. Title.

HG172.A2 C76 2000
332'.092'2—dc21
[B]   99-085978

ISBN 0-8129-3267-6

10 9 8 7 6 5 4 3 2 1

First Edition

For Harry,
with everlasting love

ACKNOWLEDGMENTS

Many people helped inspire, encourage, and advise me in writing this book, and the following acknowledgments only begin to express my gratitude. First, Stephen Adler and Lawrence Ingrassia, editors at *The Wall Street Journal,* produced a superb report on the second millennium that included a list of the fifty wealthiest people of the past one thousand years. That roster, compiled by an incomparable reporter, Rachel Silverman, told the larger story of how and why people were able to get rich through the ages. Rachel became the researcher for this project, and Steve its counselor. Both were enthusiastic, faithful collaborators.

At *The Wall Street Journal,* I was supported in large and small ways by Paul Steiger, Daniel Hertzberg, and Jim Pensiero.

The steady intelligence of my editor at Times Books, John Mahaney, helped me shape the voluminous raw material of world history into interlocking narratives. His assistants, Luke Mitchell and Jonathan Slonim, good-humoredly kept the train running more or less on time.

With this work, as with all my other creative endeavors, my husband, James Gleick, remains my truest friend.

CONTENTS

INTRODUCTION
The Wealthy, Then and Now

You've heard about the extraordinary wealth of Bill Gates, J. P. Morgan, and the sultan of Brunei, but have you ever heard of Mansa Musa, one of the richest men who ever lived?

Mansa Musa was an African king who died more than 650 years ago, but he shared more than you might imagine with Gates, Morgan, and the sultan. All four built ostentatiously fabulous homes for themselves; all employed legions of fawning retainers; and all enjoyed a knack for using wealth to create more wealth.

There are differences, of course: Mansa Musa executed anyone who sneezed in his presence, whereas the intensely cerebral Bill Gates merely accuses bunglers of saying the stupidest thing he's ever heard. Mansa Musa rode camels; Morgan had his private railroad car; the sultan of Brunei drives Rolls-Royces; Bill Gates likes Porsches. But in one important way, the four are more alike than different: They became rich on a scale attained by few in history.

Let's call them millionaires and billionaires, although before currency was used widely such words were meaningless. Only in the past few centuries has a million units of local currency become the threshold of exceptional wealth, and before the late twentieth century, millionaires were as rare as barons. Yet wealth—along with its opposite, poverty—has long been part of the human tapestry. Throughout history, some people have used strength, imagination, and luck to amass greater surpluses than their contemporaries. No one secret explains their success—each wealthy person's blueprint is unique.

If there were a league of millionaires dating back to 1000, most of its early members would be royalty or men who excelled at combat. Machmud of Ghazni, the first of the ten wealthy people profiled here, was both. He lived at a time when most of the world was still poor, its inhabitants toiling ceaselessly just to stay warm and nourished. Wealth was largely a zero-sum game in Machmud's era—the turn of the last millennium—and a man with an army became rich by appropriating other people's possessions. It was dangerous and unreliable work, costly in human lives, but it was one of only a few possible paths to great fortune.

Beginning in about 1000, the circle of wealth began to widen, first gradually and then with increasing velocity. As agricultural societies began producing surpluses and the world's population slowly grew, it became possible for conquerors such as Genghis Khan in the twelfth century to move beyond simple robbery and begin taxing a conquered people—in other words, securing a steady stream of wealth rather than relying upon the irregular acquisition of booty. With their broad and absolute power, Genghis Khan and some other early despots actually made the world safer for wealth creation by imposing order on embryonic transportation and communication systems. With the steady expansion of trade, people could become wealthy as shippers, bankers, inventors, and investors, as well as pirates, swindlers, and drug dealers.

Archaeologists of the future may someday call the second millennium the Money Age. The social changes wrought by the steady creation of wealth have transformed the world so profoundly that humans on either end of the second millennium could almost be considered two different species. A thousand years ago, luxury meant having a coat long enough to cover one's knees and more than one drinking cup to a family. Today it means a $10,000 watch box in which to store a $250,000

watch. A thousand years ago, the average peasant scrimped and scraped to pay the burial expenses when he or she died, probably at an early age. By the end of the same millennium, a person could buy a one-dollar lottery ticket, randomly choose six numbers, and become a multimillionaire.

A simple and enduring truth about wealth is that money begets money. There are occasional exceptions—one was Andrew Carnegie, who washed up on America's shore with nothing but pockets full of gumption yet became one of the wealthiest men in America. But the vast majority of millionaires, from Mansa Musa to Bill Gates, got a head start from their parents or grandparents, even if it was just a good plot of land or some sturdy weapons.

Mansa Musa, for example, inherited a small African kingdom through which one of the world's great trade routes passed. Neither producer nor inventor, Mansa Musa was an early broker, greasing the wheels of intercultural trade. He created wealth by making it possible for others to buy and sell. For him, political or religious considerations were secondary to the business of business.

Many children of fortune have dispersed their money rather than increased it. Cosimo de Medici's son Piero frittered away a big hunk of his Italian dynasty's riches while earning the sobriquet "il Gottoso" ("the gouty one"). The famously weird American millionaire Doris Duke, heiress to $300 million of tobacco profits, once gave a coming-out party for two pet camels. Tommy Manville, who was bankrolled by the Johns-Manville corporate fortune, married thirteen times and was nicknamed by a newsmagazine "the patron saint of chorus girls."

But in the fourteenth century, Pope Alexander VI, the Borgia-born Renaissance cleric, adroitly used his dynastic privilege to reach the highest plane of earthly wealth and success. Like most of the very rich, Alexander had both a distinctive gift and a receptive society in which to exploit it. In Alexander's case, he had the ability to rule the spiritual world and manipulate the political world while reveling in sensual luxury. His society was one of the most corrupt in world history.

Regardless of how they assembled their fortunes, the millionaires of the second millennium were men and women who harnessed great determination to their pursuit of wealth. Early millionaires prospered by maiming or killing their enemies, so they may seem to have nothing to teach the modern wizards of spreadsheets. But successful warriors, like prosperous capitalists, were able to do what's now called "thinking outside the box." The fact that something had never been done before was a goad, not a halter to these people. Each of them understood that accumulating great wealth entailed capturing a fraction of the property or production of other people: The plunderer stole; the monarch taxed; the bureaucrat intercepted the flow of taxes to and from the state; the landlord rented the land that others farmed; the merchant took a profit when buying and selling goods. The fact that there are so many ways to become wealthy doesn't mean it's easy.

It is easier today, however, than it was one thousand years ago. Machmud of Ghazni suffered seventy-two battle wounds during his career as a plunderer. The man who became Pope Alexander VI was passed over five times for the papacy before the miter finally lay on his head. But the self-made wealthy have always been distinguished by their resolve. Self-centered and often inept in personal relationships, they are driven by a beast that never seems content, no matter how much they acquire. Although there appears to be no definitive biological imperative to amass wealth, this "purposeless drive" may be one of the most powerful known to humans.

If the wealthy of the past thousand years share one bit of knowledge, it's that money buys possessions far more valuable than big houses and old wine. Rich people know money also helps satisfy their appetites for power, status, or love—the surplus value of wealth. Take tipping, for example. Besides assuring that a known big tipper will get good service, the tip also establishes social status and control over the recipient: The tipper presents him- or herself as the dominant one who expects to be pleased. In general, the wealthy person gets more reliable service from merchants, is treated more deferentially, and is granted all kinds of small privileges the poor don't even realize exist. "A rich man has an influence not only by what he does but also by what he could do. The pure potentiality of money . . . is distilled in a general conception of power and significance."

The force field of the rich has been isolated in experiments, such as one in which college students were asked to describe the personality of a hypothetical man based on some facts they were told about him. The students were given identical information except for one difference: Half were told he was rich, the other half that he was poor. The students assumed the rich man was healthy, happy, and well-adjusted while describing the poor man as unhappy and maladjusted. As a Jewish proverb put it, "With money in your pocket, you are wise, and you are handsome, and you sing well, too."

This kind of smug authority was personified by the fifteenth-century German banker Jacob Fugger. Fugger, grandson of a weaver, became so rich that he could buy himself seats at the banquet tables of popes and monarchs. The devoutly Catholic Fugger created wealth by lending it for interest—usury, as the practice was then called. But so great was the hunger for his money that Fugger became richer than the grandees who borrowed from him. An early capitalist, Fugger found his attempts to buy power generally successful, although even he couldn't crash the gates of Europe's landed aristocracy.

Where there is wealth, there is almost certainly poverty, too. If there ever was a time before rich and poor, it was when humans spent all their time looking for food and shelter. As soon as they stopped foraging, settled down on plots of land, and started raising crops, some people accumulated more and better seeds, tools, and land than others. Archaeologists have found evidence of economic classes as early as 4000 B.C.E., the age when copper was discovered. Some tombs from that time held gold artifacts, demonstrating that society already had classes. In the graves of wealthy people who lived around 2800 B.C.E., archaeologists found bodies of servants, buried alive with their masters so they could accompany them to the next world. Great wealth could be found in early Egypt, where pharaohs competed over the size of their pyramids. Recalling ancient Rome, Horace noted "the smoke and wealth and din."

The march of wealth in Europe ended abruptly around the fifth century C.E. as the debauched Roman Empire fell—due, some have said, to the Romans' idolization of money. Hordes of anarchist barbarians rode into Europe, throwing the continent into the so-called Dark Ages. While China and its eastern neighbors were thriving, European society became virtually moneyless for several centuries. Bread was so scarce that the Anglo-Saxon term *hlaford* ("keeper of loaves") came to mean "master" or "lord." Affluent people scratched out lives almost as harsh and tedious as those of the poor; the leading "consumer durable" during the Middle Ages was armor. Except for those of royal birth, luxury meant a full stomach. Furthermore, wealth could be a two-edged sword: Rich people were able to buy more medical care than the poor, but that might mean a "curative" potion of white wine and horse dung.

After centuries of misery, wealth started creeping back into the Western world around the beginning of the second millennium. Europe's steadily increasing population started to overflow the continent's feudal estates, while trade was expanding the world's horizons. With too many people sharing the land, some wanderers packed up their meager belongings and went looking for other ways to make livings. Towns and trading sprang up together across Europe, and the gates of international trade opened wider as ships and security improved. Coin by coin, shekel by ducat, florin by *weisspfennig,* wealth began flowing not only to kings, feudal lords, and conquerors but also to people with ideas, passions, or knacks. The river of wealth branched into streams and gullies. As social relationships changed from ones between superiors and inferiors to ones involving payers and payees, the new distribution of cash also changed the allocation of power, and new classes were created.

Connections between wealth, power, and status may have been rearranged in the second millennium, but they certainly weren't obliterated. Political leaders still try to charm the wealthy, and the wealthy still expect legislators to pay special heed to their opinions. It doesn't take a princess to buy a $600 handbag today, but the ability to do so still confers a certain distinguishing status. A thousand years ago, when many of the world's 250 million people were living on the precipice of starvation, a rich person was a rarity whose situation inspired wonder. Money wasn't a guarantee of good taste any more than it is today, but it was a useful gauge of political power and social standing. The earliest wealthy were nearly always heads of state—no coincidence when force was the primary mechanism for getting rich—and most of their positions were hereditary. For the very poorest slaves, there was no way up or out; they were lucky if they didn't die of starvation.

By the end of the second millennium, you could be an obscure, not terribly bright grandson of a man who owned a chain of shoe stores in Texas and be as rich as Croesus. You might be the chief executive officer of a company on the verge of bankruptcy. You might be an athlete who never finished high school or a rock star who enjoys wrecking hotel rooms. You might have appeared on *Who Wants to Be a Millionaire?* and answered a few trivia questions. You might have won a frivolous lawsuit or pocketed some money intended for the school or church where you were treasurer. You could be anybody! There are, after all, some 4.1 million millionaires in America alone now. No wonder the people sitting in the first-class sections of jets look much like the people sitting in McDonald's. For better or worse, wealth is nearly losing its value as an index of anything but the ability to spend. Although democratic, this takes some of the fun out of the status game: "When everybody is somebody, nobody is anybody."

Many of the late twentieth century's millionaires are youthful beneficiaries of the protracted boom in America's financial markets. They made their fortunes sitting in front of computer screens, tapping in orders to buy and sell exotic financial instruments issued by companies whose products they have never seen, let alone made or used. Money is less tangible now, a social ethicist noted in 1999. "It used to be property or gold. Now it's a blip on your computer screen. It appears and disappears. It becomes more a way to keep score, more a game in its own right, the way athletes compete with each other to make the most millions, when each additional million can't possibly matter to the way they live."

Yet as the story of John Law, the pied piper of paper money, suggests, the idea of funny money is almost as old as money itself. Law, who took over France's treasury after Louis XIV's death, understood that money is an abstraction, an agreement among people, a social contract not requiring any physical foundation. He was right, although his theories led the French national bank to disaster and disgrace. Law unleashed a system that no one knew how to control. Now his idea that there doesn't have to be a nugget of gold set aside for every dollar in existence is almost universally accepted.

The fantasy of being rich, for those who aren't, usually involves spending money. Today, more than ever, wealth is synonymous with consumption, partly because there is so much more to buy. The early wealthy had few material goods to choose from—a ribbon, a little statue, a box of pepper. The modern wealthy can buy a house with its own movie theater, wine cellar, and bowling alley; they can buy a Boxster, a weekend in Paris via the Concorde, personal assistants, and cashmere socks. Money is a third party at every engagement between human beings. "In mobilizing wishes, money sets people and matter in motion," wrote James Buchan. "It is one of those human creations that make concrete a sensation, in this case the sensation of wanting, as a clock does the sensation of passing time." Marshall McLuhan called money "a vast social metaphor."

A thousand years ago, being rich involved very little money per se. A person's wealth was calculated in land, slaves, chunks of gold, and jewels—the wealthy commanded respect and obedience through the ostentatious display of their things. Today, wealth is almost always expressed in terms of currency, whether dollars, pounds, marks, or yen. Money is more efficient for satisfying wishes and needs, noted the German philosopher Arthur Schopenhauer. Food is good only for the hungry, wine for the healthy, medicine for the sick, fur for use in the winter. "Money alone is the absolute good, for it confronts not just one concrete need but need itself."

Unquestionably, wealth makes daily life easier, removing a source of stress that weighs heavily on most people. Money gives people freedom and security; it might confer feelings of self-esteem or act as an aphrodisiac. Money controls access to precious possessions—only the wealthy can afford $2,300 pillows or $160,000 Porsches—and in the case of fine art collections, it deprives others of access to those pleasures. For some people, money gratifies their need to assess their value in relation to others. "Money never meant anything to us," the Texas oil millionaire Nelson Bunker Hunt once said. "It was just sort of how we kept the score."

Naturally, the objects of ostentation have changed over the millennium, from well-equipped armies and palaces hung with immense tapestries of hunt scenes to bodyguards, electronic security systems, and abstract oils. Personal assistants do their masters' labor. Rarely is anyone buried covered head to foot with precious jewelry. Yet the bar stools on Aristotle Onassis's yacht were upholstered with the soft foreskins of sperm-whale penises. The lingerie purveyor Victoria's Secret offered a Diamond Dream Bra priced at $3 million. And Ira Rennert, reputed to have a fortune of $500 million from his business conglomerate, built a palace in the Long Island Hamptons that would have given Machmud of Ghazni a pang of jealousy. The house was designed with more than fifty thousand square feet of space, thirty bathrooms, a twenty-car garage, and two bowling alleys.

In some historical periods, it has been wiser to conceal than to flaunt one's wealth. In the late 1980s and early 1990s, wealth became such a target of a backlash that some of the wealthy were cowed into practicing "stealth wealth"—eating at rough-hewn tables in their country kitchens, wearing Swatches instead of Rolexes, and driving Jeep Cherokees instead of BMWs. But as the overall level of prosperity continued to rise and corporate America did more hiring than firing, wealth came back in style in time for the turn of the millennium—indeed, one Manhattan resident tried to rent his apartment for the millennial weekend for $10,000.

Perhaps most appealing, though potentially most frightening, about wealth is that the rich have so many choices—the choice not to work, for example, which distinguishes them from all but the youngest and oldest members of society. Some rich people—the "idle rich"—don't work, and boredom has historically been an occupational hazard of the wealthy. "Leisure, like money, is a form of power, which people covet without necessarily having any clear idea of what use they wish to make of it."

Other wealthy men and women work long, arduous hours simply because that's what they most enjoy doing. Richard Arkwright, one of the forefathers of Britain's Industrial Revolution, continued to put in fifteen-hour days at his textile factories even after becoming one of the wealthiest people in the world. He wanted to push the boundaries of the possible, and that re-

quired his undivided attention. Arkwright enjoyed the trappings of wealth but not the indolence; money was part of the game, and whoever died with the most won.

Whether they have jobs or not, the wealthy don't immediately correlate money with time spent at labor. Their labor is voluntary, their ability to spend almost unlimited. Wealthy people "do not understand the more or less painful weighing of alternatives which constitutes daily business for the rest of us," wrote Roger Starr, a former housing administrator for New York City. It "permeates our view of the seriousness of life, since we know that choices are not usually refundable."

Wealth can also animate idiosyncrasies better left unfulfilled. "To be truly rich is to possess the means of realizing in big ways one's little whims and fantasies and sicknesses," wrote the historian C. Wright Mills. For a time, the eccentric millionnaire Howard Hughes would consume only milk, Hershey bars, pecans, and bottled water, which an aide delivered each day in a brown paper bag and presented in a formal ritual. "Money is the measuring rod of power," said Hughes, who once made a typist type the same letter for him two hundred times. Those without much money are forced by the high cost of eccentricity to give it up.

If money can buy just about anything, then consumption is limited only by the imagination of the rich. A nineteenth-century Indian maharaja expected his farts and belches to be met by applause, and when he yawned everyone around him snapped their fingers to discourage flies from landing in his mouth. Displeasing a third-century Roman emperor would result in him presenting you with a dead dog. Aztec merchants could buy humans and sponsor their sacrifice, then invite other merchants to a banquet featuring the victim's flesh. John D. Rockefeller moved trees around his estate "as an interior decorator would move chairs." Ivana Trump so hated footprints on carpets that she insisted every room be freshly vacuumed just before she entered it.

Such behavior offers everyone else opportunities to feel su-

perior, even while gorging themselves on another episode of *Lifestyles of the Rich and Famous*—the sexless porn of the twentieth century. The rich are viciously maligned and avidly ogled. This ambivalence has existed throughout history—in the Middle Ages, people both worshiped and despised their lords. The eighteenth-century English poet Alexander Pope wrote, "We may see the small value God has for riches, by the people he gives them to." Honoré de Balzac, a nineteenth-century writer who was in debt his entire life, coined the oft-quoted phrase, "Behind every great fortune there is a crime." Yet one of the most admired heroes of American history, George Washington, was a very rich man in his time, leaving an estate valued at $530,000 in 1799. Loved or hated, wealth is at least compelling, and most people can't resist an opportunity to get close to it, on the chance that a chunk will somehow fall into their hands. As Michael Lewis, author of *Liar's Poker,* put it, "[A] rich person is a walking piñata. He strolls through life stuffed with surpluses while the rest of us bash away at him with little sticks."

Sigmund Freud put the primeval ambivalence about wealth into modern language. Someone who has accumulated so much is somehow abnormal, and his or her drive is pathological. The ancient legend of King Midas—whose touch turned everything, including his daughter, into gold—suggests that the rich not only fail to enjoy their riches but are destroyed by them. Some early tribes accorded the greatest prestige not to those who accumulated the most wealth but to those who disbursed it most lavishly. The potlatch, for example, was a ceremony of competitive gift giving, in which people who had once fought by hand now fought with property. Occasionally, prestige was earned by the outright destruction of wealth. "We have seen fine canoes demolished with an ax in a few moments of time," wrote an observer of the Alaskan Tlingits in the 1890s, "dishes, stoves and other household goods smashed by their proud owner, just that he might be considered a greater man than some other."

Undoubtedly most rich people prefer having money to not

having it. Rare indeed are the people who give away so much money that their lifestyles are significantly altered. Millionaires from Machmud of Ghazni to Richard Arkwright to Donald Trump have conspicuously flaunted their financial superiority. If rich people have occasional strained encounters with their consciences, they spend the rest of their days openly wearing, eating, driving, donating, living, riding, and flying their money.

But it is also true that the rich are criticized harshly if they do not brandish their money. Hetty Green, the early twentieth-century queen of the stock market, was rebuked widely for not spending her millions. Green had little interest in the variety of material goods that money can buy. She used money to manipulate the world, like a god pulling human levers. She was a gambler, as early stock-market investors had to be. No rules governed the first securities markets, no lawsuits punished their crimes. Making money meant taking it from others, even when the country was booming. Everyone was betting on the future: railroads, the telegraph, oil, and steel. It was the Wild West on paper, and the victors, like Hetty Green, took no prisoners. ·

For all the fascination wealth has held for scholars over the past thousand years, no one has been able to explain why some people become rich while most do not. Historians, psychologists, economists, philosophers, sociologists, and novelists have put their minds to it, sifting through maddeningly incomplete and incomparable data and arriving at theories about the characteristics of rich people, invoking everything from unhappy childhoods to excessive narcissism. Despite these studies, however, no one has isolated the mental or physical traits that predict whether a particular child will grow up to become rich. The most reliable prediction of a person's eventual wealth today is the same as it has always been: "The best way to make money . . . [is] to have some to start with," wrote a fifteenth-century man named Claude Carriere about Barcelona.

That's why the American myth that hard work leads to

great wealth exasperates some historians and economists. "No man to my knowledge has ever entered the ranks of the great American fortunes merely by saving a surplus from his salary or wages," wrote C. Wright Mills. "In one way or another he has to come into command of a strategic position . . . and usually he has to have available a considerable sum of money." Indeed, from the 1870s on, most important business leaders have been native-born Anglo-Saxons of "high status" Protestant religions and the well-educated sons of native-born businessmen and professionals, according to Harvard University's Research Center for Entrepreneurial History.

Over the millennium, the counterpart of the wealthy has been the millions of people who were born and died knowing nothing but hunger, cold, terror, and plague. Most of them had little, if any, control over their destinies. Trapped by time and place, only the unlikeliest stroke of luck could lift any into wealth. Although there is a lamentable gap between rich and poor in America, the chasm has often been wide. In 1436, the wealthiest people in England—barons—had annual incomes of 865 pounds, while merchants earned only 12 pounds a year. In 1688, a lord's family income was some 3,200 pounds a year, a servant's only 15. England's King Richard I had an annual income equivalent to the combined wages of twenty-four thousand serfs, who were paid a penny a day.

Some economists have suggested that if all the money in the world were redistributed in equal shares to every living person, it would gradually drift back to its original owners. Accepting inequality as inevitable is one thing, but what role should society play in perpetuating that inequality? For example, most people agree that while those with great abilities should be rewarded, their children and grandchildren, who did nothing but be born, shouldn't necessarily be entitled to those rewards. This attitude is reflected in the federal tax system, which distinguishes entrepreneurs from heirs by looking more kindly on accumulating wealth than on transferring it to the next generation.

Although wealth seems unquestionably desirable in America today, it has little correlation with happiness. For example, the level of happiness reported by Americans in 1970 was not much different from what it had been in the late 1940s, although average income, even allowing for taxes and inflation, could buy 60 percent more. Wealth does buy better health care, nutrition, and healthful habits (fewer rich people smoke; more of them exercise), so it's not surprising the wealthy have longer life expectancies than the poor. However, beyond a certain point, there's no evidence suggesting that happiness increases proportionately with wealth. The case histories of wealthy men and women are filled with stories of nervous breakdowns, family conflicts, alcoholism, and suicide. Barbara Hutton inherited $42 million from her grandfather, Frank Woolworth, on her twenty-first birthday in 1930 and then went on to marry seven times. Her marriage to Porfirio Rubirosa lasted seventy-three days. It was for her that the media coined the phrase "poor little rich girl." The breakfast cereal king Charles William Post had a nervous breakdown and eventually committed suicide, as did the photography merchant George Eastman.

Some psychologists call their wealthy clients "emotional zombies." Free of worries about mortgages and tuition payments, rich people nevertheless have afflictions that don't trouble the less fortunate. Simply having so many choices can heighten a sense of frustration with the world: "The less limited one feels, the more intolerable all limitation appears," noted Emile Durkheim. With their many advantages, the wealthy are often held to higher standards than other classes are. Behavior increasingly viewed with compassion in members of other social and economic groups—alcoholism or drug addiction, for example—seems more abhorrent in the rich. What's their excuse? Further, they might not seek psychiatric help, afraid of being labeled "whiners," which would put them in violation of the American canon of cheerfulness.

The inability to afford something seems like a terrible limitation to many people, but in an age when consumption choices are almost infinite, it can also be a godsend. The ability to buy *anything* turns buying into an irrational exercise governed by whim. The world becomes an enormous shopping mall, where nothing is automatically ruled out by financial limits. The rich acquire multiple homes, fine art, jewelry, fast cars, yachts, and clothes, and their acquisitions become essential parts of their identities. Their self-esteem is exposed on many fronts. "It is clear that between what a man calls me and what he simply calls mine, the line is difficult to draw," wrote William James in *The Principles of Psychology*. "[A] man's self is the sum total of all that he can call his, not only his body . . . but his clothes and his house, his wife and his children . . . his land and horses and yacht and bank account."

Whatever a person has, a person can also not have—the wedge of insecurity that torments the wealthy. "If I am what I have, and if what I have is lost, who then am I?" asked Erich Fromm. "Because I *can* lose what I have, I am necessarily constantly worried that I *shall* lose what I have. I am afraid of thieves, economic changes, revolutions, sickness, death, love, freedom, change and the unknown."

That fear of change certainly troubled the nineteenth-century Chinese trader Howqua. His great wealth was built on an archaic system of trade that was buckling under the assaults of unscrupulous free traders from the West. China was contentedly isolationist; its people were doing fine without the rest of the world's surpluses. But wealth stokes change, and change stokes wealth—China had a destiny. As the country opened more of its harbors to global trade, Howqua and the other gatekeepers were left overseeing the collapse of the old world.

Unlike everyone else, the wealthy can't blame life's inevitable disappointments on lack of financial opportunity—a rationalization that has soothed countless other egos. If money isn't the root of their discontent, what is? "An income large enough to give a man what he wants when he wants it apparently can't make as much for happiness as a smaller one," the publisher Henry Holt once said. "Champagne everyday ceases to be a luxury. A thing can be best enjoyed when it is barely within occasional reach, and when its selection involves a dash of sacrifice." Indeed, researchers have found that when people suddenly get rich, the pleasure quickly wanes and their general satisfaction with life reverts to its previous level.

A study of six hundred millionaires done in 1925 found that the richer a man was, the more likely he was to be divorced. Indeed, self-made rich men often lack warmth and are unable to form close, lasting relationships with anyone. "The typical self-made man often thinks of his wife the way he thinks of his money. She is a jewel, a bauble. He has married her to increase his apparent worth. He wants the world to judge him by the prettiness of his jewel."

The psychological study of wealthy people has never quite recovered from Sigmund Freud's early analysis. Freud speculated that people who loved money were like children loving their feces, and that people's reactions to money, from revulsion to desire, were similar to their reactions to feces. Take a look at myths, fairy tales, superstitions, and dreams, Freud wrote: "Money has been brought into the closest connection with filth." Studying the childhoods of subjects who were particularly miserly or economical, Freud concluded that "the most extensive connections seem to be those existing between the apparently so disparate complexes of defecation and interest in money."

The mind behind this seminal theory belonged to a working man with money problems of his own. Although Freud and his large family never went hungry, he worked hard for his income, analyzing patients at the rate of ten dollars per session. In his later years, Freud was earning enough money to start acquiring antiquities, and he amassed some 2,300 of them, yet he never seemed secure about his financial position. A recent psychoanalytic study of the rich concluded that Freud had a "poor-house neurosis"—however much he had, he feared he wouldn't have enough.

Wealthy people often describe themselves as victims rather than masters of their money. Of himself and other wealthy men of America's Gilded Age, Jay Gould said, "We are all slaves, and the man who has one million dollars is the greatest slave of all, except it be he who has two million." A tenth-century Muslim ruler wrote, "I have now reigned about 50 years in victory and peace, beloved by my subjects, dreaded by my enemies and respected by my allies. Riches and honors, power and pleasure have waited on my call. . . . In this situation I have diligently numbered the days of pure and genuine happiness which have fallen to my lot: they amount to fourteen."

Others are dubious of the idea that it's hard to be rich. "The idea that the millionaire finds nothing but a sad, empty place at the top of this society . . . is, in the main, a way by which those who are not rich reconcile themselves to the fact," C. Wright Mills wrote. "If the rich are not happy, it's because none of us are happy."

The popular ambivalence toward wealth that has characterized so many cultures over so many centuries is less apparent today than in the past. In America, this change began with the promulgation of a new philosophy of success in the late nineteenth century articulated by a hugely popular Baptist minister named Russell Herman Conwell, who traveled around the country giving a speech called "Acres of Diamonds." "I say you ought to be rich," he exhorted his 6,100 different audiences. "Love is the greatest thing on God's earth, but fortunate the lover who has plenty of money. Religious prejudice is so great that some people think it is a great honor to be one of God's poor. . . . You ought to spend your time getting money because of the power there is in money." Failure to thrive became a failure of nerve, self-confidence, and initiative.

Today, when wealth is so comparatively widespread, failure

to succeed is more disdained than ever. The phrases "I can't afford it" and "I don't need it" have all but dropped from common parlance. To be unable to afford something reflects stupidity (for not getting into the financial markets at the right time) or lack of sophistication (why not just borrow the money?). As for need, how is that defined in a time when the average American family has three television sets?

The nine men and one woman whose stories tell this history of wealth were almost certainly not the richest ten people of the millennium. It is impossible to compare wealth today with wealth that existed before currency became the primary medium of commercial relations. In the past few hundred years, currency has become almost global, but money prices belong in their times and cannot be compared across centuries.

The ten subjects sketched here were—besides being rich, ambitious, and distinctive—representative of the mechanisms of creating wealth in their eras. Overall, the biggest difference between the rich of a millennium ago and of today is that where physical strength was once the sine qua non of wealth, it has now become all but irrelevant. The fingers will do the fighting in the third millennium, using bits and bytes of data as weapons. Bill Gates commands the computer marketplace from a bosky corporate campus near Seattle, and his net worth is measured largely by what the value of his Microsoft stock would be if he converted it to money. He created what is probably the largest fortune in world history by skimming a portion of the extraordinary growth in computer technology in the late twentieth century.

Humans have always had a choice in how they regard wealth: They can produce much or desire little. From the vantage of present-day America, the past looks harshly impecunious, short on luxury, and long on blood, sweat, and tears. It is widely assumed that people have always wanted more, that acquisitiveness is natural and austerity is unintentional. But the anthropologists Mary Douglas and Baron Isherwood told of the Nuer people of the Sudan, who in the 1930s would not trade with the Arabs because the only things they had to sell were herds of cattle, and the only things they wanted from trade were more cattle.

Ultimately, the best answer to the question "Who is rich?" may be "Those who think they are."

The
Rich
and
How They Got
That Way

ONE

When Thieves Were Kings

❦

Machmud of Ghazni (971–1030)

One thousand years ago, a man named Machmud of Ghazni was as rich as anyone on earth. By modern standards, it was highly difficult to create, defend, and exploit wealth in the eleventh century. For one thing, there wasn't much around. Almost everyone spent their lives struggling for survival against the cruelties of nature and other humans. Virtually everything that was produced was immediately consumed—little excess remained from day to day, still less from year to year. Commerce was all barter in goods and services. Hard work and good ideas could mean the difference between life and death but not between wealth and poverty.

One of the only ways to become fantastically rich one thousand years ago was by the large-scale robbery of the few regions where people had begun to accumulate caches of gold, silver, and jewels. The citizens of these small towns and villages still worked their fields to survive—their wealth couldn't buy food. They couldn't afford to hire armies to defend their precious objects against determined and well-equipped predators. Plundering was a tremendously lucrative business if it was done well, and few people have done it better than Machmud of Ghazni.

In his mountainous homeland in what is now Afghanistan, Machmud lived in the splendor befitting a conquering hero. At his palace, prudent guests carefully observed court protocol. A beefy fireplug of a man, Machmud once became so angry at a visitor who spoke out of turn that he smacked him on the side of the head, deafening him for life.

Machmud sat on a golden, jewel-encrusted throne, which local artisans spent three years building. Attending him were hundreds of guards wearing flamboyant brocade uniforms and jeweled sashes and carrying gold maces. A crowd of retainers, probably eunuchs, fluttered around him. In the corners of the court, a staff of poets composed verses in Machmud's praise. He dabbled in wine, women, and song, but mostly he worshiped gems and gold. Machmud's crown, also studded with jewels, was so heavy it was suspended above his head by a chain.

In Machmud's era, war and wealth, Mars and Ploutos, always stood together. He and his army could crush anyone in the region, but it was as important to appear fabulously wealthy as to appear invincible. Machmud's palace was his power and success made tangible. He had as comfortable a domestic life as any person could have enjoyed in his time and place, and yet evidence suggests that Machmud was never satisfied with the size of his fortune.

Throughout much of human history, the most effective way to acquire part or all of other people's wealth has been to declare, "That's mine!" and kill those who disagree. Only in the last millennium, has wealth creation become less about force than intelligence. For thousands of years, there was no demarcation between war and pillaging, and no gains were considered more just than those from war. The wealthy—almost exclusively men—were born strong, of prestigious parentage, or in many cases both. In hunting and fighting societies, the brawny survived, and the brawniest and meanest got the best land. Intelligence helped little without biceps or soldiers to back it up. Negotiations between rivals frequently ended in homicide or suicide. To the extent that parents harbored any hopes for their children besides survival, it was to grow up strong and aggressive—the kind of personality now often found in prisons. For everyone else, the best way to survive was to swear allegiance to a bully.

Like most empires of his time, Machmud's Ghazni was essentially a military machine. Anyone who intended to plunder on a significant scale needed an army, and, indeed, the armies of thousands of petty lords and predatory tribes kept the world in a state of constant guerrilla warfare. Ordinary people watched armies sweep through their territories and felt fortunate if they lost only their crops, livestock, and water. If a peasant lived to be forty, he or she was lucky (although many people didn't actually know the year of their birth). The death of children was common. Killing another person for his or her belongings was not a crime. The world was brutally indifferent to suffering, but even if anyone had cared there was little medical care or drugs to alleviate pain. Around the globe, most humans in 1000 were sedentary farmers whose most precious household good might have been a metal pan.

The history of the early Middle Ages is easier to research about Europe than Ghazni, China, Africa, or the Americas, especially for those who understand only Western languages. Large, prosperous societies were born and died virtually unrecorded. The lives of Machmud's subjects must be imagined through those of other people of the time.

The most detailed portrait of ordinary life in 1000 comes from Europe, where 80 percent of a farmer's effort was expended raising food to sustain his or her family. Peasants worked harder and sweated more than their animals did. Pesticides, fertilizer, and field rotation were unknown, so crop failures were common. One poor harvest could decimate a community; three in a row would obliterate it. Because transportation was so crude, a starving farmer and a well-fed one might live only a few miles apart. People rarely owned a change of clothes, and they waited for others to die to get a new pair of trousers. If there was no work, a family's only hope for survival was charity. Poor sanitation and malnutrition abetted a succession of lethal epidemics. Superstitions and legends explained the mysteries of nature; trolls hid under bridges. Across Europe, famine sometimes resulted in cannibalism, even parents eating their children. Unimaginable as it is, only one thousand years ago human flesh could be bought at the marketplace in some parts of Europe.

With so little surplus of anything, it was all but impossible for ordinary people to better their lots. Most were rooted to a plot of land, the fruitfulness of which determined their very survival. Without literacy or communication, they couldn't even imagine another way of life. If they owned a particularly fertile field and were industrious, fecund, aggressive, and lucky, they might become wealthier than their neighbors. But wealth meant little in those days, when it bought only an extra layer of clothes and a few candles. The houses of the rich might have fireplaces, but in cold weather the tiny rooms filled with smoke. Rarely did even a lord and lady have a bed to themselves. Many wealthy people counted their riches in heads of cattle, pigs, or goats, "money that could walk on four legs." Because wealth was displayed not so much by possession as consumption, the rich ate heaping platters of meat and drank giant flagons of wine or beer in a display of "pantagruelic excesses." Their gluttony often resulted in gout, which required frequent bloodlettings. Overall, being rich was better than being poor one thousand years ago, but the differences were smaller than they are now.

Rich or poor, people had no concept of property rights: Possession was ten tenths of the law. At any moment, a peasant might see dust on the horizon, hear the roar of hooves and yelps of horsemen, and that might be the last thing he or she ever heard. There were no central governments whose armies might defend the common people from barbarians; in fact, from the ninth to the eleventh centuries, business that would now be considered governmental was handled primarily by the church. Peasants sought asylum within the fortress walls of nobles.

There, they tended the feudal estates for the lords who protected and exploited them while fighting a lifelong war with scarcity.

There was no currency and little trade, and control of land was the primary marker of wealth. From the end of the eighth century, everyone from the emperor to the humblest serf lived on the products of the soil. Each small district, regardless of its geography and climate, strove for self-sufficiency. Even in the midst of such a struggle, trade of surpluses between manors and villages never entirely ceased. A trickle of luxuries from the East made its way to Europe's wealthy—silk, ivory, spices, and enamel—but exorbitant transport costs put them out of most peoples' reach.

The idea of profit had not been born. For a great medieval landowner, who might control ten thousand acres of scattered land, the notion of intentionally producing a surplus was incompatible with the feudal system that supported him. Because the extended feudal family could not sell excess produce, there was little incentive for the lord of the manor to extract more from his land or workers.

For European serfs in 1000, wealth was not only unattainable but also incompatible with their notion of heaven. The church was the great moral authority of the age, and it preached that land was a gift from God, the only purpose of which was to allow humans to survive until mortal life passed into life eternal. The object of labor was not to grow wealthy but to maintain oneself in the position to which one was born. Seeking riches betrayed the sin of avarice. Economic concerns were secondary to religious ones. Serfs had neither the opportunity nor the desire to get ahead. There was no such thing as saving for the future; indeed, the very notion of the future was a hazy and optimistic abstraction.

Few people anywhere in the world could read or write, which further limited most people's exposure to other ways of life. Movable type was not invented for another four hundred years, and hand-printed books were expensive—in Spain in 800, a book cost as much as two cows. The church provided Christian Europe's few scribes, but their language was Latin. Almost no one recorded the prosaic details of ordinary life, and even accounts of great rulers were often distorted by political or religious biases. It is recorded, for example, that in one battle Machmud of Ghazni killed so many enemy soldiers that his hand was welded to the hilt of his sword by blood and could be loosened only by hot water. Whether this is literally true or a fawner's chronicle will never be known.

The embellishment of legend makes Machmud and others who lived before widespread literacy seem unreal, like a super race instead of humans with clay feet. No one recorded what Machmud's wives, servants, or children thought of him. His illiterate subjects expressed their grievances to no one but one another. Exacerbating the problem of understanding Machmud was his use of religious zealotry to camouflage his savagery. Some of his biographers took him at his religious word, others doubted his sincerity; either way, they persistently sneaked small gestures of animosity or admiration into their accounts.

The works of Muhammad Nazim and Mohommad Habib, two biographers of Machmud, are good examples of how historical relativism found full expression in the Machmud archives. While Habib disdained Machmud for his greed, barbarity, and administrative mediocrity, Nazim insisted that Machmud was an upstanding man: "It can be stated with certainty that [Machmud] was not tainted with the licentious sensuality which often disgraced the life of Oriental despots," sniffed Nazim. Stitching these two accounts together, supported by other historical material written with poetic license and religious hyperbole, it is possible to paint a portrait of Machmud as people wanted him to be: invincible and rich beyond dreams— exactly what people have always wanted their rulers to be.

Born in 971, Machmud grew up in a family that was relatively affluent for the time and place; his father was a powerful and militant soldier. Machmud was educated by a tutor and drilled in the military arts. He excelled at wielding spear and bow, and he could twirl a mace over his head and throw it with deadly accuracy. When he was fifteen years old, Machmud joined his father in a pitched battle against an unrecorded enemy. Perhaps because Machmud's father witnessed his son's ferocity in this battle, he designated a different son to succeed him. But soon after his father died, Machmud launched and handily won a civil war, wresting the throne from his brother.

Fortune had smiled on Machmud: His country adjoined India, then one of the world's wealthiest societies. A trade imbalance and the production of Indian mines had produced a massive amount of gold, silver, and other wealth. Generations of devout Hindus had sent gifts and offerings to the country's temples. At the same time, India was fragmented politically by feuding rajas, subrajas, local chiefs, and village leaders. By Machmud's time, India had developed such a widespread reputation for wealth that its riches had become a serious national danger.

Machmud and his army became the inevitable menace. Seventeen times between 1000 and 1026, they ravaged India's plains. With fifty thousand or more men, horses, and elephants, Machmud's forces rode into India, capturing towns, temples, and forts, devouring the land "like a cloud of locusts." In 1010, commented a historian dryly, Machmud spent the summer "bringing some presumptuous inhabitants of Ghor to a sense of their insignificance." He left behind a decimated town, its streets covered with pools of blood.

In forty years of nearly constant warfare, Machmud never lost a battle. He employed, at enormous cost, a well-trained standing army—among the best fighters of their time. The soldiers were highly mobile: "They ascended the hills like mountain goats and descended them like torrents of water." They rode through a thick forest "like a comb through a head of hair." Machmud's preferred strategy was a fast cavalry charge, a feigned retreat to set a trap, and then an ambush. But when necessary, he could also besiege. In one attack, he catapulted sacks of snakes into the enemy stronghold to terrorize the defenders.

Unlike many of his successors in plundering, Machmud was not interested in occupying or annexing the country he repeatedly invaded. At the end of each campaign, Machmud rode back to Ghazni, his pack animals straining under the weight of stolen goods. "He is a stupid fellow," a Muslim mystic remarked of Machmud. "Unable to administer what he already possesses, yet he goes out to conquer new countries."

But Machmud did not need to control India's people to be rich, and his army was not large enough to occupy it. He could not have administered the collection of a steady, long-term revenue stream, such as a tax. Like his ancestors, Machmud preferred hit-and-run warfare. Once he had raided a town or fort, it wouldn't be worth plundering again for years, perhaps decades. In the city of Kanauj, Machmud's army murdered all the inhabitants, destroyed 10,000 temples, pocketed gold, silver, and jewels, and captured 55,000 slaves and 350 elephants.

Even for a rich man, Machmud had an exceptional appetite for wealth. Apparently, a man named Isfaraini had been Machmud's loyal tax collector for ten years. The job involved squeezing Machmud's subjects in Afghanistan to pay for the army that stole the precious objects for his treasure-house. Finally, Isfaraini told Machmud he could wring no more out of the people, and he refused to make up the deficiency from his own pocket. Machmud tortured him to death. Other tax collectors who came up short were broken on the rack or had their hands and feet amputated.

With most subjects, Machmud didn't have to resort to physical abuse; they knew his reputation. Machmud wanted to be the only wealthy man. Once, hearing that a subject had become rich, Machmud ordered the fellow brought before him. Machmud accused him of being a heretic, a charge the rich man denied vigorously. But the rich man offered to pay Machmud for a document vouching for the soundness of his religious views. Machmud, awash in gold and jewels, agreed to the bribe.

Machmud's rapaciousness seems perverse, yet it raises the question of whether there is some normal level of acquisitiveness built into humans. Some people revel in buying and owning things; others are indifferent to gold and jewels. Does everyone have a minimum level of rapacity coded in their genes, or is the desire to accumulate and acquire culturally indoctrinated? Are acquisitive people inherently neurotic and insecure, or are they actually long-term winners in terms of natural selection?

It's generally believed that animals stop acquiring when their basic needs are met (although apparently some dogs will eat themselves to death). Chimpanzees have been trained to "work" for money, using currency to operate food-dispensing machines. But having gained two or three pieces of money, the chimps quit. Unquestionably, animals have possessions: nests, territory, or hoarded food, for example. But a comprehensive 1931 study of possessive behavior of insects, birds, rodents, apes, and other animals concluded that acquisition among animals is limited to items that represent an instinctive reaction to possible future scarcity. There are not fat seagulls and thin seagulls in the same location. Or as Adam Smith wrote in *The Wealth of Nations,* "Nobody ever saw a dog make a fair and deliberate exchange of one bone for another with another dog."

Right from its moment of entry onto the world stage, however, *Homo sapiens* seemed to have a different relationship with its possessions. Prehistoric humans made whatever they owned, and their possessions were the tools of their survival. Things were seen as extensions of themselves; indeed, people often took their tools to the grave with them.

Other than food, the early hunter-gatherers needed little—

skins for clothing and stone, metal, or wood to fabricate implements. Foragers usually lived in bands of a few dozen people, often blood kin, moving with the season, climate, or better prospects over the horizon. The first permanent objects of affluence were probably bronze and iron, and control of these scarce resources could lead to power. But the incentive to accumulate surplus—and to bear children, for that matter—was considerably dampened by the knowledge that if you owned it, you carried it. "Of the hunter, it is truly said that wealth is a burden."

Because hunting was hit or miss, generosity was expected within the band. If a hunting party came back with meat one day but another hunting party didn't, a week later it might be the reverse. As anthropologists quip, "A selfish hunter-gatherer is a dead hunter-gatherer." Among foragers, strong men who were good providers gained the most respect, but they had no coercive power, and generally there were only minor differences among members in terms of prestige. There were no class differences in either production or consumption.

Hunters and foragers worked only a few hours a day and rested much more than a modern worker does. If they suddenly acquired more food than they needed for the day, they ate it all anyway—most of it would spoil if they didn't. Ironically, the earliest humans may have perceived the world more optimistically, or at least with a trusting surrender to nature: They would find more tomorrow. "The individual was more self-reliant; less of a unit in the crowd. Moving over large stretches of country, the nomad took a wider view of life."

From the pinnacle of twentieth-century abundance, the hunter-gatherers, who sometimes went two or three days between meals, appear to have lived on the edge of privation. But that says more about twentieth-century values than about what hunter-gatherers actually felt. Hunter-gatherers took the "Zen road to affluence." Unlike societies of unlimited wants and limited means, foraging societies adjusted to their limited means by entertaining fewer desires: Want not, lack not. With enough to eat and drink, they experienced "affluence without abundance." Epicurus himself later wrote, "Wealth consists not in having great possessions, but in having few wants."

If these societies were unacquisitive, perhaps acquisitiveness isn't natural at all but results from people settling down in larger communities. However aspirations to ownership arose, anthropologists tend to romanticize tribal "communism," which seems to prove that humans can live cooperatively and without economic hierarchies, sharing plenty or poverty with their clans. Yet when viewed without rose-colored glasses, the communal system may have only suppressed natural acquisitive tendencies:

> The tribal member is neither free nor secure. He is the slave of every member of his tribe stronger than himself. . . . The rights of property not being recognized, no one can possess anything he can call his own. If he cultivates a plot of ground, he cannot be sure he will be allowed to reap the produce; if by superior toil and ability in hunting and fishing, he lays up a stock of provisions, he cannot be certain he will not be compelled to share them with a stranger. . . . The gratification of immediate wants is the sole object of exertion, and anything beyond this is unprofitable, because it is an unsafe, accumulation.

Sometime as early as twenty thousand years ago, people began to find sufficient resources in small enough areas to allow them to settle down and start producing their food. In 6000 B.C.E., such a settlement may have been a village of a few hundred people, mostly related. Working the fields together, they produced grain held in common store for all. As they learned more about farming, they gradually began to produce occasional surpluses, which they might trade with neighboring villages for flint or semiprecious stones. Living in one place, people could accumulate possessions without worrying about transporting them.

In most climates, shelter is worth the expense and effort needed to build it, so people began to fabricate houses, often of mud bricks. Some people built larger or more decorative shelters than others, a distinction of the wealthy that remains as true today as one thousand or more years ago. In early agricultural communities, people began passing material goods to their children, a practice that remains widespread among all economic classes today. Tools and livestock became critical to the survival of the next generation.

Early agricultural communities often established themselves in areas where farmers could at least partially control the water supply, usually by irrigation. And just as many of the wealthiest people today prefer views of the ocean and the sound of crashing waves, the wealthiest people one thousand years ago wanted proximity to major rivers, where their fields would be better drained and more easily irrigated. With the installation of complicated irrigation systems, valuable but immovable, people lost the option of fleeing from violence. Communities now needed armies to defend their land and resources. Thugs could still be rewarded for aggression, but now some citizens would sponsor them in armies. Humans began making weapons from metal, an improvement over the stone-based arms of earlier warriors. The scale of warfare began to rise.

A career in combat is never painless, but imagine a skirmish in 1000: Men maneuvered lances, crossbows, and swords from the backs of agitated horses, while furious elephants trumpeted and thrashed around the field. Soldiers fought to the death, and why not? The hacking blows of medieval warfare, where armor protected the vital parts, were more likely to cause mutilation than death. There were few medics on the battlefields, and the surgeons of the day were also the barbers.

Simple firebombs, made from naphtha, were used to set fire to battlements and terrorize enemy soldiers and animals. Stirrups were not yet used widely, which meant that "your slashing horseman, taking a good broadhanded swipe at his foe, had only to miss to find himself on the ground." There was a constant danger of being crushed by a horse, especially one's own. In some military operations, if an army was forced to march, the wounded soldiers were killed rather than evacuated.

One of Machmud's tactical advantages was his force of some 1,300 elephants. In battle, elephants allowed field commanders good vantages, while doing double duty as battering rams. Placed in front of the battle line, the elephants, spurred on by their riders clanging their metal headpieces, charged into the enemy ranks. A wounded elephant is apparently a terrifying sight: At one time, elephants were exported to Rome to fight with gladiators, but the spectacle of the mammoth animals struggling and dying was so appalling that the practice ceased.

Machmud's army fluctuated in size from 50,000 to 100,000 men, most of whom traveled with two horses. Maintaining a force that large required a massive amount of cash, which was why regular tax revenues from Machmud's subjects were critical. Besides their salaries, soldiers often received bonuses in the form of booty, particularly weapons and slaves. Slaves had been a concomitant of wealth for thousands of years; instead of material objects, which were scarce, the wealthy bought themselves leisure and protection. Many of Machmud's troops were slaves, often acquired at an early age and molded and trained for warfare. His bodyguards, too, were slaves. They were often more loyal to their masters than free men were. Cut off from homelands and families, slaves' only allegiances were often to the master who had allowed them to live. In a world where factionalism was endemic and family members often went to war with one another, loyalty was a rare and precious commodity.

For both the vanquished and the triumphant, Machmud was simply the latest in a timeless chain of men who dominated other people by force. The ordinary peasant would be no more or less loyal to Machmud than they were to his predecessors. His economic demands were as much a force of nature as monsoons. Most peasants had fatalistic religious attitudes toward worldly wealth; they immediately started rebuilding their homes and farms, and in a matter of years their lives returned to normal, until the next attack.

With his reputation as a warrior spreading, Machmud easily attracted to his banner tens of thousands of recruits, many of them eager to fight the Hindu infidels and, if fortunate, become martyrs to the cause of Mohammad. Machmud's soldiers weren't sacrificing their own prosperous farms or businesses in any case. "The mountaineers were as poor as they were brave, and covetous as they were devout. The treasures of India, heaped up round the colossal figures of idols, appeared irresistible to these hungry fanatics." That combination of religious and financial motives was soon to fuel Europe's Crusades.

For his first big battle, fought around 1000, Machmud's army consisted of some 32,000 cavalry troops and 140 elephants. By the time the skirmish was over, 2,000 soldiers were dead, and Machmud's army had taken 2,500 enemy troops prisoner. These statistics must be taken as extremely rough guesses; an English historian noted the "penchant of Muslim historians for round numbers and their tendency to exaggerate."

In 1008, Machmud's army faced the combined forces of many Hindu sects. Machmud set up camp and some weeks later sent forward a large corps of archers. The archers were to be followed by soldiers carrying swords and lances. The archers, however, came dashing back to camp, pursued by a mob of Gakkars carrying daggers and spears. The Gakkars went to work on Machmud's troops, and "in the twinkling of an eye, three or four thousand Muslims had tasted the wine of martyrdom." But then, a stroke of luck hit Machmud: The elephant carrying the enemy leader unaccountably fled the scene, and the enemy troops dispersed. One of the Hindu ceremonies of peace involved the defeated monarch cutting off a fingertip and giving it to the victor as a trophy. Machmud, it is said, had quite a number of fingertips.

Machmud fired on one temple for seven days until its defenders finally opened the gates. Machmud had never seen so much gold, silver, and jewels, and he took it all. Among the booty was "a house of white silver, like to the houses of rich men, the length of which was thirty yards and the breadth fifteen," wrote an Islamic historian named Utbi. "It could be broken to pieces and put together again." The riches were so magnificent that "the imagination of the accountants failed to grasp it in their number." Returning to Ghazni, Machmud put his plunder ("diamonds in size and weight like pomegranates") on public display.

On some of Machmud's expeditions, towns surrendered without fights; Machmud would then demand a tribute from the inhabitants for the privilege of remaining alive, their homes standing. If those in the garrison defended it, however, Machmud followed the time-honored custom of slaughtering not only the enemy soldiers but also innocent men, women, children, and even dogs. Traveling with thousands of grazing horses, camels, and elephants, Machmud's forces also decimated the agriculture of their victims' territory, eating and drinking every scrap of food and drop of water, sometimes resulting in famine.

Another common practice among pillagers was to destroy what they couldn't take. It wasn't enough for Machmud to get richer; others must be made poorer, too. If something valuable was too large or heavy to carry back to Ghazni, regardless of its value it had to be destroyed so that no one else could enjoy it. In the city of Mathura, even Machmud was struck by the architectural beauty, "full of temples, solidly built and of exquisite design." After the temples had been stripped of their treasures, Machmud burned them to the ground.

It had long been common everywhere for some people to regularly take other people's possessions by force. The notorious

Huns of the fourth and fifth centuries were trained from infancy to kill without pity, and they became superlative plunderers. In 410, the Huns and Goths captured Rome, slaughtered wealthy men, raped women, and melted down works of art for metal. Only a few decades later, the Vandals, whose name has come to mean wanton destroyers, seized Rome and spent fourteen days systematically plundering it. The Vikings, spurred by over-population and famine, mounted regular hit-and-run raids along the northern coasts of Europe from the ninth to eleventh centuries and were said to be exceedingly cruel and rapacious; it was their custom to burn the house of an enemy with every living creature inside.

After Machmud's era came the Thugs of fourteenth-century India, who insinuated themselves with passersby and then, when the victims' guards were down, strangled them according to ancient and rigidly prescribed forms. The Pindaris, soldiers in the Muslim army of eighteenth-century India, were allowed to plunder instead of being paid. And as recently as World War II, "trophy brigades" of German and Russian forces were responsible for seizing cultural artifacts from conquered nations. American and other Western forces took their share of European plunder less formally.

Plundering has largely died out as an occupation, succeeded by looting and kleptocracy. Looting today is opportunistic theft usually following war, random bombings, or civil unrest. A kleptocracy is a government that plunders from its own people, transferring wealth by threat of force from commoners to the upper classes, such as Ferdinand and Imelda Marcos or, a century earlier, King Leopold II of Belgium. Both practices are relatively rare. Taking things by force is dangerous and unreliable, and people are less resigned to violent exploitation. In the twenty-first century, there are thousands of ways to get rich that don't involve physical risk. In Machmud's time, there were almost none.

*   *   *

At the beginning of every summer, Machmud returned home to Ghazni to enjoy the splendor appropriate to a powerful chieftain. When not on the battlefield, Machmud luxuriated in his huge palace, surrounded by wives, gold furnishings, and a well-stocked library of, among other items, erotic manuscripts.

Plunderers were almost by definition materialists—they measured their own value by the value of their possessions. They had no interest in importing the culture of their victims, however superior it may have been. They didn't measure wealth in love, gratification, or health; they measured it by material objects, the more the better. There was no such thing as too much ostentation. Machmud and his fellow plunderers felt none of the ambivalence toward wealth that the Roman Catholic Church successfully inculcated in Christians. So was materialism the natural human condition or a by-product of civilization?

It's difficult to investigate this question empirically. By the time people are old enough to have attitudes toward their possessions, they have already been contaminated by culture. The term *materialism* describes a spectrum of reactions people have to worldly possessions. Early research about materialism focused on collecting, which particularly fascinates psychologists because objects in a collection are things that have not entered people's lives casually or coincidentally. Some psychologists believe collections are a way that people legitimize their acquisitiveness.

In a late-nineteenth-century study, 217 adolescent boys were asked whether they collected stamps, coins, or anything else. Ninety-two percent had at least one collection. In 1900, a similar study found that California schoolchildren of both genders were collectors. These results confirmed the researchers' belief that to collect is "wonderfully universal," as one wrote (although Freud described his own collection of 2,300 antiquities as an addiction second only to nicotine). It was comforting to believe that possessiveness was instinctive, since social inequality could then be explained as natural and intractable.

As attachment to things became an unquestioned norm during the twentieth century, the issue of how people became materialists lost its urgency. Wanting more and better things came to seem universal, making materialism the natural rather than the abnormal state. Indeed, today, poor people who are satisfied with their lots are described as victims of the "satisfaction paradox," which psychologists attribute to "adaptation and learned helplessness produced by long experience of being unable to control their situation." How people arrived at a condition of permanent desire didn't matter as much as how it affected their behavior.

Gradually, the study of materialism moved from the origins of acquisitiveness to its gradations and how to measure them. Researchers gave the field a proper-sounding name—possession attachment research—and called their area of study possession meaning. They began to develop standardized assessment instruments. The test questions they used suggest the extent to which material possessions have developed into another language.

Test subjects of the Richins and Dawson Materialism Scales respond to such statements as "I like a lot of luxury in my life" or "I'd be happier if I could afford to buy more things." The Dittmar Possession Rating Scales asks subjects to apply to a particular possession such remarks as it "gives me social status" or "improves my mood." The Belk Materialism Scales test people's "nongenerosity," possessiveness, envy, and preservation (collecting and keeping mementos).

Although the word *materialism* carries a pejorative taint, it is actually healthy for people to feel some attachment to their possessions—instrumental materialism, as it's called. "Things are our ballast. They stabilize us by reminding us of our past, by making the past a virtual, substantial part of our present." Possessions are part of a social communication system that helps people sort out cultural categories and allows them to give visible reality to their identity and character.

But if people are too attached to possessions, they become vulnerable to feeling anger, anxiety, or guilt about them; as in any addiction, the cure is also the disease. Because consumption is so important to materialists, they may have higher expectations for how much happiness a new possession will bring them. Materialism can also lead to consumption pathologies, such as compulsive buying, in which the thrill is in acquiring rather than possessing a thing.

A person's degree of materialism does not remain static over the course of his or her lifetime. Small children are intensely possessive ("Mine!") and covetous ("Gimme!"). In adolescence and young adulthood, action and behavior seem to be more important components of identity than possession. In adulthood, possessions bring comfort and security. After midlife, people see their material objects primarily as links to memories or other people. Finally, in old age, people often give possessions away. Of course, not all possessions are the same: "We are unlikely to swap pets, wedding rings or children even when the alternative offered is demonstrably superior to our own."

Machmud's devotees make much of his cultural aspirations, and, thanks to his lavish generosity (and the occasional use of force), he drew a galaxy of cultural heroes to his court— scientists, dramatists, and poets, among others. In every affluent civilization from Athens to Timbuktu, the rich have sponsored creative endeavors, paying composers, painters, and poets. Machmud had four hundred poets in constant attendance at his court; some specialized in poems about wine. Although few of the verses have survived, poets who composed the most fulsome songs of praise for Machmud were thanked generously. Machmud once expressed his gratitude by filling a poet's mouth three times with pearls.

Likewise, Machmud used some of his wealth to improve the

infrastructure of Ghazni, building not only several palaces for himself but also mosques, bridges, aqueducts, and irrigation channels using the free labor of his subjects.

Machmud's personal morality is another of history's toss-ups. Muhammad Nazim believed Machmud lived more or less in accordance with the Muslim code of morality. He didn't seem to have exceeded the prescribed number of wives, and his wine drinking was a "pastime," not a "besotting habit." But Mohommad Habib argued that Machmud had an unseemly fondness for "war and wine and women." Furthermore, Machmud became particularly attached to a Turkish slave boy named Ayaz, who had a good build and light coloring and was, a contemporary reported, "mightily endowed with all the arts of pleasing." In love poetry, Machmud was described as "a slave of his slave."

Machmud was not a handsome man, even by the standards of 1000. Smallpox had left his face scarred so badly that on catching sight of his own features in a mirror once he noted dejectedly that looking at a king should improve a person's eyesight but looking at him "will probably injure the onlooker's eye." As Ovid wrote, "So long as he is rich, even a barbarian is attractive," and Machmud's self-consciousness did not discourage him from enjoying and sharing the sensual pleasures of life. At his banquets, it was said, "enormous quantities of largesse were distributed." Gift giving, or "necessary generosity," was how wealth was redistributed in Machmud's era. "Savage society was dominated by the habit of plundering and the need for giving. To rob and to give: these two complementary acts covered a very large portion of exchanges."

Yet all Machmud's considerable plunder never seemed to satisfy him and, indeed, weighed on him. "A rich man carries a heavy load up the slope of a hill," the Chinese sage Chuang-tzu once observed. Like most men who prosper by overthrowing others, Machmud could never relax his guard. In any state where property and plunder were so intertwined, possession lacked moral legitimacy and security. Machmud employed numerous spies in his households, who kept secret watch even over Machmud's own sons. When Machmud wanted to pass a verbal order to an officer, he usually sent two men, one to watch the other and vouch that the message and its reply were delivered correctly. The cost of affluence often includes mistrusting other people, who are presumed to be jealous and resentful. "Affluence makes acquisitive types independent from other human beings at the cost of overdependence on material things."

Nor could anything Machmud owned compare with the thrill of riding into Ghazni at the head of a caravan heavy with the enemy's possessions, a string of captured slaves trailing behind. Indeed, long past the time Machmud was fabulously rich, he was riding out to the deserts and mountains of India to pilfer some more. For those who devote themselves to getting rich, it's hard to rest: There is no ceiling.

So it was with Machmud, and so it has always been with some of humankind. Although there have been historical periods of comparatively little affluence, for most of recorded history the world's wealth has been climbing steadily. So far, people have not been content to rest after achieving a certain level of wealth. Most people want more even if they couldn't say exactly why. Fortunately for them, the ways people use and enjoy money have also never stopped increasing.

The first civilization to be wholly transformed by lust for wealth was Athens in the fourth century B.C.E. "The love of wealth wholly absorbs men and never for a moment allows them to think of anything but their private possessions," wrote Plato of the Athenians. But a relative shortage of luxury goods— no his-and-hers helicopters as there are today, for example, or diamond-studded dog collars—may have spurred the Greeks to "invest" in sports, art, philosophy, and science. Even so, the people so revered for their great contributions to civilization also dressed in showy clothes, relied on platoons of slaves, and ate and drank gluttonously.

The Athenians, however, were amateurs at conspicuous consumption compared with the upper class of the Roman republic a few hundred years later, when the phrase "money makes the man" originated. Ancient Rome was "steeped and saturated" in wealth. It was "a milieu which for sheer cupidity and money-madness has seldom, if ever, been equaled."

The Romans traded with China, India, and Arabia for ebony, ivory, drugs, parrots, dancing girls, lions, and gladiators. But they also discovered that money could be used as a tool for making more money—a kind of perpetual-motion machine that had nothing to do with the exchange of real things. The Romans had no word for *business,* but they knew money could be used to speculate, to buy and sell land, to do favors for friends. "Money was young in human experience and wild," wrote H. G. Wells. "Nobody had it under control."

A possibly apocryphal story about the Roman emperor Caligula illustrates the tenor of the times. Caligula is said to have once demanded that his subjects bring him an offering of money, throwing it onto the floor of his palace from outside. When they had all tossed their coins in and departed, Caligula took off his slippers and sloshed through the great heaps of gold. Then he lay down and rolled his whole body in it.

Another account of ancient greed involves the noble but venal Brutus, who made a loan to a Cypriot town at 48 percent interest. When the town council balked at paying back the money, Brutus's agent shut them up in their own town hall until five members starved to death.

Marcus Licinius Crassus, who lived in the first century B.C.E., was the richest man in ancient Rome. As wily a money-maker as any in the next two millennia, Crassus was involved in ventures all over the city. Among his most profitable schemes was his fire-fighting business, in which he trained brigades of slaves to put out the conflagrations that often flared up in Rome's wooden houses crowded shoulder to shoulder. Rome had no public fire department, so Crassus seized the day. When a fire broke out, his five hundred firefighters, equipped with ropes, ladders, and buckets, rushed to the scene and then stood idly around until Crassus bargained with the owner of the burning house or adjoining properties over a price for putting out the flames—or for buying the property itself.

Even in the giddy days of early wealth, before Christianity put its moral clamp on greed, some people were ambivalent about it. They could see that money incited in some people strange, unlikable behavior. "Beware of ambition for wealth," wrote the wealthy Roman statesman Cicero, "for there is nothing so characteristic of narrowness and littleness of soul as the love of riches; and there is nothing more honorable than indifference to money."

Crassus himself found that money couldn't buy him the thing he craved most: the respect of the Roman elite. He vented his frustration on the battlefield, throwing himself into war whenever he could. No man should consider himself rich unless he could feed an army, Crassus avowed. But when he died in battle, he was recognized and punished for his wealth: He was decapitated, and then, so the story goes, molten gold was poured into his mouth. "Thou has thirsted for gold, therefore drink gold," the enemy commander said. Writing in the first century B.C.E., Horace clucked, "People were wont to say that the many virtues of Crassus were darkened by the one vice of avarice." But Horace also advised, "If possible honestly, if not, somehow, make money."

Wealthy Rome became so decadent that Roman senators "lounged in bed till noon and seldom attended sessions. Some of their sons dressed and walked like courtesans, wore frilled robes and women's sandals." Fortunes were spent on interior decoration—walls were plated with gold and dotted with gems. Eating became the chief occupation of upper-class Rome. For dinner there would be sows' udders, boar's heads, fish, ducks, teals, hares, fowls, oyster pastries, songbirds, and sweets. Affluent men and women hung gold jewelry on themselves like Christmas tree ornaments, every finger encircled by several gold rings.

Ancient Rome was living on borrowed time; it was producing almost nothing while consuming practically everything. Wealth in the ancient civilizations came by "gouging and scooping, seizure and force, political advantage or public exploitation. Society had not yet integrated the search for wealth with the production of goods." Indeed, the essential role of production in creating and maintaining wealth had yet to be recognized. To the ancients, and to Machmud of Ghazni, the world's wealth was finite and becoming wealthy was a function not of producing or creating but of taking and using.

Machmud of Ghazni fought his final battle and brought home his last plunder in 1026. The following year he contracted malaria, which became chronic and turned into consumption. As he lay on his deathbed, he asked to have his jewels and gold laid out so he could see them. He died at the age of fifty-nine.

Machmud had never been a gifted administrator, and his empire—a huge agglomeration of different peoples including Indians, Afghans, Turks, Tartars, and Persians—was held together by force of his personality and army. After his death, the vast wealth that he had brought to Ghazni fostered luxury, and the court was weakened by excesses and corruption. Plunderers rarely succeeded in founding dynasties, and Machmud's wealth soon dissipated, as did his fame.

The heyday of chieftains like Machmud, trained to fight and little else, was coming to an end. New war technology reduced the importance of soldiers' physical prowess. With the stabilization of settlements, communities gradually became more peaceful, and, as the twentieth-century economist Thorstein Veblen noted, brute force inevitably gave way to "shrewd practice and chicanery" as the road to riches. For his time, Machmud was the ultimate rich man: fearless, arrogant, and rapacious.

While most of his successors among the very rich wouldn't need to wield a crossbow from the back of an elephant, they shared Machmud's determination to prevail over others in their quests for wealth. The only differences were in how they got it away from others.

TWO

The Raider Who Came to Stay

Genghis Khan (1162–1227)

Before there was money, before there were ships to move goods or even many goods to ship, before there were Internet stocks, precious works of art, ceramic plates, or indoor plumbing, the greatest marker of wealth was control of land. No one in the history of the world controlled more land than the legendary conqueror Genghis Khan.

Since the beginning of human history, land has been the world's greatest resource for the creation of human wealth. Land was and is the source of food, whether it is hunted, fished, or farmed. Even in societies where land has been abundant relative to the population, some people have always tried to seize land from other people; even the earliest humans recognized the superiority of some pieces of property.

Because land can't be transported, however, ownership has always entailed maintaining control of a valuable good that can't be safeguarded with lock and key or a few hundred guards. There were few legal deeds or titles to land in the twelfth century, and none in the territory where Genghis Khan grew up. Land, like plunder, belonged to its possessor, but only until another powerful force took it away. To realize the wealth of conquered land required a military and administrative presence, to protect its borders and tax its inhabitants. While Machmud of Ghazni and other plunderers contented themselves with such portable wealth as jewels, gold, and slaves, Genghis Khan's ambition was nothing less than to own the world. By the time he and his fighting machine stopped their conquests, they ruled almost five million square miles.

Genghis Khan's raids were the last and greatest of the nomadic assaults on developing civilizations in both the East and the West. He and his heirs captured the land now called China, Iran, Iraq, Myanmar, and most of Korea and Russia. Alexander the Great, by comparison, conquered only 2.2 million square miles. A product of central Asia's brutal steppe culture, Genghis Khan learned from an early age that aggression was the key to survival, and survival was a relentless battle against everything and everybody. Once he took possession of land, he imposed a system of tyrannical discipline designed to keep the people meek and obedient.

The by-product of establishing order and common law over ever larger areas is almost inevitably a growth of trade, as merchants from other regions discover safe routes over greater distances. Indeed, Genghis Khan's totalitarianism enriched the world far beyond his realm. To conquer and unify China, Genghis Khan's troops used a collection of caravan routes called the Silk Road, which linked China with the Mediterranean. After gaining control of these passages, he and his heirs restored and protected them and established a system of post stations and hostels. Garrisons of Mongol cavalry were posted at strategic points to assure security. Other major routes through Asia were also substantially improved by the steady horse traffic of the Mongols.

Although their primary motive for improving transportation and communication systems was governing their far-flung subjects from a great distance, the Mongols also actively encouraged international trade. Genghis Khan himself welcomed western missionaries and traders. For several decades, the curtain between east and west lifted, and the intercourse of the world diffused. People's horizons expanded, and their desires were stimulated. The Silk Road played a major role in transferring culture and technology between the two worlds, and its safety allowed the Italian wayfarer Marco Polo to travel from Venice to Beijing, visiting Genghis Khan's grandson Kublai Khan along the way.

Even in modern America, where owning real estate is practically a birthright, land retains its power as a symbol of wealth and status. Most of the very wealthy own multiple homes, at least one surrounded by hundreds of acres of land, for privacy. In earlier centuries, the landed gentry, even if heavily in debt, outclassed any other kind of wealth. Today, that distinction has almost disappeared, but some rich people still like to see their wealth in the form of land. Ted Turner, for example, owns 1.4 million acres of land in the west, and Robert Redford owns 5,500 acres in Utah.

Love of land goes back to the ancient world. About 2350 B.C.E., Sargon of Akkadia imposed such a heavy tax on his citizens that they were driven to borrow at interest rates as high as 800 percent a month. To make their payments, families might sell first their daughters, then their sons; only then would they sell their land. In other parts of the world, land has been considered such a precious commodity that transfer of ownership required a public ceremony. The seller handed some token dirt to the buyer, who placed a token coin in the hand of the seller. Ceremonies of transfer were also performed in medieval Europe, and to record them for posterity young boys who were present had their ears boxed so they wouldn't forget the occasion.

In America, land was at the center of many of the country's greatest fortunes: John Jacob Astor's speculation in nineteenth-century New York and Marshall Field's in Chicago being among the most sensational. Even in a country as enormous as America, land is finite, and land sitting under a booming town or city becomes gold. In twentieth-century America, people came to expect a profit on any sale of real estate; indeed, speculation on

31

land in Los Angeles and Florida early in the century ruined many small-time investors.

In Genghis Khan's time, however, land was not an investment: It was a matter of life and death. Whether planting barley or raising sheep, most people around the world depended on land for food and shelter. Until about 1050, land in Europe was plentiful relative to the population—humans were thin on the ground. Few peasants who worked the land considered it theirs in the modern sense, any more than landlords did. Land was seen as the source of subsistence for a larger group than the individual who owned or cultivated it. On the steppes of Mongolia, where raising herds of sheep, goats, and horses was the main occupation, there was no such thing as property rights. Land, the source of all wealth, could not lightly be consigned to private selfishness.

As nomadic societies gradually turned into agricultural societies, men like Genghis Khan were forced to refine the plunderer's traditional hit-and-run methods. For centuries, food-growing societies had been sitting ducks for nomadic marauders. But as their surpluses increased, sedentary people began pooling money to hire professional security. Defensive armies refined their techniques for fending off nomads, making the cost-benefit ratio of sieges less attractive. Defensive walls became thicker and stronger. As towns grew, they built second and even third sets of walls. Indeed, in Genghis Khan's time, and for centuries afterward, more resources were invested in defensive walls than in all other public works combined. (That many still stand is testament to their solidity. During World War I, a German advance was delayed for a week by the walls of Liege, Belgium.) In Genghis Khan's time, sieges against walled cities might take months rather than days, and even in the best circumstances such assaults were difficult to provision.

Furthermore, a raider's sovereignty endured only as long as the memory of his last raid. In an empire as enormous as Genghis Khan's, battles on one border almost inevitably drew invaders to another. Economically, it made more sense to subjugate a people than to conquer them repeatedly. Over time, raiders became rulers, collecting a steady stream of tax income instead of depending on the jackpot of plunder. Taxes were, after all, the collection of booty made orderly and normal; in return, the taxpayer received protection from rival plunderers. From the taxpayer's point of view, the desirability of substituting certain taxes for uncertain plunder depended on how much he owned and how frequently plundering bands were likely to appear.

As many rulers over the centuries have learned the hard way, the power to tax is also the power to destroy. Some sovereigns, greedy and shortsighted, have taxed their subjects to death, killing the geese that were laying the golden eggs. Taxation is a difficult balancing act between exacting the maximum amount possible while keeping subjects alive long enough to gather another harvest.

Although Genghis Khan's power depended on his soldiers' backing, his trajectory demonstrates that intelligence was becoming more important in wealth accumulation. In Genghis Khan's case, intelligence took the form of collecting, controlling, and strategically disseminating information. Indeed, one reason Genghis Khan was so enthusiastic about open trade was that the merchants who swapped armor, weapons, and clothes for the Mongols' wool, fur, and horses also brought information about other parts of Europe. Genghis Khan's army was relatively modest—despite being described as hordes, they were almost always outnumbered—so as a military leader Genghis Khan was canny and cautious rather than brave or adventurous. His daily routines—bad food, no beds, quick and violent death—may sound more like Machmud of Ghazni than Bill Gates, but Genghis Khan already knew bigger was better and that leverage could turn little to big. That made Genghis Khan more like a nineteenth-century robber baron than a thirteenth-century barbarian.

In Europe, meanwhile, real-estate speculation was becoming one of the chief sources of capital accumulation. In the late Middle Ages, Europe's population began to outgrow its fields and pastures. Although there were efforts to cultivate formerly wild and unsettled areas, some of the superfluous laborers headed for cities, where they became merchants and artisans. All over Europe between 1200 and 1400, cities were founded and enlarged, and rents steadily climbed. Merchants and traders converted cash into land for prestige and security. "The medieval real-estate operator, who bought up property and rented it to artisans and laborers, had nothing to learn from his modern counterpart."

More than 750 years after Genghis Khan's death, his name—an honorific variously translated as "strong ruler," "universal ruler" "world conqueror," "invincible prince," and "rightful ruler," among others—still resonates through world history. People who couldn't say when or where Genghis Khan reigned use his name synonymously with cutthroat terrorism, often in a tone of "horrified romanticism." But Genghis Khan's story is far more complex than his legend might suggest.

Unlike most of history's wealthiest people, Genghis Khan suffered the bite of poverty as a child. Outside his family's tent on the Asian plateau, neighboring tribes regularly attacked one another in an endless quest for more and better grazing land. Chronic warfare meant widespread poverty, anarchy, and insecurity. In their poorest days, his family survived by fishing, hunting small game, and picking wild onions and berries. Meanwhile, moral decline among the steppes tribes became so acute that robbery and sexual offenses were regarded as emblems of masculinity. The kidnapping of marriageable women from other tribes occurred constantly.

The one advantage of the plateau tribes' internecine warfare was that it created a reservoir of superb fighters, virtuosos of the art of ambushing. If they could be persuaded to stop attacking one another and unite against bigger game, they would be a force for the world to reckon with. Over the course of several years, Genghis Khan began assembling his empire by vanquishing nearby tribes, such as the Tartars and Merkits, whose captured soldiers were expected to join his army. They did, often with gusto, and a few of them even rose through the ranks to become officers. Genghis Khan's soldiers were mostly unpaid except for their plunder and were expected to supply their own food, horses, and weapons. Yet if ordered to do so, a Mongol man would, on the spur of the moment, pack up his tent and ride a thousand miles to fight for his leader.

Genghis Khan's empire was a classic command society. Wars were fought, taxes were collected, and public works were built by order. The enforcement mechanism was coercion, not tradition, and society's economic and political goals as a whole were those of its leader. There was no leisure class; everyone was expected to work. Genghis Khan's subjects wouldn't have known what to make of the words *individualism* or *freedom*; they, like most peasantry of the era, almost totally lacked egos. They probably owned their own tools and weapons, but their lands and animals were held collectively. Their anonymity was close to absolute, which also made them largely indifferent to privacy.

Genghis Khan himself also lived relatively humbly. "I have only one coat," he once wrote to a Taoist sage. "I eat the same food and am dressed in the same tatters as my humble herdsmen." Genghis Khan had a splendid tent, thousands of slaves, and a personal guard of some ten thousand soldiers that was one of the most feared military units in history. But he didn't have gold umbrellas or jeweled scepters. Owning precious objects wasn't important to him. "[He] will take from the dress he wears and give it away; he will dismount the horse he rides and will give it away." Writing about the Chinese in a way also applicable to Genghis Khan, a historian noted, "A cult of poverty haunted many Chinese thinkers and poets; it was an expression of solidarity with the poor, a lingering of an old spirit of brotherhood."

Far more important than money to Genghis Khan was the absolute loyalty of people to their superiors. He believed fidelity to the chain of command was so essential that he executed any soldier or servant who betrayed his master, even if the master was Genghis Khan's own enemy. "Is it possible," Genghis Khan once asked rhetorically, "to leave alive men who have betrayed their own lord? Let them be put to death, with their sons and grandsons."

A rigid hierarchy defined each person's status from birth. People's parentage determined their futures far more than what they knew or could do. Revenge was a reasonable excuse for murder, and no insult was ever forgotten. Genghis Khan once offered one of his daughters in marriage to a prince. "Your daughter looks like a frog and a tortoise," the prince said to Genghis Khan, and that was the last thing the prince ever said.

Even as a child, only one person ever frightened Genghis Khan, and that was his mother. "When I have caused my mother to be wrathful, I tremble before her," he once confessed. But anyone else who irked him felt terror flowing the other way. Genghis Khan didn't call himself the "flail," "punishment," or "scourge" of God for nothing.

Like all Mongol children, Genghis (then named Temuchin) learned to ride at an early age—boys were typically tied onto a horse when they were three years old. A year or two later, a Mongol boy would get his first bow and arrow; from then on, he was expected to spend his days on horseback, practicing archery by shooting at birds.

When the future Genghis Khan was nine years old, his father, a minor chieftain of noble descent, decided to seek a bride for him. Riding back from the future bride's home, Genghis Khan's father stopped to get some water from members of an enemy tribe, who recognized him and poisoned his drink. He died shortly after arriving home. Temuchin, his mother, and his six siblings were forced out of their tribe to live in privation.

Little more is known of his boyhood; if he talked about it, no one wrote it down. Genghis Khan himself could neither read nor write, nor did he ever learn any language but his native Mongolian. But historians agree that when Genghis Khan was fourteen, he ambushed and murdered his half brother. Some say Genghis Khan was angry because the older boy was withholding his rightful share of fish and game. Others suggest Genghis Khan was nipping future competition in the bud. Whatever the reason, Genghis Khan's adolescent fratricide became part of his terrible legend. His mother was initially furious (how he must have trembled!) but eventually forgave him, and no one else cared. Murder was common on the steppes, and a murderer was not a criminal, even, or especially, if the victim was his brother.

In the winter, Genghis Khan's homeland was dark and frigid; its summers were so hot the soil dried up and vegetation withered. There were no trees and little rainfall at any time of year. The climate of the land demanded regular migration, and the natives needed thousands of acres to feed their herds. Because they moved so much, the nomads developed no technologies, manufactured no goods, and learned little mining. They had no architecture, not even a concept of settled towns. "The nomad was not simply an uncivilized man," wrote H. G. Wells, "he was a man specialized and specializing along his own line."

By race, the Mongols were kin to the Japanese, Chinese, and other Asians, but their bodies were stocky and tough, with big trunks and short limbs. Their features were probably nothing at all like the Mongoloid type named centuries later. Their clothes were made of sheepskin or the skins of dogs, and their diet consisted of mice, foxes, dead animals they found along the trail, or the afterbirths of mares. If hungry enough, they would eat their own dogs or cats. They bought so few manufactured goods that iron spurs were considered to be signs of a wealthy man. A religious taboo forbade them from washing their clothes in the spring and summer, and they had to wear them until they were rags.

By all accounts, the Mongols were dirty, loudmouthed, ferocious, foul smelling, and argumentative. The Mongols "were always noted for their extreme improvidence and laziness," wrote one historian, "for the whole life of the pastoral nomad, with its ignorance of any kind of continuous labor, predisposes him in that direction."

Yet the standard of living for any peasant in the world at the time was not so much higher. There's a story of a medieval peasant in a European city who walked through a lane of perfume shops and fainted at the smell. He could be revived only by someone holding a shovel of excrement under his nose. In winter, peasants often shared their living quarters with their livestock. The very wealthy, who could afford footmen, wiped their noses on the footmen's sleeves. Prostitutes had the cleanest bodies in Europe, but a young girl's life expectancy was only twenty-four.

The same conditions that made the Mongols' existence so grueling also turned them into fighters who would rather die than capitulate. "Here there was no margin for error. The sparseness of the land and the ferocity of the climate worked on man and horse and equipment to remove all that was not essential, to produce a warrior as cruel and free from ceremonialism as he was self-sufficient."

The Mongols' other great military advantage was their equestrian agility—it was said that their nation was the backs of their horses. The muscular Mongol pony was spry, immune to cold, and unsurpassed for stamina. Although bad tempered, it wouldn't stray if left untied. It could wheel and charge with great nimbleness—"just like a dog," marveled Marco Polo. Mongols ate, drank, and slept on their horses. A Mongol, alone and desperate in the desert, might open one of his horse's veins and drink its blood. But then he would bind up the wound, because his horse was a Mongol's most prized possession.

Fortunately for Genghis Khan, in his time wealth couldn't necessarily buy battlefield victory, since the Mongols made their own equipment. Their short, strong compound bow, crafted of horn, sinew, and wood, made the horse archer the most lethal weapon system known to man, unmatched for range, penetration, and rate of fire. The Mongol cavalry carried two bows, three quivers full of arrows, an ax, and ropes for hauling. They wore light chest protectors and carried shields but were otherwise largely exposed to their enemies.

By contrast, the armies of Europe and Russia at this period, equally dependent on horses, had become glorified head bashers. A European horseman wore so much armor and carried such massive weapons that his equipment alone weighed more than one hundred pounds, an enormous additional burden for a horse's back. The Mongol soldier, outfitted in lighter gear, was more mobile and so could try more intricate maneuvers. Even after the invention of firearms, it was years before the crude, inaccurate, and slow-loading handgun could match the compound bow in range or penetration. It wasn't until the sixteenth century that artillery significantly reduced the effectiveness of a cavalry charge.

Mongol horse archers represented speed and surprise at a time when everything else moved slowly. "Mongol and horse became a single, centaur-like entity." Because they used stirrups, the archers could fire arrows or use the lasso at full gallop, often while lying flat on their backs along the horse's spine. The steppes were ideally suited to cavalry charges, unlike Europe's thick forests or towering mountains. With no such natural barriers, China, the favorite target for the "Northern Horse-barbarians," as the Chinese called the Mongols, built the Great Wall.

In 1206, in an unprecedented display of unity, the clans and tribes "who dwell in tents of felt" gathered to proclaim Genghis Khan, then forty-four years old, the king of kings and ruler of the steppes. Although every Mongol chieftain had the title of khan (prince), Genghis was known as khaghan (khan of khans). His career was advanced further by a much-revered shaman of the time, who announced that Everlasting Blue Sky, the Mongols' pantheistic divinity, had endorsed Genghis Khan. The king of kings quickly agreed: "The Sky has ordered me to govern all peoples," he said. From then on, his duty was clear: to lead his army to victory so they could all enjoy beautiful captives, good horses, and plentiful hunting grounds.

"Man's greatest good fortune," Genghis Khan once said, "is to chase and defeat his enemy, seize his total possessions, leave his married women weeping and wailing, ride his gelding, use the bodies of his women as a nightshirt and support, gazing upon and kissing their rosy breasts, sucking their lips which are as sweet as the berries of their breasts."

Tall, with a muscular build, broad brow, and long beard, Genghis needed his enemies' women as a desert needs sand. He had, standing in readiness, four chief wives, numerous junior wives, and countless concubines and servant girls. Indeed, if Genghis had a weakness for any self-indulgence besides conquering, it was sex. Even on his military campaigns, he always traveled with "seventeen or eighteen beautiful damsels." On one march, he is said to have been followed by twelve thousand virgins selected for him from prisoners. Genghis Khan occasionally gave one of his wives or concubines to a particularly deserving general.

Soon after becoming supreme khan, Genghis Khan ordered a literate adviser to scribe an elaborate legal code for the Mongols, which became the empire's institutional foundation. Although no complete copy of the code survives, medieval scholars have reconstructed it. Among other things, it prescribed the death penalty for desertion, theft, and, in the case of a merchant, being declared bankrupt three times. Since adultery could lead to feuds among soldiers, it, too, was outlawed. For obvious reasons, nomads didn't like to keep prisoners, so execution was the most common punishment, as it was for both male and female adulterers. The code dealt with matters as trivial as the proper number of times a month a man could get drunk (three) and as broad as a commandment to treat people of different religions with respect. It decreed death to anyone who urinated in ashes or water. Applied with ruthless severity, the legal code made the Mongols "the most obedient people in the world toward their chiefs," wrote John of Plano Carpini, a Franciscan monk who visited the Mongol empire in 1246. "If [the khan] ordered a son to kill his father, he would have to obey."

But at the same time, Genghis Khan's take-no-prisoners management was transforming the lawless society of the plateau into one in which no one needed to guard their tents or carts. Petty wars and surprise raids on neighbors disappeared. Genghis Khan's military establishment demanded their attention. All males between the ages of fifteen and seventy were conscripted into the army; there was no such thing as a civilian. Men were expected to keep their weapons and horses prepared for war, their bowstrings tight and their quivers full of arrows. Women assumed far-reaching responsibility for their families' possessions. Nomad women and children were already accustomed to a migratory life in tents, so the army could advance or retreat with little dislocation of society. Nevertheless, constant warfare took its toll on the Mongol economy: The perpetual campaigns diverted the tribesmen from raising animals, and battlefield deaths decimated the population.

For the conquered territories, of course, the economic impact of Genghis Khan's invasions could be catastrophic. Prolonged military campaigns interfered with spring planting and autumn harvesting. In cities, houses were razed, libraries burned, irrigation systems destroyed. For the peasants who didn't cross paths with the Mongols directly, however, life wasn't so different under their new leaders. The settled Chinese population sowed, reaped, and traded during this change of masters without lending its weight to either side.

Historians often remind us not to judge people of five hundred or one thousand years ago by the moral standards of the present. Threats of nuclear conflagration notwithstanding, the world today is a far more secure place than it was early in the second millennium. The most dramatic difference is in the value of a single human life. When men such as Machmud of Ghazni and Genghis Khan ruled the world, the possibility of dying suddenly and brutally was an ordinary though no less dreaded event. In war, especially "holy wars," killing was noble and virtuous. "Like other great conquerors of all times and nations," wrote a historian, "[Genghis Khan] was capable, if he considered it advantageous or useful to his ends, of massacring the civil population of a city." But even in his greatest military campaigns, his "cruelty or his bloodthirstiness never surpassed that which was displayed by contemporary soldiers of other nations."

Genghis Khan didn't, for example, build a tower out of two thousand live men and then cover it with brick and mortar, as a later Asian conqueror, Tamerlane, once did. He didn't enjoy watching enemy prisoners have pegs driven into their ears—another favorite entertainment of some victorious warriors. Historians doubt Genghis Khan really ordered the slitting open of women's stomachs, in case they had swallowed pearls before their capture. And if he once executed enemy prisoners by boiling them, it was only because this would prevent their spirits from returning to exact revenge.

But Genghis Khan had no respect for the sedentary people whose settlements he attacked. To him, people who worked on their knees were less valuable than horses. In this contempt for the simple laborer, he resembled other preindustrial elites, whose heroes were military, religious, or royal. Those who had to work with their hands were despised on principle. Wrote Cicero in the first century B.C.E., "The toil of a hired worker . . . is unworthy of a free man and is sordid in character." But if Genghis Khan could get a cut of what the menials produced, they became worth slightly more alive than dead.

Genghis Khan's army was both a means of production and a complex business organization. Its size mandated a vertical chain of command, and Genghis Khan was one of the first military leaders to divide his army—100,000 men—into units of 10,000, 1,000, 100, and 10. He organized and disciplined his troops to follow orders with blind and absolute obedience, to strike fearlessly, and to fight to the death. Giving orders to one of his officers, Genghis Khan said, "If anyone disobeys you, if he is a man I know personally, bring him to be tried by myself; if he is not, execute him on the spot."

In battle, if one or more of a group of ten ran away, all ten would be put to death. If a group of ten ran away, the entire one hundred would be put to death. Before one battle, Genghis Khan told his soldiers, "Who, having retreated, does not resume the advance, will be beheaded." If one of his commanders made a mistake, "no matter how great a distance—even from sundown to sunrise—separates him from the Khan, the latter will send a single rider to administer the appropriate punishment: if his head is forfeit, the messenger will behead him."

Military training was based on the Mongols' well-honed hunting skills. In one military exercise, thousands of mounted soldiers formed an immense ring. At a signal, they slowly started moving inward, maintaining their precise position regardless of the terrain, while herding every animal before them without using weapons. A hunter who allowed an animal to escape the ring was punished. When a huge accumulation of game had been driven into the center, Genghis Khan would give the sign, and the soldiers would attack the agitated tigers, boars, and bears. Soldiers demonstrated their courage by approaching the beasts with only a dagger—or even bare-handed.

In other parts of the world, peasants didn't have to prove their strength and dedication by wrestling tigers. Otherwise their bosses weren't much gentler than Genghis Khan. Feudal serfs in Europe were usually not allowed to choose their crops, marry without permission, leave the land they farmed, or bake their bread anywhere but in their lords' ovens. In fact, the only significant difference between Genghis Khan's subjects and Europe's feudal serfs was that one group paid taxes and the other paid rent. The essence of the feudal system, wrote R. H. Tawney, was "exploitation in its most naked and shameless form." In most peasant societies, the ruling class further exploited the workers by forcing them to build roads, defensive walls, and irrigation systems and to move grain that had been collected as taxes. Called corvée, the free labor thus extracted by the state built the pyramids, as well as China's Great Wall.

The Mongol nation was relatively small compared to its neighboring states—the Mongols' total population was some two million, compared with one hundred million Chinese. To balance the scales, Genghis Khan developed an arsenal of psychological deceptions. Coming against numerically superior forces, for example, the Mongols might send troops behind their own lines to stir up dust with branches tied to their horses' tails. This sometimes fooled the enemy into thinking reinforcements were on the way. Other times, Mongol soldiers, each of whom brought several horses on their campaigns, put wives, children, and even dummies on reserve mounts to make the army look bigger. At night, each soldier lit five fires. "They are not trustworthy and no nation can rely on their word," wrote John of Plano Carpini. "They are full of deceit in all their deeds and assurances."

Genghis Khan understood instinctively what is now an article of faith: Information, power, and wealth are three strands of a single braid. The scope of the world was enlarging in Genghis Khan's lifetime, as civilizations encountered one another in trade and war. The more cultures interacted, the more the world's growing population exchanged knowledge and resources. Given the earth's prodigious natural resources, this led to the creation of more wealth.

Of course, Genghis Khan didn't have electricity, let alone

e-mail. His communication system was based on arrow riders, tough soldiers who bandaged their heads and bodies against the bruises caused by riding full gallop for days. In battle, his armies used signal flags to communicate by day, blazing arrows by night. Genghis Khan established a network of spies, paying travelers to be his eyes and ears. Mongol armies were rarely surprised.

Messages between the illiterate Genghis Khan and his officers were conveyed orally by men with good memories. To make the messages memorable, they were often composed in verse. The Yam, or pony post, initiated by Genghis Khan and perfected by his son was an even more sophisticated system. At regular stages along imperial highways—roughly every twenty-five or thirty miles apart—stations were built to provide riders with supplies and fresh horses, although riders sometimes changed horses at full gallop. The riders wore bells or blew horns to alert the stations of their approach so a horse would be saddled and ready. The service, free to ambassadors and to Genghis Khan's messengers, made it possible to travel as far as 250 miles in a single day.

Armed with advance information and propaganda, the Mongol troops attacked cities that should have been impregnable. In 1217, the Mongols laid siege to a Chinese city, Chung Tu, the walls of which were eighteen miles around, forty feet high, and fortified with nine hundred towers and three moats. Chung Tu's stubborn inhabitants remained behind their ramparts, eventually lapsing into cannibalism when supplies ran out. Surrendering at last, their worst fears were realized: Mongol soldiers burned down the city and put thousands of civilians to the sword. A visiting ambassador reported that when the Mongol troops were finished, the bones of the slaughtered formed mountains, and the streets were greasy with human fat.

Slaughter on a grand scale was an efficient way to demoralize future enemies. The Mongols excelled at this technique, although Emperor Basil II, in the eleventh-century Byzantine

Empire, conceived perhaps the grisliest medium for a message: He ordered the blinding of 99 of every 100 Bulgarian captives, leaving each hundredth man with one eye to lead the others back home. Genghis Khan's widespread reputation as a monster was effective; in 1218, Koreans who had heard stories of the Mongols' attacks in China submitted without a fight, agreeing to make substantial payments of tribute.

Genghis Khan used war to repopulate and revitalize his empire. He and his officers sorted through captives as if they were used clothes. Lucky prisoners were allowed to assimilate into Mongol society. Indeed, highly civilized and able Chinese were absorbed by the Mongol government, as were well-educated people from conquered Turkistan and Persia. Genghis Khan also singled out artists, artisans, laborers, and warriors who would switch allegiance to him. As in nomads' herding methods, the flock of humans was thinned to foster better harvests in the future. Old, young, sick, or defiant captives might be killed or, unluckier still, be put out in front of Mongol troops when they stormed the next city.

Genghis Khan allowed his subjects and captives one freedom: They could worship in whatever faith they liked. The Mongols' own religion was a form of shamanism—worship of human links to divinity—but unlike zealots such as Machmud of Ghazni, the Mongols allowed other people to worship other gods. Their tolerance was motivated not so much by high-mindedness as by a suspicion that any religion might turn out to be right, so why not have them all on the same khan's side?

Other economies around the world were producing surpluses, and the range and scale of trade was slowly expanding. Most things that were bought and sold were small "luxury" items—candles, tableware, figurines, jewelry—that could be transported less expensively than bulky items such as food or fuel. Large fairs across Europe brought people together to exchange goods, and the earliest bills of trade were created. Pockets of wealth were created by agricultural surplus. But wealth was never secure—a devastating natural disaster or plague could strike without warning.

An economy like the Mongols', however, in which nothing was produced and no surplus created, demanded continual geographic expansion. So did Genghis Khan's army: If his soldiers' aggression wasn't directed against a common enemy, they would start squabbling with one another. Genghis Khan knew the best way to unite his troops was a full-scale assault on China.

To the steppe horsemen, China was a rich quarry to be plundered at regular intervals. Although the Chinese economy was almost exclusively agrarian, the people also produced beautiful luxuries—silk, lacquerware, porcelain, paper, and ornaments of gold, silver, or copper, to name a few. But most of China's inhabitants intensively cultivated small plots of land, usually no more than two or three acres, in what is sometimes referred to as "garden agriculture." There was not much storage of food or carryover of crops, so, as in Europe, a serious crop failure was a catastrophe.

For much of China's early history, several regional governments ruled the land instead of one central government. This factionalism left China disorganized against its neighbors' aggression and lacking a superior army. The Chinese were sparsely settled in most parts of the country and tended to take a defensive posture against raiders. They might try to buy peace by offering tributes in the form of iron, grain, fruit, slaves, gold, and luxuries. But if all else failed, they hunkered down in their walled settlements and hoped the people they called "the uncooked" would go away. Genghis Khan, unlike their former attackers, didn't go away. His raid turned into an occupation.

Stories of Genghis Khan's battlefield prowess are so fantastic they defy credulity. One legend tells of the time Genghis Khan advised the commander of a fortified town that if he and his men received a tribute of one thousand cats and ten thousand swallows, they would leave without a fight. The payment was made.

(Imagine the logistics.) Then Genghis Khan's soldiers tied tufts of wool to the tails of the cats and birds, lit them, and let the animals go. As the birds and cats returned to their homes in town, smoke began to rise, and soon the whole settlement was on fire.

The Mongols' typical strategy on an open battlefield was to send ahead a corps of suicide troops, which charged straight at the enemy line. As they got within range, they suddenly broke ranks, turned, and fled. "The sight of the Mongols in flight was a temptation that most enemy commanders could not resist." The enemy often gave chase—right into the lap of the rest of the Mongol army. The Mongols shot light arrows from a distance, followed by heavier, armor-piercing arrows as they approached. Finally, they pulled out swords to slash their foes to death.

Coming to a fortress, the Mongol army surrounded it, sometimes even building a fence around it. If there was a moat, they filled it in, carrying rocks and dirt by the handful. They attacked with catapults, battering rams, and arrows all night so the inhabitants couldn't sleep, lobbing pots of flaming naphtha and huge rocks into the fortresses. One witness said the Mongols took the fat of the dead, melted it, and threw it on the houses, making fires that were practically inextinguishable.

If even this didn't work, and a river was nearby, they would dam or divert it to submerge the fort. Should this fail, they would dig under the walls and try to enter underground. And if even this wasn't effective, they might build their own fortress facing the enemy's and try to entice the inhabitants with false promises of leniency. In very mountainous areas, where forts were often built on heights that no assault could reach, a blockade was put in place until starvation had done its work. In one instance, a Mongol army besieged a fort for twelve years. "Walls are as strong as the courage of their defenders," Genghis Khan once said.

Their efforts were supported by detachments of forcibly recruited Chinese engineers, who taught them how to use explosives. They packed these into rockets and fired them into enemy lines, causing great confusion. To grasp the scale of these on-slaughts, consider that for one siege, Genghis Khan's army set up 3,000 catapults, brought 2,500 loads of rock from the mountains, erected 700 machines for throwing firebombs, and built 4,000 ladders for scaling the walls.

Genghis Khan didn't live to see the day when a column of mounted Mongol soldiers no longer struck fear into the hearts of anyone who saw it coming. He became ill while subjugating the Tanguts. On his deathbed, he told two of his sons, "My descendants will wear gold, they will eat the choicest meats, they will ride the finest horses, they will hold in their arms the most beautiful women, and they will forget to whom they owe it all." He died in August 1227 at the age of sixty-five.

His body was placed in a cart, and the long trip home began. He had ordered that his death remain a secret, so anyone unlucky enough to encounter the cortege was executed "to serve their master in the other world." For his official funeral, forty "moon-faced virgins of sunny disposition and unblemished character," bedecked with jewels and rich ornaments, were sacrificed to the spirit of Genghis Khan.

Genghis Khan's heirs went on to conquer more territory, most notably Russia, but the empire Genghis Khan assembled at such a high cost in human life lasted only forty years beyond his death. After two or three generations, the comforts of civilization sapped the hardihood of Mongol garrisons. In 1294, when Kublai Khan died, the Mongol empire was split into four parts, and the four chiefs quarreled it into ruins.

If Genghis Khan could see the world now, he would likely be astonished by how the relationship between humans and land has evolved since his era. The land he controlled was his, but it wasn't his if someone else could force him off it. The idea that land could be controlled by people who neither defended nor occupied it would have struck him as not only unnatural but nonsensical. Acquiring land today is a matter of exchanging paper;

it is assumed that virtually every piece of land in America is owned by someone and that the only "free" land is that owned by the government.

In the modern world, the concept of land as private property is taken for granted. The idea that land should belong to those who need or use it disappeared in America in the nineteenth century and now seems quaintly idealistic. But, taking a longer view, the modern attitude toward land ownership seems illogical. As William Blackstone wrote, "We think it enough that our title [to land] is derived from the grant of the former proprietor, by descent from our ancestors, or by the last will and testament of the dying owner; not caring to reflect . . . that there is no foundation in nature or in natural law why a set of words on parchment should convey the dominion of land; why the son should have the right to exclude his fellow creatures from a determinate spot of ground because his father had done so before him."

In 2000, land can be bought and sold, rented and leased, borrowed and loaned. But it can almost never be conquered. Even Genghis Khan and his powerful army would find it impossible to become wealthy by seizing other people's land. Land remains a route to wealth, as well as an object of desire. Now, however, it must be acquired by a different kind of force than the cavalry of Genghis Khan.

THREE

The Man in the Middle

Mansa Musa (d. 1332)

People have always been travelers, riding beasts of burden from settlement to settlement, carrying bits and pieces of other worlds to barter for local surplus. Despite nearly impassable routes and constant attacks by bandits, these streams of trade flowed ever farther and wider. People did not rest until every corner of the world had been found. More societies were creating surpluses, and the wealthy were becoming aware of the variety of goods available from distant lands. It became possible to make a fortune by taking a cut of the purchase and sale of goods in exchange for moving them. When Christopher Columbus bumped into the Americas in 1492, he was hoping to get rich by trade, not to become a celebrated but penniless explorer.

At the same time, another age-old force in human commerce was growing more potent: the lust for gold. Although humans had always worshiped gold, the rising population and prosperity of Europe in the Middle Ages was pushing demand to new heights. Europe's wealthy could buy land, furs, fine cloth, and gemstones, but gold was the ultimate possession: It held its value whether shaped as a goblet, figurine, or necklace.

The more people wanted gold, the less there seemed to be. In the fourteenth and fifteenth centuries, Europe's primary sources were mines in Saxony, the Tirol, and Hungary, but primitive technology limited production. Moreover, the ancient trade imbalance between east and west sucked gold eastward: Asians didn't want European goods, so they demanded metal in exchange for theirs. The scarcity of gold created a vicious circle: Once people acquired gold, they tended to hang on to it, thereby taking it out of circulation. Precious metal came to be in such short supply that one European church melted down its crucifix to use as money.

Gold, like trade, inspired adventurers to head off in perilous new directions. The risks of such expeditions were high, but so were the rewards. In the fourteenth century, a clever trader could become wealthy, and so could a clever gold dealer. A trader in gold could become one of the richest people in the world.

Mansa Musa was such a trader. Although the empire he ruled was as large and about as cultured as western Europe, Mansa Musa is less well known today than many inferior leaders of the western world. In Mansa Musa's West African realm, peace reigned, people could travel and trade freely and securely, and churches and schools were built. When he died in 1332, Mansa Musa left behind an empire "as remarkable for its size as for its wealth."

Western history may slight Mansa Musa, whose name means "the ruler Moses," because he was African; most early history of the African interior comes from a handful of Arabic authors whose only previous encounters with blacks had been with slaves. "I have not described the country of the African blacks," wrote one medieval traveler, "because naturally loving wisdom, ingenuity, religion, justice and regular government, how could I notice such people as these."

Alternatively, Mansa Musa may be history's stepchild because he was only an opportunist, a man lucky enough to have been born at the right time and place. Where some lucky children today use their money to bet on horses, play extreme sports, or just to live securely and comfortably, however, Mansa Musa used his to become a middleman. Neither inventor nor producer,

Mansa Musa realized that merely by bringing buyers and sellers together and ensuring that their transactions took place in a controlled fashion, a person could become very, very wealthy.

The job of middleman in early global trade demanded a generalist who could juggle organization, diplomacy, finance, and management. Mansa Musa, whose African land was remote from most of the world, had to bridge the vast cultural and linguistic gulfs between African, Arab, and European traders. Even wider was the geographic gulf: the Sahara, one of the world's most inhospitable settings for human commerce. In order to trade salt, slaves, and, most important, gold, Europeans had to survive a three-month journey across the sandy plains of hell. Along the way, traders were prey not only to death by thirst but also to every conniver and marauder from the Sudan to Timbuktu. A good middleman made sure traders arrived at their destination with lives and wares intact. That guardianship was worth a fortune.

Reconstructing the life of a fourteenth-century African is a hard lesson in history's limits. Little material has survived human dereliction and natural disaster, and what has endured is often tainted by ancient prejudice. Texts have been translated at least once and sometimes several times. The stories tend to be what modern nonfiction writers might call "too good to check." The world's storytellers were often literally singing for their supper, and a little hyperbole, even outright invention, was good for another helping. To the extent there is historical truth, it is lost in the case of Mansa Musa. So here is what the storytellers say.

Mansa Musa was a child of good fortune, at least by the standards of his time: His grandfather was the twelfth of twelve brothers in a ruling clan; every one of his eleven siblings had been murdered by an enemy tribe. As sole survivor, Mansa Musa's grandfather inherited a kingdom of farmers, ranchers, and a handful of traders, which gradually expanded into the empire of Mali. Grandfather and, eventually, his son, Mansa Musa's father, also exploited the gold trade. Using profits from its early trickles through their territory to expand their army, they rode farther and farther afield to subdue—and then tax—farmers and shepherds, further enlarging their kingdom.

Their land was on the fertile floodplains of the Niger River in the western reach of Africa. Mali lay roughly halfway between the continent's north coast, where European and Arab traders had established a beachhead, and the Sudan, more than one thousand miles to the south, where mines produced nuggets of gold as big as pineapples. It was said there was a nugget of gold so big that the king could tether his horse to it. The Sudanese gold fields were technically part of Mali, but nobody ruled the clannish miners, who simply decreased production if annoyed.

No greater catastrophe could befall the world's leaders and traders than a reduction in their gold supply. Europeans were desperate for gold; without it they couldn't buy luxuries from the east, support big armies, and pay the tax collector. All societies appreciated gold, but in Europe it was a passion and, for some, a growing addiction. The wealthy wanted gold plate on their walls, gold thread in their upholstery, and gold rings around their fingers.

In the Sudan, a land rich in gold, the miners were poor in something every human needs to survive: salt. In the modern world, salt is cheap and plentiful. But in the centuries before salt could be easily transported, people who lived in a region without its own salt deposits struggled to survive. In the sultry Sudan, where the miners sweated prodigiously, salt was as valuable as gold. The exchange rate between the two substances was sometimes one to one. In some regions of Africa, cubes of salt served as both food and money. In fact, the modern English word *salary* is derived from the Latin word *sal*, meaning salt. Only those who have seen the phenomenon understand how intensely people crave salt if they are denied an adequate supply.

However strongly the Europeans wanted gold and the miners wanted salt and other goods, the two sides were geographically incompatible. Africa presented extraordinary obstacles—both desert and jungle—to long-distance travelers; the least painful way for the two parties to meet was in the middle, at an entrepôt. The Europeans landed on Africa's north coast and trekked south across the Sahara, while the gold traders or their agents paddled north on the Niger. The two met in Mali, in one of several cities, the best known of which was Timbuktu. Nothing was manufactured or grown in Timbuktu, a barren settlement of sun-baked brick buildings, yet for several decades it was the largest, most prosperous transit market in the African interior. It was known as the City of Gold.

Mali and its small cities had traditionally been ruled by "big man" redistributors: Generous and benevolent to their subjects, the big men held monopolies over the weapons to maintain law and order and wage military campaigns. In 1307, Mansa Musa became Mali's big man. Soon he became Africa's biggest middleman.

From their earliest visits to Africa, Europeans realized they would need help from native brokers. The geography of the entire continent made it difficult to penetrate from any direction but north. Shallow coastal waters prevented ships from approaching the shore in many areas, and rivers to the interior were protected by furious rapids and waterfalls. The Europeans had been honing their naval skills for centuries but found them worthless around most of Africa. Meanwhile, African diseases such as malaria and yellow fever, which were particularly lethal to Europeans, provided other effective deterrents to outsiders.

For a brief time, Europeans tried to negotiate for gold themselves rather than allow others to share the prize, but they found the miners eccentric and unpredictable. The Sudanese preferred what was called silent trading or dumb barter. Traders would arrive at a shore on the Senegal River, spread their goods on the ground, and retire from sight. The natives then emerged, inspected the wares, laid down as much gold as they thought the material was worth, and went back in hiding. If the merchants were satisfied when they returned, they took the gold and retreated, beating their drums to signal the close of the deal. If not, the hide-and-seek continued.

Although dumb barter got the job done, it was costly, not to mention inefficient. The Europeans made numerous attempts to locate the gold mines. But the Sudanese were aware that people would kill and die for gold, and they kept their sources mysterious, saying gold grew in the ground like carrots or was brought from under the earth by ants. The traders once tried to find the gold by kidnapping a native. He died without disclosing anything, and the miners refused to resume trade for three years, dropping their embargo only when they became desperate for salt.

Western traders eventually resigned themselves to employing middlemen. Initially, they tried to train their own, shipping some Africans back to Europe to learn their language. But before long, a new class of native brokers was born in Mali and elsewhere in Africa. They were agents, outfitters, and caravan chiefs whose job was to alleviate the three greatest obstacles to trading across cultures: security, currency, and transportation.

In the fourteenth-century world of factionalism and weak governments, security was a terrible encumbrance on long-distance trade. Although no reliable data from the early centuries of the millennium survive, some historians believe protection costs were greater than the cost of transport itself. When rich merchants carried valuable stock through a poor region, they were an attractive and often irresistible temptation. Robin Hood's gang has been glorified for stealing from the rich to give to the poor, but in less romantic terms they were poor woodsmen stealing the goods of itinerant merchants on their way to market. Merchants had to choose between hiring armed guards or bribing highwaymen to allow them safe passage.

The normal threat of robbery rose sharply if the substance being shipped was gold. Gold not only was the most valuable and liquid commodity in the world, it was relatively easy to carry and conceal. In Mali, theft of gold was discouraged by Mansa Musa's army of one hundred thousand soldiers, most of whom were armored cavalry. Stealing was punishable by death or enslavement. "Neither traveler nor inhabitant has anything to fear from robbers or men of violence," wrote the adventurer Ibn Battuta about Mali, describing a rare state of affairs in the mid-fourteenth century.

Trade was also stymied by the currency problem, which continued to hinder economic expansion for centuries after Mansa Musa's time. Although increasing amounts of currency were flowing around the world, there were no generally accepted monetary standards. Indeed, cowrie shells were still being used as currency in many places, including Mali. Coins were heavy, difficult to transport, and easily stolen. In 1338, it took a shipment of coins three weeks to travel four hundred miles from the north of France to the south. Along the way, the shipment faced the possibility of being lost, attacked by robbers, or embezzled by its carriers. Much trade still involved barter, which resulted in negotiations over how many logs equaled a teapot or how many piles of salt bought a young slave.

The greatest hindrance to trade in the fourteenth century was the physical difficulty of moving things from place to place. In most places in the world, including Africa, there were few roads or bridges, practically no four-wheeled wagons, and virtually nowhere to stop for supplies or shelter. On some routes through mountains or jungles, there was only one possible vehicle for moving goods: the top of a human head. Even in Europe, where Romans had built roads centuries earlier, transport came to a virtual standstill in winter. Heavily traveled routes became quagmires, and there were reports of people drowning in potholes and horses sinking up to their bellies in mud. Some bridges were only as wide as a single pack animal—most often mules, which carried up to 350 pounds of cargo. The Romans had built their roads for marching soldiers, not merchants' wagons. Meanwhile, many of the paving stones had been pilfered for building material. Maintenance of what remained was haphazard at best. Furthermore, over a journey of a few hundred miles, a traveling merchant might pass through several different sovereignties, each with different rules, weights, and money.

Water travel was more efficient but also more expensive. Ferry operators would hold up passengers midstream, and travelers were sometimes charged simply to wade across a stream. Without good navigational equipment, ships had to hug the coasts, despite increasing their chances of meeting pirates. (Indeed, the North African countries of Morocco, Algiers, Tunis, and Tripoli became known as the pirate states.) Tolls on rivers and highways were ubiquitous and crippling: At the end of the fifteenth century, there were sixty-four tolls on the Rhine and seventy-seven on one stretch of the Danube alone, most controlled by local princes. The high cost of transport discouraged trade in bulky, low-margin goods such as grain or simple textiles.

Crossing the Sahara desert in the Middle Ages was as treacherous as crossing an ocean. The Sahara's three million square miles, part mountains and part sand, are so barren that desperate travelers have been known to kill their camels for the water in the beasts' stomachs. Sahara days are hot (a temperature of 136 degrees Fahrenheit was once recorded in the shade), but nights are cold, and ferocious winds sweep away trails and landmarks and bury people and animals alive. Deep-cut water channels are subject to flash flooding. The Sahara does contain a few dozen main oases, and some forms of life have always existed there. In fact, some Saharan animals can survive for months, even years, without water, and a few do not drink at all from birth to death. Human travelers might have to wait eight days for an opportunity to refill their waterskins. Even as late as 1805, five centuries after Mansa Musa, a shortage of water killed 2,000 people and 1,800 camels on a caravan to Timbuktu.

One of the earliest ways traders moved goods through large,

hostile territory was by caravan. Known as "men on a string" economic organizations, caravans were as crucial to the opening of Africa as railroads were to the American West. Caravans were seen most commonly in the Middle East, but they also crossed Europe. Merchants banded together and, armed with swords or bows, they surrounded their packhorses, which were loaded with sacks, cases, and casks. Private travelers and pilgrims sometimes joined the caravans for protection—and occasionally merchants tried to pass themselves off as pilgrims to avoid paying tolls.

In the eighteenth and nineteenth centuries, large trading caravans crossed the American West from Missouri to Santa Fe and then south to Mexico. In the 1820s, a party crossing the Great Plains ran out of water and cut off their mules' ears, hoping to assuage their thirst with blood.

The complexity of organizing a caravan going any distance, let alone across 1,500 miles of desert, is staggering. The journey lasted between seventy and ninety days, and the caravan might link together as many as twelve thousand camels. On average, each merchant was accompanied by four camels—three for merchandise and one for food and water. Although as pack animals camels were both swifter and less thirsty than horses, oxen, and donkeys, the speed of a caravan of tired, loaded camels might be two miles an hour. Crossing the Sahara was dangerous regardless of how well prepared a caravan was: "Any trip across the wasteland was like a new throw of the dice."

As long-distance trade continued to expand and flourish, the profession of adventurer-merchant began to split into two specialties. Some merchants no longer wanted to accompany their goods everywhere, particularly on hazardous journeys through the bush. They were willing to pay others to bring the goods to them. With the help of middlemen like Mansa Musa, traders were able to regulate and calculate their transit and protection costs for the first time. Trade was becoming more manageable, which could only promote more of it.

*　　*　　*

The Catalan Atlas, produced in 1375, illustrated Mansa Musa's realm with the picture of a large-featured black king holding a scepter in one hand and a baseball-size nugget of gold in the other. The caption reads, "This negro lord is called Musa Mali, Lord of the Negroes of Guinea. So abundant is the gold found in his country that he is the richest and most noble king in all the land." The picture and legend bring to mind Jonathan Swift's lines, "So geographers, in Afric maps / With savage pictures fill their gaps / And o'er unhabitable downs / Place elephants for want of towns."

In the few surviving accounts of his life, Mansa Musa is stereotyped as a pious but somewhat buffoonish newly rich tribal chieftain. In fact, western cartographers attempting to draw him were stymied by the gap between their conception of monarchy and the scantily clad Mansa Musa, so they dressed him up and added a long beard.

Mansa Musa did have certain comical aspects, at least from a modern perspective. He expected his subjects to demonstrate humility in his presence by kneeling down and beating their breasts. Thereafter, they were supposed to greet everything he said with murmurs of wonder and approval. In his presence, people were allowed to do only what was asked of them, like grownups playing Mother-may-I. An unexpected sneeze was an impertinence punishable by death, and if Mansa Musa himself sneezed, all those around him were supposed to pound their chests. Mansa Musa communicated through a spokesman, who repeated his words in a loud voice. After his subjects spoke to their ruler, they poured dust or ashes on their heads to prove their unworthiness. Like his ancestors, Mansa Musa would not allow anyone to see him eat, lest they mistake him for human.

Mansa Musa's absolute control over his people was critical to his success as a global middleman. Like most sovereignties of the time, Mali was neither tight-knit nor cohesive, and its subject provinces demanded careful supervision. To accomplish that, Mansa Musa required a top-notch army. He kept his officers loyal by rewarding them richly with slaves, gold, horses, even villages. Successful cavalry commanders were rewarded with ever wider trousers; there was even a prize called the National Honor of the Trousers. Wider trousers marked higher distinction, but the king's trousers were always the widest.

Land around trade routes always increased in value simply because merchants passing through could be coerced into leaving a portion of their goods behind. Some landowners charged itinerant merchants merely for the privilege of being left alone. Others demanded right of first refusal for any merchandise carried through their territory. In Europe, some towns demanded "staple rights" for allowing ships to pass through their domain: Ships had to unload and put their goods up for sale, sometimes for as long as two weeks. If no one bought the goods, the traders were free to reload and go on.

Mansa Musa had the most valuable franchise of all in the fourteenth century: a cut of all the gold that changed hands in his empire. It's said that Mansa Musa reserved all nuggets for himself, allowing the traders to keep the dust. The gold trade flourished, trading systems improved, and the flow of gold from Africa became so extensive that at one time two thirds of the metal for European mints was coming from the Sudan. Yet no amount of gold could satiate the world's boundless appetite, which is why Mansa Musa's fortune never stopped growing.

Gold, the oldest precious metal known to humankind, is mentioned many times in the Old Testament. It is an almost mystical substance with an allure that seems disproportionate to its real value. In 1860, John Ruskin wrote, "Lately in a wreck of a California ship, one of the passengers fastened a belt about him with two hundred pounds of gold in it, with which he was found afterwards at the bottom. Now, as he was sinking—had he the gold? Or had the gold him?" Centuries earlier, young Etruscan girls accumulated dowries of gold by working as prostitutes before marrying, valuing the gold more than their chastity.

Throughout history, gold has been associated with power, success, and health. In the Middle Ages, food was sometimes gilded or served in gold or silver sauces because these metals were thought to strengthen the heart. Gold dissolved in acid— "potable gold"—was a remedy for virtually any illness. Objects and people of authentic virtue came to be considered "as good as gold," and *golden goose, Golden Fleece, golden mean, golden rule,* and *golden opportunity* are expressions of superlative quality. Gold coins have always been a standard against which other money has been measured. Mankind "consented to put an imaginary value on gold and silver, by reason of their durableness, scarcity and not being liable to be counterfeited," wrote John Locke.

Besides its beauty and indestructibility, gold is also useful for industrial purposes. It doesn't rust or corrode, which means it can lie at the bottom of an ocean for centuries without losing its luster. Although it's heavy, it's so pliable that artists can pound it into delicate shapes. It can be flattened into razor-thin sheets or microscopic wire, and it melts easily, so it can be recycled.

The quest for gold not only motivated people to explore land and water but also stimulated generations of amateur chemists to try to synthesize it from base metals. The one who discovered the philosophers' stone would not only turn metal to gold but also restore youth to the aged. Some alchemists were better at flimflam than science—they might coat a piece of gold with quicksilver and then, adding a chemical that washed the quicksilver off, purport to show the cheap metal transformed into gold. Others, at least the ones who survived their sometimes hazardous experiments, helped to develop the science of chemistry, along the way discovering alcohol and mineral acids.

Alchemy represented a transitional stage between magic and science, between the irrational and the rational.

But an obsession with gold has driven people to mischievous and criminal acts, too. Samuel Johnson called it "the last corruption of degenerate man," and Shakespeare described gold as "poison to men's souls." A young Roman emperor loved to throw gold and gems among milling cattle and watch people get trampled to death as they rushed to pick it up. Another of his favorite games was tossing gold coins from the top of a basilica and watching the citizens below kill one another to get it.

Two centuries after Mansa Musa's era, the gold of South America began to pour into Spain, and the Spaniards demonstrated that the craving for gold is truly unlimited.

> They applied gold to window frames, mirrors and wall hangings. They used gold leaf on doors and balustrades. They covered their coaches with gold, and they applied it to the wooden frames of chairs, sofas, beds, chest and cabinets. They dripped it on their hunting guns and knives. They made dishes and snuffboxes from it. They covered their books with gold filigree and added golden hinges for their bindings. They embroidered golden threads into their clothing and upholstery, as well as tablecloths, draperies and tapestries.

A few centuries later, the discovery of gold at Sutter's Mill, California, in 1848 triggered one of the greatest population movements in history. Tens of thousands of people descended on California in usually futile efforts to get rich quick. In 1845, some 700 Americans lived in California; three years later, the territory's population had exploded to 14,000, and by 1849 there were 100,000 people prospecting for gold in California.

It was Mansa Musa's gold that won him a modest place in world history—specifically, the gold he spread along his path as he and some sixty thousand companions traveled to Mecca in 1325. The Koran requires every Muslim to make a pilgrimage to Mecca at least once in his lifetime. As Mansa Musa prepared to go, he consulted an elder for the right day to set off on his journey. He was told he should wait for a Saturday that fell on the twelfth of the month. The first such opportunity came nine months later.

Mansa Musa took with him thousands of porters, five hundred servants, and what one writer of the time called "a pleasantly memorable supply of gold"—some eighty to one hundred camel loads of it. Mansa Musa's senior wife came along, too, with her own retinue of five hundred maids and slaves. In Cairo, Mansa Musa "flooded [the city] with his benefactions." Indeed, he left so much gold there that twelve years later, the market was still depressed. The Egyptians were naturally predisposed to a man so generous, but Mansa Musa's pale complexion, variously described as red or yellow, may also have smoothed the way. "There was no trace of the traditional contempt of sophisticated orientals for the negro," wrote a British historian in the early twentieth century. "He was, in fact, the first to penetrate the iron curtain of colour prejudice which shut off the negro from the civilized world."

Gold was the most lucrative business for Europeans and Arabs in fourteenth-century Africa, but they soon found another commodity to buy and sell at enormous profits: slaves. Like gold, slaves were in demand by the wealthy in many parts of the world and were bought to serve in armies, palaces, mines, and fields. Although slavery was not introduced to Africa by outsiders—indeed, some African tribes had their own slaves—the constant demand from the Middle East and, eventually, the New World turned slaves into one of Africa's principal exports.

From its earliest known appearance, some ten thousand years ago, slavery has been a symbol of economic surplus. It's unlikely that hunter-gatherers would have had enough food to add another mouth to the family in exchange for more leisure time. But as soon as people settled down and began distinguishing themselves by what they owned, land and slaves became the two most common tokens of affluence. Nothing conferred status like a palace full of slaves consuming food, space, and clothing while producing nothing but relaxation for their masters. In fact, among some North American Indian tribes slaves were considered so expendable that they were occasionally killed in potlatches in a display of wealth or to demonstrate contempt for property. The traffic in slaves was one of people's earliest forms of commerce and almost certainly the greatest human cost ever exacted by surplus wealth.

Until the past few centuries, however, slavery was an accepted and ordinary part of human life, and a slave was given no more thought than a tool, wagon, or horse. Humans believed inequality to be divinely allotted—some people were rich, some poor, and some slaves. The abstract idea of freedom meant little in societies ruled by fear. All human life was cheap in Mansa Musa's time, and the value of slaves could be measured in grains of salt.

Like other luxury items, slaves in the early centuries were generally the property of kings, chiefs, or armies. But as the world's wealth grew, slaves gradually became affordable to more people. In Rome, some slaves even owned slaves, and in an aboriginal hill district in China, a slave could buy a half share in his own wife. For the first millennium, the primary source of slaves was war—slavery disposed of enemy troops and civilians while rewarding victorious soldiers. Some historians have suggested that slavery was a blessing for the vanquished: Before slavery, defeat meant torture and death for the men. War captives who became slaves were white, black, brown, and yellow; there was little connection between race and slavery. But for masters, slaves could present high supervision costs and, with no incentive to be otherwise, slaves could be rough on the master's tools and animals.

In Athens, the cradle of democracy, slavery was so common that some 25 percent of the city's population were chattel slaves. Aristotle himself compared slaves with wild beasts, claiming both groups were better off under some control. Greek masters were allowed to execute their slaves with impunity. In Rome, as much as a third of the population was enslaved (some three million people altogether), and some masters were said to own thousands of slaves. In 319 C.E., the emperor Constantine laid down a code on the treatment of slaves. Although masters could beat a slave to death to chastise him, they were not allowed to "pour poison into him" or have "his sides torn apart by the claws of wild beasts."

The wealthy also used slaves as entertainment, in Rome watching trained slaves—gladiators—fight to the death. Given no choice but to train or to die, slaves learned to fight; those who didn't were prodded with hot irons. Romans gathered in arenas to watch gladiators clash with other men or animals (including lions that also came from Africa), sometimes for days at a time. The sight of the slaves' blood and suffering was said to teach the audience contempt for pain and death.

In Europe, slavery, like all society, was largely agricultural during the first millennium. By the Middle Ages in England and elsewhere in Europe, agricultural slavery had gradually turned into serfdom, and serfs became the lowest rung of the social ladder—"a miserable race which owns nothing," a bishop wrote in 1025. Still, the serf did not live in a complete state of submission, as the slave did. If serfs had no more food than they had had as slaves, they did have a little more personal freedom.

Among the Sudanese, whose slaves were often traded through Mansa Musa's kingdom, the trade was robust and without stigma. The custom of stealing children to sell them into slavery was widespread. There was a constant demand for eunuchs, who were entrusted with guarding the harems and palaces of eastern potentates (although Venice was known as the "greatest eunuch factory in Europe"). The Sudanese typically gelded the most robust of the boys caught in slave raids, and in some tribes castration was used to punish crimes. Only about 10 percent of the victims survived the crude operation. Those who lived to try crossing the Sahara had a second chance at death. The track was marked by the bones and shackles of those who had succumbed to thirst or exhaustion along the way.

In Europe, the roughly three hundred years between Machmud of Ghazni and Mansa Musa were a relatively stable period compared with the previous five hundred years, which had been marked by repeated barbaric invasions. With a budding confidence in the future, people began having more children, and the population started growing slowly but steadily. Between 1000 and 1300, Europe's population doubled and in some parts may even have tripled. Agricultural productivity increased, too, as did the volume of small industry and commerce. Most of the wealthy were still members of the ruling class, but new avenues to riches were beginning to open.

In Europe's Middle Ages, luxury consumption revolved around spices, the first objects of foreign trade and the most important ones for several centuries. Spice was to the fourteenth century what copper was to the fifteenth century, tea to the nineteenth century, and oil to the twentieth. Merchant captains roved the seas looking for spices the way modern wildcatters hunt for petroleum. Spices were relatively easy to ship and commanded exorbitant prices, reflecting the long route they took to Europe. By one account, Indian spices passed through twelve pairs of hands before they got to the consumer. Yet the wealthy developed an insatiable appetite for spicy cuisine; indeed, food became little more than a vehicle for spices and condiments. In addition, spice not only preserved food but also camouflaged the taste of rot if food had spoiled. As late as the 1530s, a Portuguese king commissioned a series of expensive tapestries from a Flemish firm, stipulating that they would be paid for in pepper.

For most Europeans who lived in this period, however, the struggle to stay fed and warm consumed all their time and energy. Parts of Europe, hitherto settled sparsely, became overcrowded, as people "balled" together in towns, where they might find a church, a small school, a tavern, and some merchants. But the water in towns was often unsafe, and people hadn't yet made the connection between sanitation and disease. Even if they lived in small villages, most people worked the land for survival, making them pawns of the weather, especially rain. "The margin of subsistence became paper-thin. Medieval Europe had come to the edge of disaster."

The first great disaster of the fourteenth century was the famine of 1314–1317, consecutive crop failures that reduced people to eating the leaves from trees and the flesh of recently executed criminals. Gangs of starving people roamed the countryside searching for food. People in jails weren't fed at all.

Then came a plague unlike any seen before or since. Arriving in 1348, the Black Death took the lives of some twenty-five million people, more than a third of Europe's population, in its steady march from Italy to England. Afterward Europe was a profoundly changed land, its economics thrown into disarray. Some historians believe the Black Death marked the end of the medieval period and the beginning of the modern world. For the wealthy, money bought little advantage against the plague. Yet the epidemic redistributed Europe's wealth, creating a new class of rich.

The Black Death came to Europe from Asia via flea-ridden rats. The plague was first noticed on the shores of the Black Sea during an attack by a Mongol khan of the Golden Horde—one of Genghis Khan's successors. When the epidemic broke out among the Mongol army, the khan undertook what one historian calls the first recorded incident of biological warfare: Using catapults, the dead were hurled into town, with the hope that the stricken inhabitants would either die or stop resisting. The exercise failed as a military strategy, but some fleas and rats were infected, and they later boarded ships heading west.

The success of the European trading system in distributing goods served to distribute plague as well. As it spread across the continent, the "grisly fury" killed between 60 percent and 75 percent of those it touched (the pneumonic plague claimed 100 percent of its victims), and it extinguished kings and peasants indiscriminately. "The sexton and the physician were cast into the same deep and wide grave," wrote a survivor. "The testator and his heirs and executors were hurled together from the same cart into the same hole together."

The one advantage to wealth was the ability to flee to a place far from the population centers, the poor hygiene of which worsened the contagion. The medical profession offered little help even to those who could afford their advice: Some thought the plague was caused by corrupt vapors that entered the skin through open pores, and they forbade bathing and lovemaking. They recommended that people stay at home with their doors and windows closed. They also sprinkled perfumed water in rooms and on clothes. "Flee in haste and take much physic," one doctor advised.

Some people woke up from the plague to find that as the only survivors of their families, they were suddenly wealthy. Since land, tools, farm animals, and precious metals didn't vanish in the same proportion as the people who wanted them, the rich got richer, and so did the poor. The plague opened the doors of opportunity for many: Clerks became merchants, former workmen became employers and contractors, farm laborers became gentlemen farmers. With fewer mouths to feed, farmers could abandon their least productive land and concentrate on better soil.

Those who had been wealthy before the plague awoke to a

different set of consequences: With a significantly smaller labor pool, real wages rose some 50 percent while the value of land declined. Big landowners were forced to pay more for labor while receiving less in rent. The new system of rents and wages favored greater peasant independence. Before the plague, people had volunteered for such demeaning and backbreaking work as being galley oarsmen. After the plague, only slaves or convicts would do that job.

The psychological effects of the plague on survivors also changed the way people thought about the future. If survival was a crapshoot, why not live for the moment? Luxuries became necessities, and there was a wild orgy of expenditure on furs, silks, and jewels. The old nobility was superseded by the nouveau riche. Manners decayed, and the wealthy began to dress in garish costumes and flashy jewels. But their celebration was short-lived. Once the excess had been absorbed, Europe became much poorer as production virtually ceased for months.

In every society where there were opportunities to become rich by luck or skill and not just birth, there emerged a class of people variously labeled as parvenus, upstarts, or pretenders. They confounded the established social order by jumping class, and, if judged on appearance alone, were indistinguishable from those who had been born to wealth. This was unacceptable to a world that depended on social discipline for its stability. Hence, the odd practice of passing sumptuary laws developed, which often had the secondary benefit of reducing foreign imports.

Sumptuary laws had existed at least since the Roman Empire. In 215 B.C.E., Rome enacted the *lex oppia*, which prohibited, among other things, women from wearing more than half an ounce of gold on their persons at a time. But sumptuary laws also had a long tradition of being widely disregarded. "In nine cases out of ten, if one looks a person over from head to toe, one will find that he is breaking the law," wrote an official of the thirteenth-century Song dynasty in China.

Henry III of France was a fervent believer in sumptuary laws, and in 1583 he decreed that only princes could wear pearls or bands of gold embroidery on their garments. Although French kings didn't have to justify their imperial whims, Henry did: He claimed that God was angry because he couldn't recognize a person's quality from his clothes.

Yet most sumptuary laws were intended to ensure that wealth alone didn't give a person the right to act wealthy. So, for example, in 1362 Edward III of England proclaimed that merchants could wear the same clothes as a knight, but only if they were five times richer. Yeomen and below were forbidden to wear buttons. Henry VIII's detailed laws forbade Englishwomen of any rank below countess to wear gold, silver, or purple cloth, with one exception: "Viscountesses may wear it in their kirtles."

By the time Mansa Musa died in 1332, other routes through Africa were becoming more popular, other tribes more powerful. But the trade Mansa Musa had helped to promote continued. Trade offered opportunities for getting rich that didn't require high birth, standing armies, or big muscles. Overseas trade was a great practical school of entrepreneurship—not only for those who, like ships' captains, the supercargo, and the merchants, actually went overseas, but also for the merchants, insurance agents, shipbuilders, reexporters, victuallers, and other employees of companies that took part. Furthermore, with wider markets, people could get rich on an ever greater scale.

If the early part of the second millennium was the age of the plunderer and lord, the middle part was to be the age of the entrepreneur. Increasing surpluses of wealth made it possible for some people to save or borrow the capital to invest in a shipment of goods, commission new vehicles, launch expeditions, and find new markets of buyers and sellers. Financing armies on the scale needed in the more populated and technologically sophisticated world was becoming prohibitively expensive for all but kings. It was easier and cheaper to become wealthy by trading than by fighting. Mansa Musa was a link between thief and trader, between plunderer and packman. Before long, the traders were to run the thieves out of business. For the first time ever, the big man would no longer have to be big.

FOUR

Ungodly Rich

Pope Alexander VI (1431–1503)

The power to tax has created many large fortunes in history, and one of the greatest was that amassed by the canny and corrupt pope, Alexander VI. To take small amounts of money from many people, Alexander used an authority even more effective than brute force: divine imperative. As leader of the Roman Catholic Church, the largest financial institution of the time, Alexander had at his disposal a huge pool of wealth to skim. Furthermore, he was resolutely unashamed of his cupidity; he was God's representative on earth—it would be disrespectful not to live magnificently. "Alexander VI showed, more than any other pope that ever was, to what extent the Pontiff could make his will prevail, using both money and force to this end," wrote Niccolò Machiavelli in his treatise on statecraft, *The Prince.*

Alexander VI and his epoch of daggers and poison now seem too grotesque to be true, but Alexander was as real as Billy Graham and the Dalai Lama. Alexander simply lived at a time when wealth could buy lucrative offices for friends and grisly assassinations of enemies. Using the wealth he appropriated during his thirty years as a cardinal, Alexander at last succeeded in buying the most powerful position in the world. No one expected moral rectitude from the leaders of the church. A high-ranking official in the administration of Calixtus III, who became pope in 1455, had sold a bull that gave permission to a French count to have sex with his sister.

Fifteenth-century Europe, especially in commercially precocious Italy, was giddy with prosperity and indifferent to laws and rules. Emerging from the wreckage of the Black Death, Europe's population and affluence had begun to rise again. Advances in human knowledge quickened the pulse of trade around the world. There were better roads and maps; larger, more seaworthy ships; and sturdier wagons. Improved agricultural techniques provided the surplus that allowed more artisans, merchants, and traders to gather in cities. Subsistence remained the standard of living for most people, but now they might have a few copper pennies in the bottoms of their shoes. Small cottage industries were already growing to the point that they required division of labor. Everywhere, there was more to buy and more money to buy it with.

For the rich, the world was a novelty shop, a dazzling exhibition of luxury goods from distant and exotic lands. They could buy ermine-lined robes and silver fireplace hoods, candied capers and unicorn horns. Wealthy people living close to one another in cities were mindful of competitive display and would pay large sums for particularly rare and unusual goods. They might want water-lily ointment, trotting donkeys, or anything else from axes to zithers. "To be 'magnificent' was to be someone with the means to acquire all those coveted possessions which expanding trade made available, someone who proclaimed that purchasing power by the public ostentation of his or her apparel and furnishings."

While most of the wealthy were enjoying the new money economy, the world's richest institution—the church—was caught in a terrible predicament. Ever since Saint Peter, the church had been preaching the virtues of poverty and humility. Yet throughout the Middle Ages, each successive pope lived more like a prince. While gouging peasants for their tithes, popes and cardinals collected precious cameos and threw extravagant parties. The church was no longer a spiritual society; it had become a money machine, collecting and spending like a drunken lord. "The church was coming to resemble a business which, secure from competition, ploughs its profits into directors' salaries and leaves its sales force slack or despairing." Even some meek and illiterate peasants of fifteenth-century Europe were wondering if something was rotten in Rome.

Actually, many things were. Rome had become a sinkhole of corruption where, Dante wrote, "Christ was sold everyday." Syphilis ravaged all classes of society. Prostitution flourished under the tolerant eye of the papacy, which collected taxes from the city's distinguished courtesans. An earlier pope's illegitimate son scandalized the city by being "a crapulous debauchee of the very worst sort," and one cardinal was said to have died "of excess" at the age of twenty-eight. There was an undercurrent of violence at all levels of society. Convicted criminals were mutilated and butchered publicly. Fear of the night was universal; night was the devil's day. All men of means, including ecclesiastics, carried weapons—daggers, usually—when venturing out. There was little that couldn't be bought.

The clergy were supposed to be celibate, and they were forbidden to marry, but many lived openly with mistresses. The stigma of illegitimacy faded as many clerics spawned children. Alexander himself attended orgies, had several mistresses, including one who was a third his age, and sired as many as nine illegitimate children. One daughter was Lucrezia Borgia, whom Alexander pimped to advance his political career. Only once in his life, when his eldest son was brutally murdered, did Alexander seem to have a crisis of conscience. Otherwise, he was a man without shame.

The Roman Catholic Church controlled a piece of more people's money than any organization in history. Subjects from across Europe, even Iceland and Greenland, paid taxes to the papal treasury, beginning with a tithe (tenth) of a man's annual income. Local church officials saw to it that every household paid its share. Ecclesiastics at every level—of whom there were tens of thousands—were taxed at even higher rates: They sent the papacy half their first year's income and at least a tenth every year thereafter. Often, there were additional assessments, such as for the Crusades.

In addition to this enormous influx of cash, the papacy also held vast stores of precious items that had been given to the church for safekeeping by owners who never returned from wars or pilgrimages. In other cases, troubled souls on their deathbeds turned to the church for last-minute "fire insurance" against purgatory by bequeathing money or property to the church. Since the clergy were the only people who could read and write in the Middle Ages, they conveniently ended up drafting most wills.

The papal treasury also collected revenue from customs, tolls, salt monopolies, mines, grain-export licenses, and dues on the seasonal moving of livestock herds from hills to pasture. It's estimated that by 1250, the church owned three fifths of all arable land in England and a third of the land in Germany, much of it effectively withdrawn from commerce. The papacy owned an alum mine—alum was used for making both cloth and leather—and forbade Christians to buy the substance elsewhere. By 1480, alum profits made up a third of the church's secular revenue. Afloat in wealth, the church had begun to worship it.

In the early Middle Ages, popes started to outspend their extensive revenues. The palace of the popes in the French town of Avignon, where the papacy had resided for most of the fourteenth century, had a prison, an arsenal, a butchering room, and the so-called tower of latrines—a two-story-high lavatory attesting to the vast staff in residence. A German chronicler noted that prelates' hands, "loaded with costly rings, are placed proudly on their thighs. They preen themselves on the finest horses and are followed by a numerous train of domestics in splendid liveries. They build themselves fine palaces, where, amid sumptuous entertainments, they give themselves up to a life of orgy."

After decades of such lavish spending, the church went into debt, and debt became a useful method for financing even greater extravagances. But debt needs servicing, and to do that Alexander transformed the church into a commodities market, where spiritual positions and favors were sold to the highest bidder. With his money, Alexander bought an enormous palace and decorated it with red satin furniture, gold brocade, silver vases, and massive tapestries. Affording a spectacle was a way of ruling. "It did not occur to them that their role of serving God could be fulfilled without ostentation. They had but one economic attitude: to spend for the glory of God."

This couldn't have been more contrary to the original spirit of Christianity, which held that private property, by definition, was stolen property because a person couldn't have more except at someone else's expense. True believers didn't mind the conditions of this world—"sufficient livelihood" was the goal. The peasants' job was to be worthy of the next world. Avarice was one of the seven deadly sins, in the same category as laziness, jealousy, and adultery. Wealth beyond one's needs belonged by moral right to God's poor. "No man can serve two masters," warned Matthew in the New Testament, "for either he will hate the one and love the other, or else he will stand by the one and despise the other. You cannot serve God and Mammon." By Alexander's time, the church seemed to have repudiated Matthew's dictum. It had become not just the keeper of Europe's wealth but also its greatest champion.

Since 380, when Christianity had become the official religion of the Roman Empire, the pope and the church effectively ruled many parts of people's lives. The church's court administered all legal matters involving oaths and vows, so it controlled wills, matrimony, charitable bequests, and contracts. The pope "can deprive anyone of his right, as it pleases him . . . whatever pleases him has the force of law," wrote a fourteenth-century Franciscan. The church also monitored people's behavior—and learned their secrets—by mandating confession of even venial sins.

The church's authority came partly from its power to excommunicate, which damned a heretic to hell while meanwhile removing him or her from any association with other Christians. No Christian was allowed even to talk to the excommunicant, under threat themselves of excommunication. As reward for ungrudging submission to the church's authority, however, ordinary people might go to heaven. Given the hardship and despair of most people's lives during the Middle Ages, that was a potent appeal.

The church also earned its subjects' devotion by giving some of the funds it collected to people in need. The church's monasteries dispensed food to the poor and lodging to travelers; its hospitals cared for the sick and destitute. Monks copied and preserved manuscripts, keeping Greek and Latin alive, and the Vatican underwrote art, architecture, and music. Most important, the church gave the West a moral code and legal system crossing all local political boundaries. During the bleakest centuries of the Middle Ages, the church was the stoutest barrier between humanity and savagery.

But by the time Alexander acquired the papal tiara in 1492, the church's grip on its people was showing signs of weakening. With most of the barbarians tamed or dead, state governments were waking from a long slumber and exerting their own authorities. Nationality was becoming a more important element of a person's identity. People were taking pilgrimages, going to war, and otherwise moving across greater expanses of the world. Buying, selling, and talking to one another, traders from East and West couldn't help but feel a new sense of cultural openness.

These changes came slowly and subtly, and the church at first didn't notice them and then tried to ignore them. Over the centuries, the church had created so many layers of bureaucracy that its leaders were blind to life outside their walls. As the church folded in on itself, its officials began to view their subjects less as lost lambs than as animals to be shorn. The comforting institution of the early Middle Ages gave way to a forbidding panel of prosecutors and financiers. Church and state competed for the same subjects' taxes, and often for the same reason: to bankroll wars in the name of territorial expansion. By spending money on luxuries and wars, people established "worth" in the political arena.

To compete with Italy's princes, the pope needed to look and act like a prince, and so did his underlings. Alexander once scolded a friar who had been appointed archbishop but continued to live ascetically, "A becoming regard for each one's rank in life is praiseworthy and pleasing to God. Try to act and conduct yourself exteriorly, in conformity to the loftiness of your station." Wearing one's status is an age-old custom of the wealthy, but in earlier centuries such display was essential to being taken seriously. A person dressed simply or unfashionably was vulnerable to rumors of financial insolvency.

In the five centuries since his death, Alexander has been the subject of the usual conflicting interpretations: He was a scoundrel, a saint, a charlatan, a Samaritan. Like some other odd historical characters—Richard III or Robin Hood, for example—Alexander makes historians irritatingly argumentative. If they generally agree about little, they agree on virtually nothing about Alexander.

Fortunately for the historical record, though not for Alexander's reputation, a witness to many of his activities faithfully recorded the details of court life in a personal diary. The diarist, Johannes Burchard, was master of ceremonies for the papal court from 1483 until 1506. Although most of the diary was written with decorous formality, Burchard told some naughty tales. At a dinner hosted by Alexander's son, Cesare Borgia, chestnuts were strewn around the floor, and fifty naked prostitutes crawled on their hands and knees to retrieve them. The pope was "present to watch," Burchard wrote. Historians refer to this occasion as the Feast of the Fifty or the Ballet of the Chestnuts. Another time, some passing mares were pulled into a Vatican courtyard where stallions stood waiting. Equine coupling was encouraged while the pope and his daughter "watched with loud laughter and much pleasure," noted Burchard.

The papal administration was rife with secret alliances and nepotism, leaving almost no dissenting voices in the inner circle. By the time priests and bishops became cardinals and popes, "they were usually oldish men, habituated to a politic struggle for immediate ends and no longer capable of world-wide views. They wanted to see the power of the church, which was their own power, dominating men."

To Alexander, of course, nepotism was as natural as genuflecting. It was, after all, his uncle's vision of a family dynasty that transformed the bright, genial Spanish boy named Rodrigo into Pope Alexander VI.

Born in 1431 into the Spanish branch of the large Borgia clan, Rodrigo de Borja y Doms, as he was then called, might have lived and died in obscurity if not for his uncle Alfonso. When Rodrigo was twenty-four, Alfonso was crowned Pope Calixtus III. Calixtus, then seventy-seven, was sickly and senile, which made him an appealing choice among the cardinals' warring factions: Competitors hoped for a quick rematch. At the time his uncle received the papal crown, Rodrigo was studying law in Bologna. He squeezed a five-year program into sixteen months, collected his doctorate, and was appointed to the prestigious, lifelong job of cardinal. A year later, Rodrigo assumed the second most powerful position in the church—the vice chancellorship—putting him in charge of collecting taxes and distributing favors.

Calixtus lived three more years, just enough time to fill dozens of church offices with Borgia family, friends, and hangers-on. At the pope's death, Rome erupted in chaos, as it typically did between popes, but this riot was particularly fervent. Angry mobs of Romans hunted down Spaniards and pillaged their homes. In the midst of the unrest, Rodrigo Borgia and his immediate family fled Rome in disguise, accompanied by an armed escort of some five hundred soldiers. When the new pope, Pius II, was enthroned some weeks later, however, Rodrigo rode back into town, still in possession of his red hat.

Even in that era of moral laxity, Rodrigo's youthful high jinks were notorious. He couldn't keep his hands off women, and women couldn't keep their hands off him. As his tutor wrote, Rodrigo was "handsome; with a most cheerful countenance and genial bearing. He is gifted with a honeyed and choice eloquence. Beautiful women are attracted to love him and are excited by him . . . more powerfully than iron is attracted by a magnet." Another historian commented dryly, "His vigorous character was notorious." On his family flag, a red bull grazed on a gold field.

At the age of twenty-eight, Rodrigo and another cardinal attended a party in Siena that was so bacchanalian that Rodrigo's boss, Pius II, heard about it and dashed off an angry letter. Pius had been told there was "dancing of a dissolute character," and "not one of the entitlements of love was withheld." Scolding Rodrigo for his "frivolity," Pius closed by saying Rodrigo had made himself a laughingstock in the church.

The persuasive Rodrigo responded quickly, claiming that he was the victim of malicious gossip. He promised to stay out of trouble in the future. Pius, who had a soft spot in his heart for young, silver-tongued Rodrigo, forgave him. Rodrigo quickly forgot his promise. As Machiavelli wrote in *The Prince*, "Alexander VI . . . never had another thought except to deceive men, and he always found fresh material to work on. Never was there a man more convincing in his assertions, who sealed his promises with more solemn oaths, and who observed them less."

*　　*　　*

If the church is seen as a corporation, the members of the college of cardinals are its board of directors. Throughout the fourteenth century, cardinals were appointed—by the pope—increasingly for their wealth and connections, not their piety. By Alexander's era, cardinals didn't even have to be ordained priests, and many had never even delivered a sermon. Few let sacred vows impinge on their pleasure. Renaissance cardinals "hunted, gambled, gave sumptuous banquets and entertainments, joined in all the rollicking merriment of the carnival-tide, and allowed themselves the utmost license in morals," wrote a nineteenth-century Catholic historian.

Cardinals and other church officials made their money by supervising regions of the papal empire, which entailed the right to take a cut of the revenue collected in that region. Each level of the church hierarchy took some of the collection and passed the rest to the next higher level. Because so many of the clergy were honest, enormous sums of money made it all the way to Rome.

An inventory of the belongings of the fifteenth-century cardinal Francesco Gonzaga illustrates the level of wealth attainable by high church officials. Cardinal Gonzaga's collection included five hundred gems, intaglios, and cameos; sumptuous clothing; goblets decorated with nymphs; gold tableware; and opulent tapestries. His belongings "bestowed upon him a reputation for splendor which contributed to the esteem in which he was held in Rome."

Rodrigo Borgia, too, dressed in expensive robes, rode fine horses, and collected rare books. On the hunt, he galloped across country, "cloaked and booted, with spirited steeds and a superb hunting pack." He loved to play cards. And he bragged that he had so many sacks of gold coins that he could fill the Sistine Chapel with them. "His lavishness was hard to distinguish from extravagance," conceded one historian. In 1457, scarlet was adopted as the official color of the cardinals' robes. "The visible expense of the cloth worn by the cardinals . . . created an effect of power and opulence."

Yet for all Rodrigo's extravagance and authority, he still didn't have the prize he most coveted: the papacy. As one pope after another died, Rodrigo suffered the agony of seeing other cardinals enthroned, each the result of political machinations so complicated that no one understood them all.

When Rodrigo was fifty-three years old, Pope Sixtus IV—who claims history's notice as patron of the Sistine Chapel—died. Another succession campaign began. For almost twenty years, Rodrigo had waited for this moment. He flooded the cardinals with promissory notes and pledges of gifts. But Alexander's enemies, leaders of other family dynasties, worked as hard for his opponents, and Alexander was unable to muster the two-thirds vote he needed to win the election. Innocent VIII became the new pope.

While the cardinals wrangled over who would be the next vicar of Christ, there were rumblings of discontent in the manors, villages, and towns of Christian Europe. For sociological, demographic, and economic reasons, people's attitudes toward authority were changing. The church still ruled people's consciences, but now a few Christians wondered why it was so costly to be a believer. The clergy remained the most learned people, but others were finding sources of knowledge and belief elsewhere, especially through the printed word. More books were published in the forty years between 1460 and 1500 than had been produced by all the scribes and monks in the Middle Ages. Vernacular versions of the Bible became available. People with some education felt nearly equal to ecclesiastics. Indeed, in 1501, Alexander felt the need to issue a papal bull instructing printers to submit their works to the archbishop for licensing. Belief in institutions was waning while individual religiosity was growing.

Into this spiritual ferment fell the spark of Girolamo Savonarola, zealous foe of big money. Savonarola, a Dominican monk in Florence, began to denounce the money madness of his city in 1490, damning the impure relations between the church and bankers. He foretold, apparently with convincing and terrifying detail, a sword falling from the sky and punishing the wicked with divine wrath. His speeches were so potent that people were reduced to "terror, alarm, sobbing and tears," wrote one contemporary. "Everybody went about the city bewildered, more dead than alive." Condemning all luxuries, Savonarola urged people to throw their jewels, paintings, and fine clothes into the bonfires of "vanities" that he inspired. Most forms of public amusement were banned.

Other seers soon joined the apocalyptic chorus, and the people of Florence, squeezed by the church for centuries, listened with interest. Then came a series of natural calamities: In 1495, the Tiber overflowed its banks and turned Rome into a muddy lagoon. Famine and pestilence followed. There were reports of a monster with the head of an ass, the body of a woman, and the bearded face of an old man on its back. Surely these were signs of a God angry with his sinning children.

The church doggedly covered its ears. To find fault with the church was to find fault with God, and that was heresy. Papal inquisitions hunted down heretics across Europe and hanged and burned them as church officials looked on approvingly. Old, impoverished women became the scapegoats for all kinds of calamities and were stretched on the rack until they confessed to being witches. In the criminal registers of a Swiss town were written the names of two women charged with starting a thunderstorm; beside each name it said, simply, *"convicta et combusta."* In Spain, a man who had blasphemed "had his tongue pinioned and a cord placed around his neck and he was beaten two hundred times with a rod." "Like all God's works, [the church] is perfect," a cardinal wrote. "It is, therefore, incapable of reform."

The papacy was further insulated by the many hangers-on who populated Rome. The city had never developed any large-scale commercial or industrial activity, except pilgrimages. A one-company town run by large-scale consumers of luxuries, Rome had practically nothing to trade but the revenue of the papal treasury. Too many Romans were feeding at the church's trough to make reform popular.

The Crusades had an unexpectedly deleterious impact on the church. Although these holy wars were instigated to reclaim the Holy Land from the Muslims, they did many other things. Preparations for the Crusades stimulated commerce and industrial crafts, as merchants and moneylenders equipped and transported the Christian army. The shipbuilding industry benefited from orders for fleets, and Pope Alexander, who sponsored the last, meager Crusade, had "nine cannon of various dimensions" and other artillery cast. Italian, French, and Spanish merchants established communications and commercial relations with the enemy, and the trade gradually overshadowed the conflict.

For an ordinary knight, the Crusades represented a chance to steal with religious approval. "Churches, shops, palaces, homes were sacked by the gold-crazed Men of the Cross." The Crusades opened the western soldiers' eyes to ways of life they had never imagined possible. Coming from their dim, drafty huts and houses, the East was one big wonderland. Just seeing it must have aroused their appetites, and they brought home with them, among many items, silks and furs. Probably no single event contributed as much to the moneymaking impulse of the Middle Ages as the Crusades.

By Alexander's reign, it was becoming more difficult to rally troops from European states. While the pope was putatively the commander in chief of the Christian armies, monarchs regularly meddled and disobeyed him. Fighting among themselves reduced the monarchs' enthusiasm for sending large contingents of armed men abroad. Needless to say, the Crusades were money pits, and, as Christian forces repeatedly failed to win a lasting victory, some of the bloom went off the rose. "In the eleventh century, the idea of the crusade must have been like a strange and wonderful light in the sky," wrote H. G. Wells. "In the thirteenth, one can imagine honest burghers saying in tones of protest, 'What! *another* crusade!' "

In July 1492, just a few months before Columbus reached the Americas, Pope Innocent VIII died. His body was still warm when the cardinals and their partisans began a round of fierce—and occasionally fatal—maneuvering. Some 220 murders were committed in Rome in the month between Innocent's death and his successor's elevation.

Once again, the cardinals convened in a small, dark, and airless part of the Vatican, where they were confined until they elected a new pope. Renaissance conclaves were hotbeds of political intrigue, and one cardinal who was later elected pope recalled extensive plotting in the lavatories.

Twenty-three cardinals were present at the conclave of 1492. Through the exhausting night, Rodrigo haggled his way to the papacy. There were reports of outright bribery—four mules loaded with silver (some say gold) were seen leaving Rodrigo's palace and arriving at the home of a cardinal who decided to vote for Rodrigo. By a bare majority, Rodrigo, sixty-two years old, was at last elected to the job he had craved his whole life. He renamed himself Alexander VI.

"Flee, we are in the hands of a wolf," warned a young cleric when he heard of Alexander's election.

Alexander set the tone for his eleven-year reign with his coronation, which was glittering, fantastic, and expensive. "Marc Antony himself was not received so magnificently by Cleopatra," exclaimed one spectator. Alexander loved any pomp and splendor, but none more than public celebrations of himself and his family. On his ride through Rome to Saint Peter's, streets were decorated with garlands of flowers, and living statues were formed by gilded naked youth. At Saint Peter's, hundreds of people kissed his feet as he sat on his golden chair.

Five days after his enthronement, Alexander appointed his

son Cesare and two nephews to lucrative posts in the church. Launching a mass hiring campaign of relatives and friends, Alexander enlarged the college of cardinals, naming eleven new ones, including the fifteen-year-old scion of another politically powerful family. In his entire tenure, Alexander appointed forty-three cardinals, including five members of his own family, and created eighty new offices. "Ten Papacies would not suffice to satisfy all these relations," grumbled an observer.

A new pope was expected to resign the many benefices he had accumulated earlier, so every pope had many gifts to distribute. But Alexander's treasure was particularly splendid. A partial list of the benefices Alexander offered to a disappointed rival included three abbeys, a monastery, a legateship, two canonries, a rectorship, a prebend, and others.

Church offices such as abbacies, bishoprics, and cardinalates could be used as gifts, but they could also be put up for sale, a practice known as simony. Simony was named for the biblical figure Simon Magus, or Simon the Magician, who offered the apostles money if they would let him work miracles. For Alexander, simony was a kind of undercover borrowing—it allowed him to collect lump sums from his officials and pay them back from revenue streams. The longer the abbot, bishop, or cardinal lived, the better his investment became.

Selling offices gradually became one of the church's most important sources of revenue, and popes became addicted to it. In a letter to Machiavelli, Agostino Vespucci wrote, "Here they have more benefices for sale than we have melons, waffles or drinking-water."

At the same time, Alexander was trying to sell other religious documents, such as decrees, bulls, briefs, marriage annulments, absolutions, and dispensations, which had the force of law. With these, too, money talked. "Alexander sells the keys, the altars, Christ himself," mocked Renaissance humorists. "He had a right to sell them, for he bought them first." Not surprisingly, in so corrupt a system, Alexander wasn't alone in selling his approval: His private secretary confessed to forging more than three thousand bulls.

Perhaps Alexander's most lucrative business was the sale of indulgences, a fund-raising technique that reached fever pitch during his administration. Less than two decades later, indulgences led to the Protestant Reformation and a fracturing of the Christian world.

At first, indulgences seemed harmless enough. In Rome's vision of afterlife, anyone who sinned on earth would spend time repenting in purgatory, even if they were eventually destined for heaven. Purgatory wasn't hell, but it was uncomfortably close. And in hell, people were told, demons with iron hooks plunged the bodies of the damned alternately into fire and icy water or hung them up by their tongues or boiled them or strained them through cloth. How much better would purgatory be?

Indulgences purported to give people the means to shorten their terms in purgatory. If they paid an indulgence salesman and said a few prayers, their time in purgatory would be reduced, sometimes to nothing. Indulgences quickly became a popular item. They were distributed by special appointees whose fee was a percentage of the gifts. This was an invitation to cheat and deceive, and, indeed, many false monks sold fake indulgences. In 1450, the chancellor of Oxford University complained that no one cared about sinning anymore because it was so easy to win remission of any penalty. "For these indulgence-mongers wander over the country and give a letter of pardon sometimes for two pence, sometimes for a draught of wine or beer . . . or even for the hire of a harlot." For the poor, indulgences had the ironic effect of robbing them of the great comfort that their earthly misery would be rewarded in heaven. Now it seemed the rich would arrive first again.

In 1476, Pope Sixtus IV had proclaimed that indulgences could be applied to souls already suffering in purgatory. Unfortunately, this resulted in some peasants starving themselves and their families to retrieve a loved one from punishment. A proverb was born: "As soon as the money in the coffer rings, the soul from purgatory's fire springs."

By long-standing tradition, when cardinals or other church officeholders died, their wealth reverted to the papacy. (They weren't supposed to have heirs, though many did.) Because Renaissance cardinals were so rich, their passing could mean hundreds of thousands of florins for the pope, as well as real estate and other precious goods that could be converted to cash. Once, when Alexander was visiting a mortally sick cardinal, he demanded an inventory of the cardinal's possessions lest any sly retainer try to intercept his booty. The death of a cardinal also had the pleasant effect of creating a vacant office, the revenue of which the pope collected until another cardinal was appointed. Of course, another appointment eventually meant another big payment to the papacy treasury.

This may explain why Alexander and his son, Cesare, were suspected in the deaths of several high church officials. When one cardinal died after two days of violent vomiting, his entire fortune went to the Vatican. Romans said it had become dangerous to be a cardinal and rich. The Borgias' murder weapon was popularly believed to be a poison they had invented. A small dose of the white powder dissolved in wine or soup was lethal, but the victim lingered just long enough to avoid suspicion of poisoning. Around Rome, the phrase "to have drunk" came to mean "to have been poisoned by the Borgias." In one letter home, an envoy posted in Rome wrote, "The Spanish ambassador . . . is gravely ill, and it is suspected that he drank."

Suspicion of poison surrounds most sudden deaths of important figures of this time, and there were probably fewer poisonings than suspected—although there were no small number of accidents. Poisoning was an inexact science. Some of the concoctions proposed as poison—saliva of a mad pig hung upside down and beaten to death—would not have been fatal. As for Borgia poison, an English statistician analyzed the death of cardinals under four popes of Alexander's era and concluded that, proportionately, there was no increased mortality under Alexander.

As pope, Alexander was the chief administrator of a bureaucracy that makes the Kremlin look streamlined. By all accounts, he was a gifted manager. After years as vice chancellor, Alexander knew every corner of the church's sprawling domain. He spent his first two years balancing the church's budget, something that hadn't been done in half a century. Under Alexander, records were strictly kept, staff salaries paid on time.

As the church's finances became more complicated, papal officials were forced to become experts at business. With money arriving from dozens of countries, the pope's money managers had to learn currency exchange. In one fifteenth-century sale of indulgences, seventy different currencies poured into the papal treasury. Not all funds were currency, however, so the church's treasurers also dealt in precious stones, spices, wines, and other commodities. Because the church needed accurate records, church officials learned bookkeeping techniques and became superior accountants.

Outside the church's front door was the impoverished and neglected city of Rome. In 1377, the papacy had returned from Avignon to its original headquarters, only to find collapsing buildings, disease-ridden swamps, and washed-out streets. The church began a campaign to spruce up its hometown, installing new roads and erecting some of the most beautiful structures in the world—"sermons in stone," as one pope called them.

Crime was also an enormous problem for the city and its surroundings. Because so many Italian states were constantly at war with one another, mercenary soldiers roamed the land, sometimes supplementing their income by theft and assassination. War must feed war, as the saying went. One ambassadorial procession hired a squadron of security guards, only to be "despoiled by their own safeguard." Like secular rulers of his time, Alexander, the official head of Rome, dealt with crime not by trying to prevent it but by harshly punishing offenders. The guilty were hanged and their houses burned down.

Alexander reformed the management of prisons as well as the Roman constitution and set aside a day when ordinary citizens could personally lodge complaints with him. He rebuilt the Roman university and made sure its professors received salaries. He was tolerant of Jews and could not be coerced into persecuting them.

Outside Rome, the church's people were becoming restive. Between Savonarola's sermons and the signs of excess around them, they felt a growing revulsion against worldly extravagances, a puritanical disgust with the corruption of the flesh. Newly created religious orders, such as the Franciscans, stressed the spiritual value of poverty instead and supported themselves by begging. People still had faith, but increasingly their beliefs were no longer the exclusive property of the Roman Catholic Church. "Indeed it was *because* genuine religious and moral feeling was still present that dismay at the corruption of the clergy was so acute and the yearning for reform so strong."

To Alexander, however, reform was a thought "terrible beyond anything else." When Alexander was fifty-nine, he began a love affair with a nineteen-year-old married woman best remembered for her blond hair, which reached to her feet. Despite the Italians' laissez-faire attitude toward their clerics' sexuality, the forty-year age difference offended some and added to a growing dissatisfaction with Alexander.

Then there was the jubilee of 1500. The jubilee was an ancient religious custom that had lapsed for several centuries before being resumed in 1300. In jubilee years, which occurred every twenty-five years in Alexander's era, pilgrims who journeyed to Rome could receive an indulgence that would wipe clean their slate of sins. In the first jubilee in 1300, so much money flowed into the papal treasury that two assistants worked around the clock "raking together infinite money" that had been deposited at the tomb of Saint Peter. Alexander hoped for similar results: He wanted to bankroll another crusade against the Turks. For those too fearful of robbery, plague, or war to make the trip to Rome, Alexander issued a bull listing "away" prices for the indulgence.

Nevertheless, the faithful poured into Rome from the farthest stretches of Europe, some two hundred thousand people in all, making the jubilee a rousing financial success. While in Rome, the pious people saw with their own eyes the materialism and hedonism of their church. At home, they told their neighbors about immoral popes, papal poisonings, and general paganism and venality.

Among Alexander's brood of children, the two most famous were his daughter Lucretia and his son Cesare. He spoiled each according to gender. For Cesare, Alexander sponsored improvident military campaigns. For Lucretia, Alexander financed three dowries, trousseaus, and weddings.

By all accounts, Cesare was at least as devious as his father but not nearly as accomplished; later, he became the model for Niccolò Machiavelli's *Prince.* Cesare, who roamed the city streets at night surrounded by a pack of guards, was considered dangerous. "Every night, four or five murdered men are discovered, bishops, prelates and others," reported a Venetian ambassador in Rome, "so that all Rome trembles for fear of being murdered by the Duke"—meaning Cesare. Cesare had a mixed record on the battlefield and died at the age of thirty-one. Machiavelli summed up Cesare's career, writing, "For twice five years the sun had shed light on these grim and ugly deeds, and looked down on the earth made red with blood."

Lucrezia's life was longer but no less difficult. She lived at a time when a woman had as much control of her destiny as did a vase. In Lucrezia's era, a bride was a piece of precious dynastic property who could be traded for money and power. Love, respect, and passion were irrelevant to marriage. Lucrezia was eleven years old when she was first engaged to be married, thirteen at the time of her first wedding. Married three times,

Lucrezia, who though not beautiful was apparently intelligent and witty, chose none of her grooms.

Four years after Lucrezia's first marriage, Alexander and Cesare found a more advantageous political match for her. The pope took the problem of her marriage to a meeting of cardinals. He explained that the marriage should be annulled on the ground that it had never been consummated due to the groom's impotence. Hearing of this, the groom vehemently denied the charge, but eventually—after a meeting with Cesare?—he came around, not only agreeing to the annulment but also returning the dowry.

The following year, Lucrezia married her second husband, Alfonso. Shortly afterward, Alfonso, concerned by a rumor that Cesare had turned against him in favor of an even more important suitor for Lucrezia, fled Rome. Alfonso and Lucrezia produced a child, so impotence wasn't an issue. Finally, Alfonso dared to return to Rome. Late one night the following year, he was set upon by five men in a public square and severely beaten. Alfonso lingered for more than a month. Then, apparently convinced that Cesare was responsible for the attack, Alfonso shot an arrow out his window at Cesare. One of Cesare's servants dashed up to Alfonso's room and strangled him. None of the original attackers was ever identified.

Lucrezia's third marriage was a partnership with the ancient and noble Este family, an advantageous connection for Alexander's political interests. But before the fortuitous match could occur, the two sides had to negotiate the dowry, which was, at the time, a contract as complicated as one in a big corporate merger today.

The marriage dowry was a common and stifling institution often present in wealthy societies in which traditional women's work was done by servants; it became part of the price a woman paid for not doing a job. But as dowry prices rose, they became a greater threat to family fortunes, leading some of the wealthy to send their daughters to convents rather than deplete their fortunes. For less wealthy families, the dowry could be crippling. In a letter to a son living in Naples, a Florentine woman wrote in 1447 about her daughter's dowry: "She is 16 years old and it was not advisable to wait any longer to marry her. We tried to place her in a nobler and more powerful family, but we would have needed 1400 or 1500 florins, and this would have meant our ruin. I do not know if the girl is pleased, for it is true that, with the exception of political advantages, this marriage has very little else to recommend it."

Alexander's contract negotiations with the Estes over the dowry were interminable and sometimes vehement. Alexander complained that the groom's father was behaving like a small shopkeeper. Finally, the two sides came to an agreement: If the Este family would accept Lucrezia as their son's bride, Alexander would pay a large cash sum, give the groom's family political control of two cities, and reduce the family's church taxes to zero.

Alexander lavished an enormous trousseau on Lucrezia: It contained two hundred chemises alone. The wedding celebration, bought with church money, lasted thirteen days. There were balls and recitals, receptions and feasts. The groom, however, did not attend; Lucrezia was married by proxy and didn't meet her husband until several days after the ceremony, when she and her party of seven hundred courtiers and servants (all on the papal payroll) rode to his home in Ferrara. Until she died at the age of thirty-nine, Lucrezia Borgia was known as a model wife, mother, and princess.

Although Alexander squandered fortunes on both Cesare and Lucrezia, neither was his favorite child. That distinction belonged to his oldest son, Juan, who, as the duke of Gandia, was on the path to political glory until 1497, when his body was found at the bottom of the Tiber, a stone tied to his neck. His throat had been cut, and he had nine knife wounds in his body.

Rather demoralized by this unexpected murder, Alexander saw it as a judgment of God against his many sins. After three days and nights without food or sleep, he announced a broad program to reform the church and began by appointing a commission to suggest changes. The group took its charge seriously and proposed a list of reforms that included not only an end to selling benefices but also reductions in the incomes of the cardinals and limits on the size of their households to eighty and the size of their mounted escorts to thirty. At meals, cardinals would be allowed to serve only one boiled and one roast meat, and they would no longer be allowed to employ youths as body servants. Whether the reform seemed too draconian or too wearisome, Alexander lost interest in the project, and the changes were never instituted.

It was August 1503. August was always a dangerous month in Rome, as the swamps around the city provided ideal malarial conditions. Alexander remarked to someone at a ceremony, "This is a bad month for heavy people." After dining with some cardinals and his son, he contracted a fever and took to his bed. Some fourteen ounces of blood were drawn from him. He continued his precipitous decline, and within days, Alexander died. Later, there was a rumor that he had mistakenly drunk from a cup of poisoned wine he had prepared for another.

Eight laborers, making blasphemous jokes about Alexander, carried his body from the church altar to its coffin. But the carpenters had made the coffin too narrow and short, so they rolled up the pope's body in an old carpet and pummeled and pushed it into the coffin with their fists. No candles were lit, and no priests attended to his body. A contemporary writer described the "incredible rejoicing" of the Romans when they saw Alexander's body in Saint Peter's: "They could not feast their eyes enough on the sight of the dead serpent . . . this lecherous monster who would indiscriminately sell things sacred or profane."

The end of the church's total and unquestioned authority was rapidly approaching. Fourteen years after Alexander's death, in 1517, Martin Luther used the issue of indulgences to incite the Protestant Reformation. Once the Christian church split in two, there was no longer a single moral voice instructing Christians on how to live. The church was still to command enormous amounts of money, but a growing number of people fell out of its grip.

In some ways, Alexander VI could be said to be a mostly nonviolent plunderer. Like other wealthy men and women of his century, his fortune came not from producing or creating something but from picking the pockets of farmers, artisans, and merchants through taxes. The world was still largely a zero-sum game—one person's wealth was another person's poverty. This made it virtually impossible to reconcile being a Christian with being avaricious.

But the world's wealth was steadily increasing, and some good Christians wanted a piece of that prosperity. The church's attitudes toward money would be forced to change. Before long, the striving for wealth was to become more universal than the Universal Church.

FIVE

Money Begets Money

Jacob Fugger (1459–1526)

Almost two decades before he died, Jacob Fugger, or "Fugger the Rich," as he was known, commissioned his own burial chapel. Glimmering with marble and gold, the Roman Catholic crypt reflected Fugger's immense pride in his ability to make money. His epitaph, which he wrote, declared that Jacob Fugger was "second to none in the acquisition of extraordinary wealth." It went on: "As he was comparable to none in life, so after death is not to be numbered among the mortal."

More than 450 years dead, Fugger now must certainly be numbered among the mortal. But the economic machine he helped set in motion is as robust as ever. Jacob Fugger was one of the first and most accomplished mobilizers of merchant banking, venture capital, corporations, and cartels. He personified a new class of wealth—the early capitalists—whose members leveraged surplus money into fortunes unlike any before seen outside royal or religious institutions. In the late Middle Ages, for the first time in history, a person could become rich and powerful without the threat of force. "The king reigns but the bank rules" was Jacob Fugger's favorite saying.

Fugger's method of creating wealth involved a relatively recent arrival on the economic scene: debt. The infinite possibilities of debt dazzled wealthy Europeans from kings to countesses, popes to princes, while the church's traditional condemnation of borrowing and lending began to soften. "Debt was as much a feature of the day-to-day life of the wealthy in the early 15th century as the accumulation of belongings," notes a historian. Desperate borrowers promised anything for an infusion of money. One emperor, who possessed what was believed to be Christ's crown of thorns, pledged it to a Venetian merchant for a short-term loan, which subsequently went into default.

The forces behind the explosion of debt in Jacob Fugger's lifetime had been building for centuries. Explicitly forbidden by the Christian church, lending for interest had long operated underground, which meant the practice was local and difficult. But by the early fifteenth century, economic demands had begun to supersede religious scruples. Monarchs and popes needed loans because their systems of taxation remained "extremely occasional and imperfect." The scale of lending became so large that interest was often paid not in cash but in lucrative franchises or trade concessions. This gave bankers like Fugger the opportunity to diversify and enrich themselves further.

For the aristocracy, applying to merchant bankers for loans was far more convenient than pledging their land to abbeys or sending plate to the mint. Although interest rates might be as high as 80 percent annually, Europe's new bankers could provide larger sums of money than earlier lenders, and they could do it faster. The "funny money" aspect of paper debt nurtured a growing disconnection between quantity of money and intensity of desire. To admire something meant wanting to own it, and the idea that happiness could be found in consumption was born. "Nowadays the rage for possession has got to such a pitch," complained Erasmus, the fifteenth-century Dutch scholar, "that there is nothing in the realm of nature, whether sacred or profane, out of which profit cannot be squeezed."

The new money economy stealthily disassembled Europe's political, cultural, and religious patterns and reassembled them to encompass the notion that every value can be quantified, every item in life reduced to a single standard. "Money allows humans to structure life in incredibly complex ways that were not available to them before the invention of money," wrote James Buchan. "Money represents an infinitely expandable way of structuring value and social relationships—personal, political and religious as well as commercial and economic."

At first, money held out the promise of being an equalizer, increasing the chance of a low-born person becoming rich from zero to slightly more than zero. Yet although the vast majority of the poor remained poor, they were inevitably drawn into the money economy as more wages and rents were paid in currency rather than through labor or barter. Most important for future wealth, money spawned a new class, the so-called third estate (after the first two estates, clergy and nobility), in the late Middle Ages. Also known as the bourgeoisie, these cautious, pious, and dutiful merchants and their families gathered in burgs where they established small businesses and began trading first locally, then across regional and national borders. To the extent possible, each tried to keep the business and its profits in the family. Heirs were trained to preserve and protect the dynasty.

By the time Jacob Fugger was born, there were second, third, and even fourth generations of affluent merchants in Europe. Fugger's father, mother, brothers, and nephews all worked in the family firm that had been founded by his grandfather. Each generation of Fuggers developed new ways of facilitating the exchange of material goods for money—and taking a bite at the same time. Or as Robert W. Sarnoff, an early pioneer of television, put it centuries later, "Finance is the art of passing currency from hand to hand until it finally disappears."

While money was transforming human relationships, Christianity was slowly but inexorably losing its power in Europe. The common people, the church's taxpayers, were beginning to see life less as an irrational melodrama of demons and disasters and more as an explicable and measurable system. The first mathematics books for popular audiences were published in

Fugger's lifetime, although most Europeans still used Roman numerals. (Mathematics and religion coexisted peacefully; a math book published in 1589 stated decisively that hell was 3,758 miles away.)

The introduction of double-entry bookkeeping in the fourteenth century allowed people to describe a business as a corporeal entity distinct from its owners. Until then, the condition of a business could be determined only by combing through many ledgers and journals kept by different clerks using different systems. The influence of double-entry bookkeeping on western thought "has been almost without parallel. Our conversation is replete with assets and liabilities, depreciations, profits and loss, balance-sheets." As one historian noted, "Every time an accountant has divided everything within his or her purview into plus or minus, our inclination to categorize all experience as this or as that has gained validation."

The new language of credit and debit was accompanied by new ideas in art, politics, and literature. The ancient belief that the greater God or community made any single person expendable was fading as individualism became more accepted. Authorities that had once been unquestioned were questioned. People wondered whether salvation should entail sheeplike adherence to someone else's rules or, rather, should be "earned" by an effort of self-transformation. The notion of sin was changing: Now it was believed to reside not in the act but in the intention, another view encouraging people to look inward for moral governance. Economic issues, too, were seen increasingly as matters of individual conscience rather than as religious commands.

Many people cursed the new individualism, especially the economic kind. Amidst the "edgy religiousity" of the period, they felt uneasy with the morality of business. Medieval business ethics, articulated in the thirteenth century by Saint Thomas Aquinas, had rested on the notion that material goods were not inherently evil if sought in moderation. What can nourish two, the saying went, should not be absorbed by one, which may explain why fifteenth-century merchant bankers of Florence were known as *popolo grosso* (fat people), whether they were fat or not. The goal of medieval economic organization was to reproduce, not enhance, the material well-being of the past. Its motto was perpetuation, not progress.

Yet material goods, being part of the world God made, were divine creations, and if used morally could bring about good. This giant loophole allowed men like Fugger, a devout Catholic, to embrace two activities condemned by the church: usury and the unrestrained pursuit of profit. Fugger and those like him were, one historian noted, "economic revolutionists, as obviously at war with the established order as the inventors of the power loom at a later day."

If the history of capitalism is a mosaic in which each tile is a risk-taking entrepreneur, one of those pieces would be Jacob Fugger's grandfather Hans, a weaver by trade. In 1367, Hans Fugger left a small German village to seek his fortune in Augsburg. There was a saying then—"town air makes free"— that appealed to people seeking something more than their ancestors had. Within a few years, Hans Fugger had stopped weaving and had begun to import raw cotton, distribute it to other small weavers, and sell the finished textile. This was the "putting out" system that eventually became widespread across Europe. As he established trading relationships, particularly in Italy, Hans Fugger began importing and exporting other goods.

Almost all big European banking houses started as small-scale trading operations of cloth, spices, wine, porcelain, copper, or any of thousands of other products. With the help of better maps, navigational devices, and ships, the volume of overseas trade was expanding rapidly, and traders were going farther afield. Although long-range trade still entailed great risks and losses, it also offered bigger profits than any other business venture.

The most skilled traders sometimes had excess cash, and

other merchants and traders needed capital to fit out their expeditions. The two inevitably found each other, and some traders ceased dealing in goods and began dealing in capital. A division between labor and money took root in Fugger's time. As Europe's contentious monarchs squandered fortunes on wars with one another, debt multiplied and multiplied again. In a matter of decades, the monarchs, once the richest and most powerful people in the world, were at the mercy of the bankers.

Jacob Fugger and other business leaders could increasingly influence political decisions that had once belonged exclusively to the aristocracy. Fugger "watched the interplay of politics, trade and finance, and judged how and when to interfere." Before long, the outcast bankers became welcome in upper-class society (though certainly not as equals). Large holdings of land still represented a higher social standing than cash alone, which explains why many overly optimistic merchants bought estates that they were later forced to sell.

Although the landed gentries were considered more refined than urban merchants, estate life could be almost barbarous compared with urban luxury. In 1518, a man wrote to a friend about his stay on a large estate:

> The castle was not built for pleasure but for defense, surrounded by moats and trenches, cramped within, burdened with stables for animals large and small, dark buildings swollen with stores of armaments and machines of war. Everywhere the disagreeable smell of powder dominates. And the dogs with their filth—what a fine smell that is! And the comings and goings of the knights, among them bandits, brigands and thieves. Usually the house is wide open, because we do not know who is who and do not take much trouble to find out.

Jacob Fugger and other urban merchants represented a new class of the working rich. He saw wealth less as a ticket to opulent houses and a well-stocked library—although he bought himself both—than as a gauge of his proficiency. He relished the pursuit of gain beyond its immediate return and psychologically thrived on taking risks. Fugger had no interest in wielding political power except as it served or damaged his business interests. However much he enjoyed hobnobbing with royalty, he also matter-of-factly denied them unsecured credit. When a relative advised Fugger to abandon a speculative enterprise and enjoy the wealth he had accumulated, Fugger shook him off, saying he "wished to make a profit as long as he could."

The Fuggers were not the first dynasty of the new money aristocracy. The Medicis of fifteenth-century Florence were lenders, manufacturers, investors, importers, and exporters, and they sustained a commercial empire for 150 tumultuous years. But it took three generations for the Medicis to become the most important banking house in Italy and five generations for their influence to be felt in other parts of Europe. The Fuggers came to international power much more quickly. When Hans Fugger died, his son Jacob—young Jacob's father—took over the prospering business and expanded it until his death in 1469, when Jacob was only ten. Jacob's mother assumed control until the next generation was sufficiently trained. Indeed, the death of a husband or father was the only way women could manage businesses in this era. Otherwise, it was considered indecent for a woman to be involved in commerce.

The new bankers, such as the Medici and Fugger families, were referred to as merchant princes and commended for bringing prosperity without violence. Their ready cash gave them the courage to behave with "merchant hauteur" in this new "cocky meritocracy." And none was more imperious than the "monstrously cool" Jacob Fugger.

Fugger was born and raised in Augsburg, which was probably much like other German towns of the time, with narrow, irregular streets raucous with noise, open sewers, and houses made of wood (the French city of Rouen burned down six times between 1200 and 1225). Many houses had room for the family's cattle, and some of the wealthiest merchants kept entire barns inside the town walls. A bathroom was a rare luxury even into the seventeenth century. Fleas, lice, and bugs could be found in rich as well as poor interiors. The houses of the rich, built in the popular Gothic style, were more forbiddingly majestic than warm and cozy. Yet by Fugger's time, the wealthy could put glass, rather than oiled paper, in their windows and buy feathers for beds, silver goblets, chandeliers, and mirrors.

Jacob, his parents' third son, was studying for the priesthood when his mother abruptly decided he should join the family business instead. At the age of fourteen, he was sent to the Venetian branch of the family firm to learn banking, finance, and so-called *Welsche Praktik*—commercial arithmetic. Five years later, Jacob became a partner in the business then called Ulrich Fugger and Brothers.

Jacob Fugger trained himself methodically: He studied every phase of business, every advance in bookkeeping, manufacturing, merchandising, and finance. His education in economic rationalism allowed him to test the accounts and balances of all the branches of the Fuggers' far-flung empire and determine the condition of the whole network. Bookkeeping, Fugger believed, should reflect the enterprise as clearly as a mirror shows a face. It was no longer acceptable to be "close enough."

Fifteenth-century Augsburg was a good incubator for the embryonic capitalist. Europe's trading centers were moving north from Italy, and Augsburg, with some twenty-five thousand people, was becoming the new Florence. Besides its extensive weaving and trading industries, Augsburg was close to the mines of the Tirol, the most important copper- and silver-mining district of the fifteenth and sixteenth centuries. Furthermore, the people of Augsburg took a progressive view of business and economic policy. "The secret of this great leap forward in productive effort was the release of ambitious individuals from political,

social and moral restraints on self-serving attempts to accumulate wealth," a historian noted. "European entrepreneurs were
the first people in the history of the world who could go about
their business without wondering if some 'internal bureau of
plunder' was about to cut them down." Augsburg's reputation
for wealth spread, and people looking for loans came to see its
bankers, first among them Jacob Fugger.

Under the leadership of Jacob and two older brothers, the
Fugger firm handled a large number of commodities, but its most
important product was fustian, a blend of cotton and linen.
Though the textile industry had started as a collection of home
businesses, it was becoming controlled increasingly by entrepreneurs such as the Fuggers—a division of labor that subordinated
the producer to an intermediary. The firm picked up raw cotton
from Mediterranean ports and brought it by mule through the
Tirol to the weavers in Augsburg. Later, the Fuggers bought the
finished product from the weavers and distributed it around
Europe. Gradually, the Fuggers began to import metals, spices,
silks, brocades, herbs, medicines, works of art, rare food, and
jewels. They were also leading players in the pepper market for
several decades. By about 1525, the Fugger firm, with eighteen
branches, was the most powerful financial force in the world.

Although Augsburg was then known as the village of millionaires, in 1471 more than 65 percent of the city's population
owned no property at all. The economic disparity between rich
and poor, which was apparent all around Europe, was wider
than at any time since that of ancient Rome. (In the fifteenth century, the wedding gown made for the daughter of an Italian merchant prince cost the equivalent of 140 days of a mason's wages;
the costume included a garland of two hundred peacock-tail
feathers, pearls, and bits and leaves of gold.) Furthermore, the
newly rich had less contact with the poor than when they had
shared a feudal estate. The rich had no traditions of responsibility or charity as the landed gentry once had. "Among the
upper levels of the bourgeoisie, increasing scorn and fear of the

proletariat went hand in hand with the relish for aristocratic manners."

The rich spent their money first on land, then on precious objects and servants. Silver plate became a common possession of the upper classes, and some families had entire tables and chairs made of solid silver. The wealthy filled their houses not only with finery—painted portraits, oriental rugs, and tea services—but also with domestic help. In addition, they hired poets, dwarfs, jesters, falconers, and doctors. In the fourteenth century, some of the rich wore gowns with sleeves that covered their hands to show they had the constant use of other people's hands. The American economist Thorstein Veblen recorded the perhaps apocryphal story of a French king who was sitting dangerously close to the fire but whose chair-moving functionary was occupied elsewhere. "The king sat uncomplaining before the fire and suffered his royal person to be toasted beyond recovery."

Despite their new finery, the rich's standards of etiquette lagged behind. Advising his well-born nephew, a sixteenth-century papal official wrote, "When you have blown your nose, you should not open your handkerchief and inspect it, as if pearls or rubies had dropped out of your skull," and "Anyone who makes a nasty noise with his lips as a sign of astonishment or disapproval is obviously imitating something indecent."

The poor, meanwhile, owned practically nothing. Their beds might be straw-filled sacks on wooden planks, and they probably ate while sitting on crude benches without a table. Their diets were mostly grain: wheat, barley, and oats. A common meal was bread floating in thin vegetable soup. Their water came from whatever source was closest, including rivers contaminated with waste, which left them vulnerable to disease. Their clothes were made of crude homespun cloth. A frivolity would be a pin or a bit of lace or ribbon.

Drunkenness increased as people turned to alcohol for cheap calories and temporary elation. Sixteenth- and seventeenth-century German engravings of peasant festivities almost always show one of the guests turning around on his bench to throw up. And medical care was still too expensive for most workers. Responding to epidemics, doctors' best advice was "flee from such persons as be infect." As late as the early eighteenth century, a doctor commented that a laborer who doesn't recover from an illness quickly must return to work still sick. "Certain things can only be done for the rich who can afford to be ill," the doctor said.

To create a constant flow of reliable wealth, Fugger and other merchants knew they had to assemble a large-scale and widely diversified empire. In the early days of commerce, traders had commonly bet everything they owned on a single enterprise, such as a shipment of pepper. At the time, many other goods were uneconomical to transport. For example, only 5 percent of the cost of delivered timber represented the forest price; the rest was absorbed by transport, in the form of tolls, tariffs, and outright bribes. But as transportation and communication improved in Fugger's time, it became possible to spread investments over more industries and a wider geographical area. Merchant adventurers became sedentary businessmen who sent agents abroad to do their trading. Foreign hosts who had entertained the merchants when they were traveling acted as brokers.

The new business class of fifteenth-century Germany demanded an end to the disorder of petty wars and feuds among lords and knights. As the feudal system collapsed, many knights had been thrown out of work, and they comforted themselves by preying on travelers on Europe's roads. The brigands became a menace to trade, and a few even cut off hands of the merchants they robbed.

Not surprisingly, merchants wanted a strong central authority to impose order on these military entrepreneurs. But the feudal barons were the very people who once provided armies for popes and emperors. Now governments were forced to hire mercenaries, who demanded to be paid in cash. There was only one way to raise enough money for such an enterprise: Borrow it. In the early days of royal loans, a king might deal with a single banker. But as the size of loans escalated, a consortium of merchants would subscribe, usually under the leadership of someone like Fugger. For the Jacob Fuggers of the world, war was a profitable business: As costs of armaments and weaponry grew, so did the size of loans.

Being a pious Christian, Jacob Fugger realized that the church did not look favorably on the practice of lending money for interest. To good Christians, a request to borrow was an expression of need from one of God's children to another. To profit from a neighbor's hardship was usury, and usury was a mortal sin. In the thirteenth and fourteenth centuries, a usurer was a pariah. By church mandate, no one was allowed to rent a house to a usurer, nor could a priest hear a usurer's confession or grant absolution. In 1311, the church's Council of Vienne declared that anyone who even defended usury was a heretic. If a deceased merchant was proved to have been a usurer, the church could confiscate his entire fortune. Such cases proved so profitable for the church that when an affluent businessman died, witnesses were usually found to testify to his guilt.

Inevitably, however, the practice of lending continued—it was too profitable to abolish. Jews, who didn't answer to the Christian church, became Europe's moneylenders. They didn't have much choice: They were excluded from most other forms of trade. Initially, Jews lent grain, clothing, raw materials, or other objects and received a greater amount of these in repayment. Gradually they began to deal in precious metals and currency. In 1400, Florence brought in Jews for the specific purpose of carrying on the forbidden business of lending. But as global trade continued to expand, merchants and sovereigns needed more money than individual Jews could supply. Borrowers faced great expense and inconvenience if they wanted to finance their activities without resorting to usury.

The church's usury doctrine influenced the development of

business in broad but subtle ways. Because the church looked more kindly on commercial loans than on those to desperate individuals, devout Christians were more likely to use their capital to form partnerships than become bankers. Interest was often camouflaged as a gift or share in the profits of a venture. It was tolerable to collect interest in the form of bills of exchange, because such bills carried a risk of fluctuating foreign-exchange rates. Lenders to the pope collected interest by overcharging on sales of silk, jewels, or other commodities. The church, in the person of Saint Thomas, had decreed that it was a sin to collect interest on a loan but not a sin to pay interest "since it is not a sin to be a victim."

Hairsplitting on the usury doctrine became ever more arcane and self-interested. Merchants decided it was a sin to "commit usury" with their own money but not with borrowed funds. Countless words were invented to stand in for the forbidden *usury,* including *fictum, damnum, gracie,* and *bene.* In 1220, the word *interest* became distinct from the word *usury;* interest was compensation due to a lender because of a loss or expense incurred by the loan. It was "damages" in the broad sense, which might also include the profit the lenders might have made if their money had been elsewhere. The phrases sometimes used to describe this payment were "trouble, danger, and expense" or "the danger of chance."

Many pious lenders knew they were sinning against the spirit, if not the letter, of the church doctrine, and some tried to make restitution for ill-gotten gains on their deathbeds or in their wills. If they didn't, they might not receive the sacraments and last rites or be buried in hallowed ground. Cosimo de Medici, troubled by his conscience, received a papal bull allowing him to atone for his business practices by endowing a monastery. The church usually agreed to exchange absolution for restitution since the money came to the church and not the victims of the usury. Indeed, Florence's beautiful churches owe at least some of their splendor to the funds received this way.

*   *   *

Few economic areas offered the opportunity to get rich fast in Fugger's lifetime, but mining was one of them. Europe's monarchs needed metal for currency and firearms, yet gold, silver, and other metals were among the few commodities eastern countries would accept in exchange for its spices, silk, and pearls. The mining of gold, silver, tin, cobalt, and iron stimulated the creation of many objects, including machines, which perpetuated their own demand.

Mining was an ancient trade, and by the late fifteenth century, it was among the world's most sophisticated industries, demanding the greatest number of workers and the largest investments of capital. Extracting metal from the earth required engineering skill, machine and natural power, and chemical expertise. The easy deposits had been tapped out by Fugger's time; to go deeper into the earth required better and more expensive machinery. Merchants like Fugger had the money to invest, though because of the scale of mining investments, merchants usually had to pool their money to underwrite even one mine. Most mines had been owned by the states, which had proved to be ineffectual proprietors, economically incapable of squeezing much from their holdings. Before long, most of Europe's mines fell into private hands. The merchants, "having become bankers by successful commerce, became industrialists by successful banking."

Some of Europe's best copper and silver mines could be found near Augsburg. They were controlled by the Hapsburg dynasty, which was then running the Holy Roman Empire— running it into the ground, that is. In 1493, Maximilian I took over the Holy Roman Empire, which Voltaire later described as neither holy nor Roman nor an empire. Two years after becoming emperor, Maximilian, desperate for money to pay his armies, asked Fugger for a loan—something he was to do dozens of times over the next several years. As security on his loans, the emperor pledged the output of many of Hungary's and the

Tirol's silver and copper mines until the debt was repaid. By 1515, Fugger owned the output of Maximilian's silver mines for the next eight years and of his copper mines for the next four.

Fugger joined forces with a Hungarian engineer named Johann Thurzo, whose family had a stake in some mines and who had made great advances in reclaiming flooded mines. To seal the bond between the two families, two Thurzos married two Fuggers—"for the furthering of the Fugger trade," noted a Fugger family chronicle. Investing in modern mining technology, Thurzo and Fugger increased the productivity of the mines. With three principal plants and several hundred workers, Fugger's mining business was one of the largest of the time and the chief source of the Fugger family's great fortune.

From his earliest days in the metal industry, it was clear that Fugger was aiming, with single-minded determination, to corner the world's supply of copper. Indeed, it is almost universally true that where there is competition, there is also a temptation to monopolize. Monopolizing a commodity is a certain way to become rich as well as powerful. The Fuggers began their monopolistic pursuit by forming a copper cartel in 1498 with two other Augsburg suppliers. The three companies pooled their copper and sold all of it at one price through Fugger's middleman in Venice.

By 1501, the Fuggers were operating mines in Germany, Austria, Hungary, Bohemia, and Spain, strictly controlling the amount and source of copper available in each region. As news of their monopoly gradually became public, Fugger was denounced by legislators and small-business owners. The smaller merchants could see that cartels, monopolies, and networks would squeeze them out of the market. The imperial advocate—the attorney general—instituted proceedings against Fugger for violating antimonopoly laws, one of the first trust-busting campaigns in history.

To fight this indictment, Fugger resorted to a frequent strategy used by business leaders under legal attack: He contacted his powerful friends in government and hired a team of lawyers. He complained vehemently to the emperor, Charles V, who ordered the attorney general to cease his prosecution. In 1525, Charles V declared that henceforth ore contracts granting monopoly rights would not be considered monopolistic.

Nevertheless, public opinion among Germans began shifting against the once-revered Fuggers. The Hungarians were even more outraged: They were starving, their country had a crushing debt, and foreign capitalists like Fugger were exploiting and draining their resources. A storm of indignation against Fugger's "usurious monopoly" swept through Hungary, and mobs sacked and looted two of his company's plants. Once more, Jacob sought help from the emperor, who threatened Hungary's king with war if Fugger's holdings weren't restored to him. And so they were.

Besides trading, banking, and mining, the Fuggers carried on an extensive money-changing business, which had been established to help merchants transfer sales receipts across national borders. Cities, princes, the pope, and sometimes even private individuals wanted to stop carrying coins long distances in belts or saddlebags. Moving money was dangerous and inefficient; for the papacy especially, it was a perpetual nuisance. In distant outposts such as Scandinavia and Poland, where few banking facilities existed, there were long delays in getting money to the Vatican—a transfer from Poland could take six months. Papal agents often had to trust traveling merchants or pilgrims to carry their money or goods.

The Fugger firm made it possible for travelers to carry letters of credit from one Fugger operation to another, where they could redeem their paper for cash. Using an intermediary such as the Fuggers, a pope or prince could get quick infusions of money rather than waiting for thousands of small coins to make their way to their treasuries.

The Fuggers also ran a reliable courier operation, whose employees could cover eighty-five miles a day. The couriers brought news of political and economic importance from large firms and halls of state around the globe to the Fuggers' Augsburg headquarters. Their reports were collected in a newsletter and published everyday. Although the Fugger news-letter may be the earliest instance of daily journalism, most people would not have been able to read it. Many of the reports were written in Italian, the commercial language of the time; scholars and clergy used Latin; and other letters were written in the language of their country of origin. The newsletters were passed along to scribes, who hand copied and sold them.

Maps, another vital source of information to trading firms, were as closely guarded—and as frequently stolen—as any trade secret. From the earliest days of civilization, the power of maps had been recognized: In the Roman Empire, it had been a crime for a private person even to possess a map, and as late as 1520 only a tiny number of Europe's people had seen one. In Fugger's time, private trading companies prepared their own "secret" at-lases. Once the world had been marked by longitude and lati-tude, every place could be located on a common scheme. With the arrival of the printing press, maps became more accurate and available. In the late fifteenth century, the lens through which Europe could see the world opened rapidly: The Cape of Good Hope was rounded in 1488, the West Indies discovered in 1492, India reached by sea in 1498, and the Pacific sighted by Balboa in 1513.

Another industry that promoted the creation of wealth boomed during the Renaissance: insurance. Insurance bordered on gambling because investors had no statistics to rely on. In-deed, no one from king to peasant could accurately guess what would happen in the future because they had no clear figures de-scribing the past. Yet insurance made it possible for people to in-vest in ventures that might otherwise have been considered too risky.

*   *   *

Despite the number and complexity of his businesses and the political and social unrest of his time, Jacob Fugger rested easy. He told his nephews that he never had "any hindrance to sleep, but laid from him all care and stress of business with his shirt."

Apart from a few often-repeated anecdotes and quotes, little was recorded about Fugger's personal life. His portrait was painted several times, and he is pictured as a wide-browed, clean-shaven man wearing a gold cap. He was pleasant but plainspoken and had relatively simple tastes, although he was hospitable in the grand style of his age. Lavish hospitality was an index of social prestige, or at least financial wherewithal. Married but childless, Fugger had four majestic houses filled with paintings and sculptures by Europe's best artists. He was a life-long collector of manuscripts and books, and at the time of his death, and for some decades afterward, the Fugger library was the most famous in Germany. In 1511, the weaver's grandson was made a count of the empire by Maximilian. Nevertheless, his new title could not crash the social gates of his hometown's snobbish aristocracy.

Unlike the wealthy of the modern era, sixteenth-century business heroes had few ways to publicize their success and fortune. Princes might use poets, writers, and artists. Other wealthy people self-published biographies of their families or erected extravagant monuments. Portrait medals in gold, silver, and bronze were also used widely. Fugger commissioned one of himself in bronze and used replicas of it as personal gifts.

Fugger's lengthy association with Maximilian was one of history's most audacious partnerships between business and state. Maximilian was an unstable leader, impetuous and extravagant. To satisfy his passion for hunting, for example, he kept a kennel of two thousand hounds. There were few laws, rules, or traditions concerning what should or shouldn't be bought—money's limits were largely untested. At one point, Maximilian decided he wanted to be pope, and he planned to ask Jacob Fugger to lend him bribe money for the cardinals. As security on the loan, Maximilian would pledge "the four best caskets with Our jewels together with Our robes of state." Maximilian's ambition, noted a historian of the Renaissance, "remained a pious wish."

As Maximilian approached retirement, he decided he wanted his grandson Charles to succeed him. His treasury was completely bare, however, so Maximilian applied to Jacob Fugger for the funds to purchase electors' votes. Meanwhile, a rival candidate, Francis I of France, was also trying to bribe the electors. The stakes rocketed.

Before the election was settled, Maximilian died, and young Charles fired Fugger and hired a banking rival. Fugger was furious. He warned Charles that without his financial backing, Charles would never be emperor. Fugger then approached the electors himself, who in turn informed Charles that unless his bribe offers had Fugger's backing, they would not feel secure. Fugger was rehired by Charles, and in 1519, after months of negotiations, the contest was decided by the vote of the margrave of Brandenberg. Francis had offered the margrave a rich French wife with a large dowry. Fugger countered with Maximilian's granddaughter and a large cash premium, a third of it payable in coin when Charles was elected. The election of Charles as Holy Roman Emperor may have been the largest business transaction of the century.

Fugger, while remaining politically loyal to the Hapsburgs, did not hesitate to demand repayment when their royal debts were due. In a letter to Charles, Fugger demanded that he "order that the money which I have paid out, together with the interest on it, shall be reckoned up and paid, without further delay." Fugger signed the letter, "Your Imperial Majesty's most humble servant," but Fugger was neither humble nor a servant.

From imperial banker to papal banker wasn't a big step, but

no other German or French merchant had ever done it; the Italian banks had monopolized church finances until Fugger appeared. Gradually, he snatched the papal treasury of one country after another—first Germany, then Scandinavia, then Hungary, and then Poland. And for almost twenty-five years, Fugger handled the bulk of the papacy's Roman coinage.

Being the pope's banker was a mixed blessing. Popes weren't always diligent about meeting their obligations, and the only recourse against them was to refuse their next entreaty. The benefit of the position, however, was the lucrative income that came from collecting and directing the flow of funds into the papal treasury. Fugger could also influence the selection of bishops in Germany.

The many anticlerical dissidents active in Germany in the early sixteenth century were tinder for a spark of fury against the church, which Jacob Fugger helped to supply. The story behind the conflagration began in 1517, when Pope Leo X announced an indulgence, the proceeds of which were to be used to finish refurbishing Saint Peter's Cathedral, a costly but beloved project launched by his predecessor. Indulgences had become almost commonplace by this time, and Leo's would have been unremarkable except that it collided with another drama then playing out in Germany.

Count Albrecht, who was already archbishop of two dioceses, wanted to add another to his treasure chest. A single person holding three archbishoprics would be unprecedented, but the Vatican was open to it. However, to secure the third diocese, Albrecht would have to pay a hefty surcharge on the usual substantial fees clerics paid for such positions.

Albrecht knew that his communicants were already staggering under the weight of taxation and that he would need to devise a fresh fund-raising plea. He and the Fuggers came up with a strategy for buying Albrecht his diocese while enriching the Fuggers. Albrecht would borrow a lump sum from the

Fuggers while simultaneously launching an indulgence campaign in his territory on behalf of Saint Peter's. Half the money collected would go to the Vatican; the other half would pay off the Fuggers' loan to Albrecht.

The two parties hired a famous indulgence preacher of the day, Johann Tetzel, who had demonstrated a gift for persuading people to give money to the church. To keep things fair and square, an agent of the Fuggers accompanied the pardoner Tetzel on his rounds, checking expenses and receipts and keeping a key to the indulgence chest. Together, preacher and money manager trekked from town to town, selling one-page documents with a blank to enter the name of the buyer. When the indulgence chest was full, it was opened in the presence of Fugger's agent, and the entire amount was sent to a Fugger employee in Leipzig, who only then forwarded the pope's half to Rome. Some people believed Tetzel was dedicated more to raising funds than to saving people's souls, and they had reason to think so: Tetzel was dispensing sealed letters of forgiveness for sins a person hadn't yet committed.

One of Tetzel's critics was Martin Luther, professor of theology at the University of Wittenberg. Several buyers of "papal letters" brought them to Martin Luther, asking that he attest to their authenticity. Luther refused to authenticate them and denounced "Fugger's cutpurses." When Tetzel heard this, he denounced Luther back, provoking Luther to compose his ninety-five theses. Indulgences had turned sin into a trivial matter, Luther preached, to be adjusted amicably over a bargain counter with the peddler of pardons. Luther's theses became the talk of literate Germans, their pent-up anticlericalism having at last found a voice. The Reformation was born.

The splintering of religious beliefs opened wider the chasm between religion and business. Some Protestant leaders expressed doubts about the biblical doctrine against usury and began defending interest and credit. Luther, who originally opposed big business and denounced interest, gradually compromised, hoping to gain the power to regulate business affairs. It was not complicity in sin to pay usury, after all, Luther decided. Private property must be respected. The Christian man was free to lend his money. Indeed, the church should dissociate itself from business and commerce, Luther at last declared, removing the last traces of moral governance over commercial behavior. From then on, people were permitted to make money as effectively as possible, grappling with their religious scruples in private.

Later, the Protestant leader John Calvin tried to control business in Geneva, putting all commercial and moral matters under the regulation of the church. Although his experiment was ultimately unsuccessful, his dogma was widely embraced: To achieve God's reign on earth, humans must be thrifty, sober, and diligent, the ingredients of business success. He justified accepting a moderate rate of interest as being harmonious with the good life, prompting a rush of converts from the business sector. "It took with the brethren like polygamy with the Turks," wrote a pamphleteer of the time. Calvinism replaced the ideal of social and economic stability that entailed knowing and keeping one's place; instead, people began to believe that it was respectable to strive for material improvement. In funeral orations of the time, the dead were increasingly honored not for having renounced vain worldly goods but for acquiring wealth through labor and industry. Everything that increased a person's power of action was good.

Profit, too, was freed from the reproach of traditional Christian teachings. "Whoever buys a thing in order to make a profit selling it, whole and unchanged, is the trader who is cast out of God's temple," Saint John Chrysostom had said. Profit was a kind of theft. The church believed that objects had a "just price" that covered material, transport, and labor. In the thirteenth century, Saint Thomas Aquinas gave Christians some wiggle room by defining "just price" as including a margin for the seller's reasonable comfort. But even Luther believed a person shouldn't say "I will sell my wares as dear as I can or desire" but "I will sell my wares as dear as is . . . right and proper."

The just price was set by craft guilds, which had evolved from bands of long-distance traders who transported their goods in caravans. As they settled into towns, guilds began to dominate and regulate commerce. Only the guilds' members could buy, sell, or manufacture goods in the town. In time, merchant guilds were supplanted by craft guilds. In return for monopolistic protection, members of the craft guilds agreed to rigorous regulations. The guild, for example, forbade a member from keeping longer hours, paying better wages, or, most significant, charging more or less for his product than other guild members. The system became enmeshed in a tangle of red tape, so that the hilts, blades, and sheaths of swords were made by three different guilds. Noted a historian, "The tone was one not of free enterprise, but of control, of equality of opportunity among members, of security rather than risk."

The craft guilds eventually fell victim to competition, and the last moral restraints on usury and profit disappeared. Traders, merchants, financiers, and manufacturers no longer had to fear the opprobrium of their neighbors or the wrath of God. The seeds of Protestantism could be found in the antipathy so many Germans and other Europeans felt toward the church's business practices. Yet the Reformation was one of the best things that could have happened to modern capitalism. Removing religious stigma from acquisitiveness meant there were no longer any moral boundaries on commercial schemes. Furthermore, material success increasingly became the measuring rod for goodness. People mired in poverty were no one's responsibility—they were simply not diligent and thrifty. For the rich, wealth was not a gift but a reward; they had earned the right to do whatever they pleased.

In his final years, Jacob Fugger was the most honored and unpopular citizen in Germany. Even the Fugger name became the stuff of mockery: In the vernacular of the time, *Fokker* or *Fucar* meant financial power, which meant war and repression, taxation and rising prices, and *to fugger* carried a connotation of unconscionable interest rates and other questionable business practices. The Fuggers were using Germany's capital resources not to finance new productive work, their critics said, but to finance war loans and government speculations. Jacob Fugger didn't let the vitriol disturb his equilibrium: "Many in the world are hostile to me," he said. "They say I am rich. I am rich by God's grace without injury to any man."

Fugger eventually relented and hired someone to help sell him and his philosophy to the public. Konrad Peutinger, a lawyer, theologian, and humanist became Fugger's chief adviser. He also drafted several progressive trade laws for Maximilian. Peutinger defended cartels, monopolies, profit, and interest; he was the first great philosophical evangelist of the profit system. "Every merchant is free to sell as dear as he can and chooses," Peutinger wrote. "For it happens often enough that merchants to their injury are forced to sell their wares cheaper than they bought them."

No one could deny that the working class became poorer and politically weaker in the sixteenth century. Workers produced the goods that were exported to pay for imported luxuries enjoyed by very few. Prices of all commodities in most of Europe rose during the sixteenth century. An amount of money sufficient to buy a whole costume in one generation bought only a pair of shoes in the next. Between 1500 and 1600, the price of wheat rose 300 percent in Germany. Peasants' revolts between 1524 and 1526 left one hundred thousand people dead. In the 1590s, a massive famine across Europe resulted in widespread starvation. A Swede wrote: "People ground and chopped many unsuitable things into bread such as bark, buds, hay, straw, peat moss, nutshells, etc. . . . Many widows were found dead with seed that grew in the fields and other kinds of grass in their mouths." The philosopher Thomas Hobbes was moved to write that humanity's natural condition was "poor and solitary, nasty, brutish and short."

Throughout the century, the Fuggers were routinely blamed for the collapse of the northern European economies. In Augsburg between 1556 and 1584, approximately seventy large companies declared bankruptcy. An antiplutocratic movement took hold in Germany, where proposals were made to restrict companies to three branch offices and a finite amount of capital. Even Luther realized that the collapse of ecclesiastic authority had led to a chaos of unregulated authority. "It is clear enough how much more greedy, cruel, immodest, shameless, wicked the people are now than they were under popery," he wrote.

Jacob Fugger died in 1526, leaving his nephew Anton to carry on the Fugger dynasty. At his death, Jacob was worth approximately $75 million. For the previous seventeen years, his firm's profits had averaged 54 percent a year. In his will, he arranged for the construction of the first low-cost, garden-apartment housing for the poor. Fifty cottages housing two families each were built in the Augsburg suburbs for under-privileged workers. Called the Fuggerei, the cottages still stand, a paradoxical reminder of the man whose monopolies cost German workers a fortune.

To Fugger, his golden countinghouse, as it was sometimes called, had an identity separate from that of its individual members. More than anything else, he sought immortality for the Fugger dynasty. After Anton died in 1560, the business was passed along to his nephew, who kept the firm afloat until 1607, when Spain's King Philip III declared his country bankrupt. The Fuggers were among Spain's largest creditors, and the firm couldn't survive the blow. It was forced into compulsory liquidation, and by 1640 it had ceased to exist. But the personal qualities that helped Jacob Fugger create so much wealth—ambition, determination, and vision—still enrich the successful capitalists of the modern world.

Six

Dreamers, Gamblers, and Suckers

❧

John Law (1671–1729)

It was only a matter of time before people realized that money didn't have to be a thing—it could be an idea. And if everyone believed and trusted that idea, then currency could be manipulated to promote production, trade, and consumption. Since the creation of money, its potential had always been limited by its substance—money was gold, silver, jewels, and land. These tangibles were finite, and the supply of them wasn't growing nearly as quickly as people's desire to use money as a way to buy and sell. It was absurd for trade and economic growth to be hindered by a shortage of metal, but that was the state of affairs in Europe when John Law surfaced. Law became one of the first people to understand that traditional doctrines about money were not immutable. Law claimed he had discovered the philosophers' stone: "My secret is to make gold out of paper," he said. Free money was an intoxicating, irresistible, and cataclysmic idea.

Born in Edinburgh in 1671, John Law lived during Europe's so-called Enlightenment, when reason and logic exorcised superstition and religious hobgoblins. The universe no longer seemed like the battleground for warring angels and devils. Nature was a mechanism governed by discoverable laws. People began to count and measure everything—population, production, trade, money—and modern understanding of statistics was born. Edmund Burke called the Enlightenment an age of "sophisters, economists and calculators," but it was also a period of optimism. People believed that social problems were soluble and that, in general, history was a chronicle of progress.

Despite their broader grasp of the world, however, people hadn't solved the problem of exchanging value. Traders used some paper currency—called bills of exchange—but most people still carried their money, usually in the form of coins, on or near their person and defended it with swords. High-stakes gamblers like John Law found it physically impossible to carry enough cash to their games. They settled their accounts by signing IOUs that were paid—by honorable gamblers anyway—in cash the next day. Traders who had to accept cash faced a bewildering variety of coins minted by different nations, princes, and cities. In exchange for a shipment of goods, a merchant might receive a sack of guilders, drachmas, guldens, marks, ducats, livres, pistoles, ducatoons, piscatoons, and other coins of which he had never heard. Since coins then were hammered by hand, thicknesses of the same denomination coin could be different, and cheaters filed and clipped the edges.

Meanwhile, shortages of gold and silver plagued even realms of prosperity. Hoarding was a problem wherever governments were unstable, which was virtually everywhere at some time. Kings and popes came and went, but metal was forever. It could be secreted underground against future hardship. Even if people didn't have to hide it, they wanted their silver close by, in goblets and platters, not out circulating in the world, where it could be seized or debased. They didn't have many choices about where to put precious metal anyway—there were few retail banks. This hoarding mentality had earlier given rise to Thomas Gresham's enduring law that bad money drives out good.

In early eighteenth-century France, where John Law then lived, Louis XIV was taxing with such reckless impetuosity that many people had begun to smuggle money out of the country. The French weren't poor—anyone could see in the aristocracy's clothes and furnishings that there was real prosperity in France. But the country didn't have enough currency, and that made it difficult to trade with other countries. Banks and governments tried to substitute paper for metal as bills of exchange, but this was of limited advantage: For each piece of paper, there was an exactly equivalent amount of metal out of circulation.

France's predicament disturbed John Law. Why should the country's economic system starve because of insufficient supplies of metal money? Why should a great colonial empire, with its own army and navy, run on the inefficient medium of coins? If people became as confident of paper currency as they were of metal, wouldn't they prefer the convenience of paper? The very word *credit,* after all, derives from the Latin for "to believe." Confidence, Law once wrote, "is nothing but the certainty of being paid." (Others have countered, "Credit is suspicion asleep.") Paper should have a claim on metal, Law conceded, but why would everyone want to convert from paper to metal simultaneously? Therefore, a government could issue paper with more value than that of the underlying metal. Creating money in the form of credit could actually create sustainable wealth, Law believed: "Credit is to business what the brain is to the human body."

Money was a function, not a surrogate, John Law decided, taking the next giant step in the progression of currency from cowrie shells to electronic bytes. Indeed, the seventeenth century marked the end of "the medieval dream of a fixed world of stable commercial and moral values, of good money and just prices, earthly duty and heavenly reward." Displacing this was "a floating world, in which land and people and things are tossed this way and that on billowing tides of money." Even as the world's prosperity increased, there remained a stubborn belief that wealth was finite and concrete. John Law and a few of his contemporaries didn't see why that should be true. Their philosophies were famously catastrophic but ultimately correct.

*   *   *

One of eleven children, John Law grew up in Edinburgh, where his father was a goldsmith who lent money on the side. As a child, Law displayed an aptitude for arithmetic, geometry, and algebra.

When Law was thirteen years old, his father died, and his mother took over the family business. Law worked for the firm for three years, learning the principles of banking, and after work he studied tennis and fencing. Before he left to seek his fortune in London, he was described as "nicely expert in all manner of debaucheries."

In the city, Law gambled, studied finance, and practiced what was then called "gallantry"—all at considerable expense to his widowed mother. He was a good athlete, quick-witted, eloquent, and fastidious in dress. He was also a great favorite among women, who called him Beau Law. The men of the city called him, less affectionately, "Jessamy John."

For reasons lost to history, Law began feuding with a man named Beau Wilson, another London dandy. The two arranged to fight a duel at midday in a public square. Their fight lasted only a few seconds: In Law's one pass, he fatally pierced Wilson's chest with his sword.

Because duels were assumed to be premeditated, Law was charged with murder and convicted. Imprisoned while awaiting a public hanging, Law escaped. Some say he drugged the guard with an opiate, filed off his leg irons, jumped thirty feet from the King's Bench prison wall, sprained his ankle and, with the help of friends, got to a boat bound for France. Less romantic versions have Law's high-placed friends arranging and underwriting his escape. An advertisement published in the London *Gazette* in 1695, offering a reward for Law's return, described him as "well shaped, above Six foot high, large Pockholes in his Face, big high Nosed, speaks broad and loud."

For the next ten years, Law drifted around the Continent, supporting himself by gambling. In Venice, Genoa, and Amsterdam, he also studied fledgling banking companies. His mathematical mind was persistently reflecting on the intricacies of high finance. At Europe's many gambling houses—Paris alone had more than sixty at the time—Law became known as an expert at calculating mathematical odds. A composed and disciplined cardplayer, Law would enter a gaming house carrying a sack of gold in each hand. He would always claim the place of "banker" at the green baize faro table—a position from which the gambler can manipulate odds.

Eventually, he was winning so much money that he commissioned the casting of a large gold coin to facilitate the handling of his stakes. He began to travel around in a polished coach attended by men in livery. Charming, handsome, and wealthy, Law was able to get letters of introduction to the drawing rooms of powerful Europeans. At one home in Paris, Law met the duke of Orleans, who a few years later became regent of France. At the time, however, not even the duke could prevent the Parisian police from ejecting Law from the city. "He knew how to play too well at the games he had introduced," explained the police chief.

Law learned the most about banking and finance in Holland, where the Bank of Amsterdam was already one hundred years old. Established as a solution to the shortage and inconvenience of metal currency, the bank had become a trusted safety net under Holland's booming economy. "The bank was the watchdog of capitalism in Amsterdam," one historian wrote. "Its overriding concern was not to generate funds for enterprise but to control the conditions under which they could be exchanged. . . . Its working motto was probity, not profit."

In John Law's time, the Bank of Amsterdam primarily handled transfers—merchants brought coins to the bank and received credit for their value in the form of banknotes. Because so much currency had been diluted, the bank judged value by weight and examination, not denomination, and the value the bank determined was referred to as "bank money." Merchants used banknotes to settle accounts among themselves. Because the bank simply transferred money among accounts, it could never be caught short of metal reserves. So trusted were the Bank of Amsterdam's notes that people sometimes paid a premium for paper over metal.

When Law first saw Amsterdam's bank in operation, he was astounded. Here was an institution that controlled much of the country's money without any of its owners feeling poorer for it. Furthermore, once coin or bullion entered the bank, it tended to stay there. Here was another way to get rich: Collect vast pools of other people's money and then maintain authority over how it was used.

Amsterdam also had a large, liquid, and unruly financial exchange, where investors bought and sold shares of the Dutch East India and West India companies, as well as financial derivatives such as options and futures, which were known as trading in the wind. The Amsterdam exchange was open only two hours a day, which contributed to its riotous atmosphere. Indeed, it was here at the Amsterdam exchange, thirty-five years before John Law's birth, that thousands of investors were seduced by one of the most extraordinary speculative frenzies in history.

Without surplus money—money not needed for bread, firewood, or shoes—speculation is impossible. In the early seventeenth century, Holland was awash in surplus. The country had become Europe's leading commercial power and financial capital, the primary world market for guns, diamonds, sugar, and porcelain, among much else. The Dutch were primarily middlemen and brokers—they "buy to sell again, take in to take out," Daniel Defoe later wrote—and they were adept at it. In 1631, René Descartes wrote from Amsterdam, "There is no one in this city, except me, who is not engaged in trade." The nation's affluence trickled down to even the lowliest workers, who enjoyed the highest incomes in Europe. But one drawback to prosperity is that people often become more credulous and less skeptical of promises of easy money.

In 1629, another stroke of good fortune fell to Holland: The

Dutch West India Company captured the Spanish silver fleet and brought home a windfall of wealth. This intensified people's belief that they could get rich by luck alone. The bounty unloaded at the wharves of Amsterdam seemed to offer a magical rather than a methodical route to fortune, and Dutch culture became suffused with "admiration for heroic materialism." As a character in a satire about speculation said, "I've wasted my life in hard work, and so did many parents with their toil and starvation." From this attitude to gambling on tulip futures wasn't such a big leap.

In a world where tulip bulbs can be bought for pennies, heated speculation on tulip futures sounds quaintly daft. But in the early seventeenth century, exotic plants and elaborate orangeries were favorite toys of the wealthy. Tulips had first come to the Netherlands from Turkey late in the previous century, and for several years they were too expensive for any but the richest—indeed, tulips grew in the Fuggers' garden in Augsburg. Unlike other rare objects of desire, however, individual tulips could also reproduce themselves, which gave them a definite, though unknown, future value.

By the 1620s, tulips had become the fashionable flower of France, Germany, and the Netherlands. New, less expensive varieties put them within reach of the common person. The tulip fad spread during the 1630s, and then it exploded. Bulbs became a national craze, perceived less as flora than as an investment. Traveling salesmen took bulbs into the hinterlands and peddled them. Everyone in the country, from nobles to chimney sweeps, yeomen to footmen, swarmed to tulip bulbs "like flies around a honey pot." Foreign money poured into the country to invest in tulips.

Tulip mania was an archetype of the greater fool theory: People knew bulb prices were entirely detached from rational value, but they believed others would be even bigger fools than they were. For a while, they were right. At the peak of the boom, family fortunes were squandered on single bulbs. People traded land, houses, furniture, horses, sheep, cheese—anything for a tulip, particularly such remarkable varieties as Viceroy or Semper Augustus. In France, the entire dowry of one bride consisted of a rare tulip bulb. Eventually, sellers sold bulbs they didn't have to buyers who didn't have money to buy them. Neither party intended to deliver anything; they were simply betting on the future price of bulbs. In early 1637, bulb prices were almost doubling every day. A tulip grower was said to have committed suicide when his entire stock was eaten by a cow.

Later that year, the bubble burst for no obvious reason except rumors circulating about a shortage of buyers. People tried to extricate themselves from the webs of credit and debt they had woven. Some investors were left with a handful of tulip futures and a heavy mortgage on their homes. There was the usual fury and recriminations that follow every financial cataclysm, and the usual inability to find a person to blame. The crowd, nevertheless, had learned its lesson: Tulips would never again excite so much lunacy. Next time it would be something else.

In the early 1700s, John Law left Continental Europe and returned to Scotland, which was then mired in an economic depression. In a pamphlet he published there, Law proposed that the government establish a council of trade, which would issue interest-bearing notes also serving as legal currency. With the money raised, the council would develop the country's mineral wealth, restore the nation's fisheries, encourage foreign trade, and abolish monopolies—a kind of eighteenth-century New Deal. But Scotland, indeed all of Europe, was littered with pamphlets vehemently proposing or opposing economic remedies. Law's plan was flatly dismissed by the Scottish parliament and the public.

While in Scotland, Law also published a treatise, "Money and Trade Considered with a Proposal for Supplying the Nation with Money." He recommended the creation of a land bank that would issue notes to landlords secured on their estates, relieving the insufficiency of "specie" by supplying a stable medium of currency. Instead of gold backing the notes, the property of the country would do so. The proposal had some support in parliament but not enough to pass it.

The approaching union between Scotland and England in 1707 exposed Law to arrest, so that year he left for the Continent again, moving among big cities, where he again gambled for his living. In his travels, Law met a married woman named Catherine Seigneur, who left her husband to run away with him. Although the two never married, Catherine took his name, bore two children, and remained loyal—though not faithful—until his death. After drifting around together, the two moved to Paris in 1715, where Louis XIV had recently died. Louis had passed France to his five-year-old great-grandson, Louis XV, whose regent, the duke of Orleans, was John Law's friend from the faro table.

The profligate Louis XIV had set the tone for a spending spree among Parisians that played into John Law's hands. In seventeenth-century Paris, there was no such thing as excess. Wealth was seen as an unalloyed good, and the wealthy pampered themselves with grotesque and silly magnificence. No one felt guilty about attending a party where the door prizes were horses. The mistress of a rich nobleman wanted to exceed the legendary Lucullus, who swallowed a diamond worth 100,000 francs, so she ate a bill worth 500,000 francs. While some of the wealthy were children of the landed aristocracy, others made their fortunes by milking the national treasury. Their grotesque appetites played out in strange ways: A man named Beaujean kept fantastic gardens but was too fat to walk in them.

Louis XIV's belief in divine right—*"L'etat c'est moi"*—turned the king's debts into the nation's. Louis had been living on loans for years, borrowing from his subjects and issuing worthless paper that went by different names to promote confusion. The floating debt was enormous—in the last fourteen years of his reign, Louis XIV had spent two billion livres more than he had collected in taxes. The coinage had been so debased that it was almost worthless—the amount of silver in the livre had been cut from twelve ounces to less than half an ounce. With his extravagant tastes—architectural historians call Versailles an example of "power architecture"—Louis XIV left his country's treasury bankrupt, the army unpaid. On his deathbed, even Louis himself had to admit, "I have loved war too much."

Meanwhile, tens of thousands of workers were unemployed, and agriculture was in distress. Peasants lived in mud houses, slept on straw, ate boiled roots and ferns, and suffered through a succession of typhoid and smallpox epidemics. Many fled to the cities, where they became beggars and vagrants. Trade was almost at a standstill. Artisans were fleeing the country; others were sending their money abroad. There was no large-scale industry, and business fortunes were made primarily by "the invisible hand"—bureaucrats diverting tax money to themselves. One study found that less than half of the taxes collected in one year reached the royal treasury.

The government's finances were clearly a shambles, but because state accountants still didn't use double-entry bookkeeping, no one realized how dire the situation was until Louis XIV died. The government considered declaring bankruptcy, but the regent rejected the idea. Instead, he cut the interest rate on state securities from 7 percent to 4 percent, devalued the currency, and reduced the size of the army and the government. He also established a chamber of justice to investigate tax collectors, financiers, merchants, and others. Like so many governmental bodies of the time, the Chamber of Justice was despotic and corrupt. Informers were encouraged, and blackmail was rampant. One financier who had been fined some twelve million livres for having taken illegal profits was told by a powerful count that the fine could be reduced for a sum of one hundred thousand crowns. "You're too late," the financier replied. "I've already made a deal with your wife for fifty thousand."

Anyone who was wealthy was presumed to be guilty of something, and the clever ones assessed themselves before someone else did it for them. Many people were stripped of their power, influence, and possessions. A few were executed, and some who felt their situation was hopeless committed suicide. But in the end, the witch-hunt of financiers had little effect except to make people more careful about where they were seen spending money.

John Law believed he could fix France with his "system." He knew the French economy urgently needed funds pumped into it, but he began by proposing a bank that would issue notes and hold and transfer deposits, much as the Bank of Amsterdam did. As an incentive to the government to endorse his bank, Law would sell shares of the new bank for a combination of cash and government securities, which, although then trading at a deep discount, he would honor at face value.

Law hoped for government backing but got only its permission. In 1716, he established a private bank called Law and Company. The original capital was six million livres, consisting of 1,200 shares of 5,000 livres each. So sure was Law of his system's promise that he invested his entire fortune in it and—ever the gambler—promised to give 500,000 livres to charity if the project failed.

Many other people had tried to replace metal with paper, but it was difficult to persuade people they should exchange coins, which had a known value, for the promise of other coins in the future. Coinage everywhere was subject to sudden and arbitrary devaluation or augmentation, making its purchasing power somewhat hypothetical. Between 1702 and 1718, the prices of silver and gold in France had changed forty-two times. But Law made a promise to the French people that their government hadn't: His notes were redeemable on demand for coin "of the weight and standard of the day of issue." That meant the value of the notes would be unaffected by future fluctuations in coinage. Law's new notes were taken so seriously by the government that altering or counterfeiting them was deemed a capital crime.

Many French people had never seen a banknote, and in Law and Company's early months the new financial instrument was the subject of derision around Paris. But gradually trust in the bank began to build. In 1717, the notes were made receivable for taxes and other royal revenues. The following year, Law's bank became the state—royal—bank. This meant its notes were guaranteed by the crown, even though Law, a private citizen, retained control of it. Many merchants and government officials vociferously objected to this arrangement, to no avail. Law and the state became one, although neither totally controlled the entity they had created. One of the nationalized bank's first actions was to change the terms of its notes to be redeemable for "current coins." Now Law's notes would be subject to fluctuating values.

Law's alliance with the French government ultimately led to economic disaster, but for a few years he was one of the most revered people in France. His past as a duelist, gambler, and refugee became irrelevant; he was a financial pied piper, and all France danced to his music. Law may have been at the right place at the right time, but he also had the creativity and guile to electrify people on a monumental scale.

Many writers and historians have puzzled over what made John Law so successful at promoting his system. Karl Marx described Law as having "the pleasant character mixture of swindler and prophet." Or maybe Law was a classic example of a "projector," a transition between alchemist and modern speculator, a man who could make gold out of bubbles. He was educated in neither science nor finance but whispered plans, often of a highly visionary character, into high-placed ears. He said what his audience wanted to hear: He could make them rich merely by printing paper. To be such a man as John Law, jeered Daniel Defoe, "you must put on a sword, kill a beau or two, be condemned to be hanged, break prison if you can, get over to some strange country, turn stock-jobber, set up a Mississippi stock, bubble a nation, and you may soon be a great man." A French writer sighed, "He is as difficult to assess as a theological proposition."

That he was an inveterate gambler tells part of the story; gamblers are often characterized by grandiosity, love of risk, and unconventionality. Although Law did not, gamblers often come from lower-class homes, where fate, chance, and luck seem to loom larger. For people who feel alienated, one study of gamblers has suggested, gambling becomes self-expression. Freud believed compulsive gamblers were driven by an overwhelming need to lose—to savor victimhood and injustice and to revel in remorse and self-pity. Others have found that gambling provides thrills, aggression behind a playful facade, and artificial and short-term solving of issues, divorced from real life. The French government was gambling as much as John Law was, although Law himself didn't see their arrangement as much of a risk. To him, it was a sure thing.

In 1717, Law proposed establishing a company that would have the exclusive rights to trade with and exploit the resources of the Mississippi River, the Louisiana Territory, and Canada's fur trade—all under French control at the time. Law persuaded the regent that such a trading company could make France the greatest commercial nation in the world. He might have noted the favorable precedents: The Dutch East India and British South Sea companies loaned money to the government in return for monopoly trading privileges. The shares of the companies were traded among merchants and used as currency to settle accounts. But Law's scheme went further: He would pay down some of the government's enormous debt from the company's profits.

The regent and parliament approved Law's plan, and the Company of the West was established. Its one obligation to the state was to settle six thousand white and three thousand non-white people in the territory. Shares in the company sold slowly at first: For nearly two years, they could be bought below par. To attract public attention, Law declared that in six months he would "call" for two hundred shares of the company at par, even though the shares were then selling at about half of face value. Share prices began to rise.

Law's company gradually began to acquire other contracts for government business, occasionally issuing more shares to finance its acquisitions. It bought the tobacco monopoly in 1718, when consumption of tobacco was rapidly escalating. Shortly afterward, the company absorbed the Company of Senegal, whose business was largely slave trading in Africa, and the French East India Company, which owned the China trade. The company commissioned twenty-four oceangoing vessels. Renamed Company of the Indies, Law's "primeval conglomerate" was popularly known as the Mississippi company. In 1719, the French government gave the Mississippi company the right of coinage. John Law now controlled the mint, the public finances, the bank, the sea trade, and the Louisiana, tobacco, and salt revenues.

At the same time, Law was encouraging holders of government annuities—whose debt financing was crippling the crown—to exchange their instruments for shares in the Mississippi company. He issued two hundred thousand shares of his company and again accepted discounted paper at face value. Several months later, he issued another fifty thousand shares. All were snapped up enthusiastically, so Law issued still another fifty thousand shares. Then, in September 1719, Law announced that he would buy the entire debt of France by issuing more shares of his Mississippi company and basically swapping dividends. By the end of the year, he had sold six hundred thousand shares in the Mississippi company.

To keep the share price rising, Law used various promotions and manipulations. He published exaggerated accounts of Louisiana's riches, mineral resources, and people. The mountains were "full of gold, silver, copper, lead and quicksilver. As these metals are very common, and the savages know nothing of their value, they exchange lumps of gold and silver for . . . cooking utensils, spindles, a small looking-glass, or even a little brandy." He distributed engravings to the masses picturing Indian women with large, dreamy eyes. He created duchies, earldoms, and marquisates in Louisiana (and gave himself the duchy of Arkansas).

The reality, of course, was quite different. Much of the Mississippi valley was still unconquered wilderness. Law offered cash bonuses and 450 acres to families that would emigrate. When that aroused little interest, Law issued an edict declaring that any servant who was out of work for four days was an idler and should be sent to Louisiana. Hospitals and prisons were combed for prostitutes because of the terrible shortage of women in the territory. Some people seized the opportunity to rid themselves of inconvenient relatives, with spouses accusing each other of being vagabonds. Squads of archers, called the Mississippi gangsters, roamed the city's streets searching for recruits. When the unwilling immigrants arrived in Louisiana, they found filthy huts and no evidence of the gold or precious stones Law had hoped might lie under colonial soil.

But in Paris, no one knew this, and no one asked or cared. The only thing the French knew with certainty was that prices of Mississippi shares would never stop climbing. Stock that had come on the market at 500 livres was selling for 10,000 livres. This price unnerved even Law himself, although he had become one of the richest men in the world. Meanwhile, the regent, seeing how easy it was to print money, ordered more money printed. In one year, the supply of money almost doubled. Inflation soared.

For a while, inflation is agreeable. More money circulates, giving people the illusion that they have more money to spend, until some months or years later they look at the debits and credits and face the cold truth. Until then, however, they giddily suspend reason and believe in magic. If they refuse to be duped,

they're regarded as oldfangled idiots. There were fewer caution-
ary precedents to warn them of the danger ahead. They were less
cynical; they hadn't heard it all.

The Mississippi company issued its shares from an office on
the rue de Quincampoix—a tiny street no more than a few yards
wide. Beset from morning to night by eager applicants, the alley
became the de facto center of financial exchange in Paris. *Tout
le monde* came to call: Dukes and duchesses, counts and countesses waited for hours in front of Law's door to buy shares. Some
took rooms or apartments in nearby buildings. Rents on houses
in the street soared. Outhouses became sitting rooms—or so the
story is told—and a hunchbacked man rented his hump as a
writing desk. A cobbler leased the chairs in his stall for stock-
jobbing. The profusion of paper brought counterfeiters out of
the woodwork, and they confused things further by throwing
false certificates into the market. For speculators without ready
cash, usurers with nearby offices offered "clock loans"—a quarter percent per quarter hour. No one regulated the speculators—
if Law and the regent did anything, it was urge them on. The
rush for speculative riches is the acquisitive impulse in its most
unfettered form, characterized by lightheartedness and rosy optimism. Who has not imagined him- or herself a sudden millionaire?

In Paris, people of every class enjoyed the novelty of making
a fortune while they slept. Rags became riches, and riches became inordinate riches. A former footman who hit the jackpot
apparently betrayed his origins by climbing up behind his new
coach instead of getting into it. So many people were becoming
rich that the French needed a new word to describe them, and
millionaire was it. Writing home, an English clerk living in Paris
noted that the Mississippi company had so gripped the French
that "to talk of anything else is to be ridiculous, and not to be listened to." Some three hundred thousand people flocked to Paris,
and more wanted to come; there was a two-month wait for a
stagecoach seat to Paris from several French cities. The visitors

spent money on places to stay, meals, and stables, and an illusory prosperity shone over the land.

To supply a new demand for luxuries, industries proliferated around the country, and labor became so scarce that workers were able to demand quadruple their earlier wages. One of the newly rich decorated his Parisian home so luxuriously that an observer wrote, "To form an idea of the magnificence of his apartments, we must have recourse to descriptions which are used of fairy palaces." All his cooking utensils were silver; he had eighty horses in his stable, and ninety servants in his home. Another new millionaire bought a gold chamber pot for his bedroom. Everyone wanted a coach, and the streets became paralyzed by traffic. "Everybody speaks in millions," wrote the regent's mother at the end of 1719. "I don't understand it at all, but I see clearly that the god Mammon reigns an absolute monarch in Paris."

John Law became a national hero. "Long live Mr. Law!" shouted the crowds that trailed behind his coach. It became almost impossible to get a minute of his time. The aristocracy fawned "like cats round a milkman," wrote the political philosopher Montesquieu. Law's servant took bribes simply to announce a person's name. One woman ordered her coachman to keep an eye out for Law while she rode around in her carriage; if he spotted Law, the coachman was to drive against a post and overturn the carriage. And so it happened. Law rushed to the spot to render assistance, and after a quick recovery the woman confessed her plan and was promised some stock. Another woman drove her carriage to a house where Law was dining and ordered her footman and coachman to yell "Fire!" Law and the other guests rushed into the street, where the woman was waiting to buy some shares. The regent's mother complained, "A duchess kissed his hands before everyone, and if duchesses kiss his hands, what parts of him won't other ladies salute?"

Although Law's popularity was unrivaled, he was prohibited from holding government office because he was not

Catholic. Law's true religion, however, was finance. He renounced Protestantism and was received into the Roman Catholic Church. A year later, in 1720, he was appointed France's comptroller general of finances, making him the de facto prime minister. The day after he assumed office, shares of the Mississippi company reached an all-time high. Using his trading profits, Law bought dozens of parcels of land and buildings in Paris, some twenty estates, jewels, a 45,000-volume library, and a wine cellar. But Montesquieu, who knew Law personally, believed that he was "more in love with his ideas than with his money."

Eventually, all financial fevers break, even if no one can explain why it happened at that particular moment. In Law's case, professional speculators had been deliberately driving the share price up, and they understood that trees don't grow to the sky. A few speculators began selling, but instead of accepting paper as payment they demanded coin. Law knew his bank would soon be depleted if this continued, but he also knew it would be suicidal not to honor his redemption promise. One large "realizer," as the speculators were called, came to the bank for his money accompanied by three wagons. The selling continued, and share prices fell.

Many factors began to conspire against Law. While he was trying to save his system, a similar speculative frenzy was turning London upside down. The English government had watched unhappily as British investors took their money to Paris to buy Law's shares. Why shouldn't they initiate a similar business in England? They already had the South Sea Company, which had been granted exclusive trade rights with the Spanish colonies of South America. The South Sea Company could be England's answer to the Mississippi. To the extent that the South Sea plan diverted money from Paris to London, it was successful. In no other sense was it a success, since it eventually left its investors with piles of worthless certificates.

In Paris, shares of the Mississippi company were steadily losing value, and attempts to convert paper into gold or jewels accelerated. Nervous investors sent their money abroad or hid it. Attempting to discourage the conversion of paper to things, the government announced a new law against wearing diamonds and precious jewels. People shifted to objets d'art made of gold and silver. The government forbade goldsmiths from making or selling any object of gold or silver that weighed more than an ounce except for archbishops' crucifixes. Yet metal continued to be taken out of circulation.

Although Law had always believed that market forces should be allowed to take their natural course, he could not bear to see his system collapse. At his urging, the government introduced a series of mandatory edicts aimed at forcing the public to use paper instead of metal. On February 27, 1720, the government ordered that no person "of whatever estate or condition" should have more than 500 livres in coins or ingots. All payments of any kind of more than 100 livres had to be made with paper. Informers on hoarders were promised a reward of half the sums recovered; sons betrayed their parents, brothers their sisters, and servants their masters. One judge supposedly informed on himself so he could keep half his fortune as a reward. The authorities commenced so-called domiciliary visits, resulting in widespread confiscations. In the cellars of an ex-chancellor named Pontchartrain were found 57,000 gold coins. On March 11, the government announced that gold and silver could no longer be used to pay debts. This made France the first country in the civilized world where a commercial transaction couldn't be conducted with gold and silver.

The public was understandably incensed. Lord Stair, a British minister to the French court, wrote that "the rage of the people is so violent that, in the course of one month, [Law] will be pulled to pieces." Lord Stair also reported a thirdhand rumor that Law had begun to get out of bed at night and run, raving mad, around his room making a terrible noise, "sometimes singing and dancing, at other times swearing, staring and stamping, quite out of himself." There's no question that Law was distressed, and even feared for his life. He was given a detachment of Swiss Guards to protect him from enraged crowds. Once when his empty carriage was recognized on the street, an angry mob attacked and tore it to pieces. The windows of his house were smashed. Yet despite this popular antipathy, Law still had the ear of the regent. He was, after all, the only person in the world who really understood the system.

On May 21, the government issued the edict that broke the system. It devalued all the company's notes and shares and fixed their prices. The value of Mississippi company shares was reduced by almost half. The devaluation destroyed the last bits of confidence in the company. "It is in everyone's mouth that they are robbed of half they were worth, that it is the most notorious cheat that ever was committed," wrote one observer. Noted another witness: "A man might have starved with a hundred millions of paper in his pocket." The public outcry was so vociferous that the edict was repealed a week after its publication. But the damage was done: The price of a share of the company on May 27 was 7,475 livres; four days later, it was 4,200 livres, a 44 percent plunge. Law submitted his resignation as comptroller general.

Crowds began appearing at the bank every day to exchange their notes for whatever metal they could get. The rush on the bank was so great that the bank closed for ten days. Seeking to stabilize the situation, the bank opened again on June 10. But so many people tried to crowd into the bank that some people suffocated or were crushed to death, and there were sporadic outbreaks of violence with guards. As each day passed, the crowds grew. On July 17, the crowd arrived at the bank to find barricades around it. This so incited them that they rushed the barriers; twelve people were killed, many others injured.

Meanwhile the price of food was rising, and shopkeepers would accept paper currency only at discounts as high as 90 percent and sometimes not at all. People began to starve. Others tried to leave the country with whatever meager resources remained to them. But the government forbade people from emigrating, and highway patrols intercepted people smuggling out plate and jewelry.

By this time, everyone realized the system was a disastrous whipsaw of greed and hysteria. The government began to withdraw paper from circulation by announcing that all notes of 1,000 livres or more were canceled unless they were used to buy government annuities or for opening accounts at Law's bank. Another edict soon did the same for all other notes. A few months later, the use of gold and silver was resumed in all commercial transactions. On November 27, the bank closed its doors for the last time. John Law's experiment with paper money had lasted less than two years. A few Mississippi millionaires had taken their profits at the right time, but most people lost everything they had invested. It would be a long time before the French would hear any more talk about financial innovations.

Law knew he had to leave Paris, and he called on the regent one last time. He conceded that he had made mistakes, but "I made them because I am human . . . you will find neither malice nor roguery in my conduct." On December 13, Law fled to one of his country estates, and two days later received permission to leave France. He left in a borrowed carriage. All his property, except a small amount of cash he carried, was confiscated by the government. Law returned to England, where he asked for and was granted a formal pardon for his thirty-year-old murder conviction. In France, however, he was widely hated, and his name became associated with the irrational behavior of crowds.

In 1725, Law moved to Venice, where he made a modest living by gambling. He died of pneumonia in a lodging house four years later at the age of fifty-eight. An inventory of Law's wealth included furniture, sculptures, and musical instruments, but his most impressive holdings were 488 paintings, including works by Titian, Raphael, Michelangelo, and Leonardo da Vinci. A satirical epitaph published in France after his death read, "Here lies that celebrated Scotsman, that peerless mathematician who, by the rules of algebra, sent France to the poorhouse."

It's easy to hate swindlers after they've been exposed. Yet before their schemes collapse, they are much-loved wizards who can create wealth without labor. No matter how many times people are fooled by a swindler's irrational blandishments, there will always be gamblers waiting eagerly for the next false promises—from the next Ivar Krueger, the Swedish industrialist who cornered the world's match production in the 1920s, or the next Charles Ponzi. Perhaps the best-known swindler of twentieth-century America, Ponzi, like Law, was a gambler and student of banking systems. Ponzi also thrived on making money and then telling other people about it.

Ponzi's scheme, to exploit postal exchange rates, became so popular that people borrowed money at high interest rates to invest. Of three police inspectors assigned to investigate Ponzi's operation, two decided to invest some of their own funds. Ponzi took his investors' money and bought a fabulous home in the country, furnished it lavishly, and laid down a cellar of vintage brandies and clarets. "You invented money!" screamed one fan in a crowd surrounding the famous Ponzi. Some forty thousand investors trusted Ponzi, and most of them lost everything.

People such as Charles Ponzi or John Law may not be welcome in the business hall of fame—as Ambrose Bierce wrote in 1906, "the gambling known as business looks with austere disfavour upon the business known as gambling." John Law's experiments, like many experiments, was a failure, even a tragedy for some. But his ideas were like smoke from a bottle: Once out, they could not be put back. Law had dealt a heavy blow to the role of gold as a single global standard of value. He had proven that the value of money is an agreement among people, not an objective standard measurable in nuggets or ingots. Although gold remained the centerpiece of most nation's finances, its importance steadily diminished. By the end of the twentieth century, investing in gold was considered risky. Gold wasn't the same as money, nor any other thing. John Law had helped to free money from its physical anchors, a separation that fostered the next great stage of wealth creation.

SEVEN

Men and Machines

Richard Arkwright (1732–1792)

When Richard Arkwright created his spectacular fortune, there was no English word to describe his occupation: It had never been done before.

Arkwright was an industrialist before anyone realized an industrial revolution was transforming the world in complex and far-reaching ways. In Arkwright's century, previous notions of wealth, productivity, work, time, and humanity itself were swept aside like so much dust. The economic and social reorganization of England in the eighteenth century, which enlarged the divide between consumption and production, soon spread to the rest of Europe, North America, and eventually most of the world. Wealth is surplus, and machines produced surplus like nothing ever seen before.

Consumer society was born in Arkwright's time—the demand side to match the supply side. A chicken-and-egg debate simmers about which came first: Did demand stimulate supply or did supply necessitate demand? In any case, the world of buying and selling changed radically. Sporadic fairs and itinerant peddlers gave way to permanent retail shops with displays in windows and cabinets. In England, a greater proportion of the population could buy consumer goods than in any previous human society, and there were more goods to buy.

Until the eighteenth century, almost everything a person

owned was one of a kind and lasted a lifetime. But as a growing population produced more of everything, prices of many items fell, and even families of modest means could buy material objects. People wanted ceramic tableware rather than pewter; metal instead of wooden utensils; cushioned chairs; carpets; wallpaper; brass door locks; framed mirrors. They bought sugar and tea regularly, and they found they liked changing their shirts more than once a week. People started to purchase, rather than make, soap, candles, and beer. Boots began to take the place of clogs, and hats replaced shawls, at least for wear on Sundays.

Advertising became widespread with the proliferation of newspapers and magazines. By 1765, some thirty-five provincial newspapers were publishing in England. This new world, Arkwright proclaimed, was committed "to the necessity of arousing and satisfying new wants." Earlier wealth had belonged to thieves, traders, shippers, and lenders, moving a limited amount of value among themselves. Arkwright's way of creating wealth was vastly different: He manufactured it.

Although Richard Arkwright lived in the epicenter of the Industrial Revolution, even he could see only a tiny part of its impact. He devoted himself to one commodity, cotton, and to one purpose: using machines to expand the scale and scope of production. Arkwright wasn't a man of complicated motives. He came from a poor family, and he wanted to be rich. He knew that the person who increased productivity by augmenting human power with machines would make a fortune. That's how Richard Arkwright, trained as a barber and a wig maker, became Sir Richard Arkwright, owner of some of the first modern factories and one of the richest people in the world.

A builder in some eyes, a destroyer in others, Arkwright was instrumental in transferring work from people's homes to places where their labor could be monitored and controlled. From one point of view, Arkwright converted autonomous workers into helpless automatons, their very survival hanging on the whims of a self-seeking owner or boss. The factory owner was allowed—even encouraged—to push and punish his workers; "enlightened selfishness" was the new economic creed. Self-interest replaced noblesse oblige, and the former vices of avarice and consumption were perceived as economically advantageous for the British empire. In 1776, Adam Smith published his influential *The Wealth of Nations,* advocating a high-production, high-consumption economy in which each individual, working for his or her own aggrandizement, would indirectly enrich the whole world. "Beneficial luxury," once an oxymoron, became the ruling ethic.

The term *industrial revolution* didn't enter the popular vocabulary until a century after Arkwright built his first factory. It was used by the British political economist Arnold Toynbee in lectures at Oxford in 1880 and 1881. Toynbee believed the essence of the Industrial Revolution was the substitution of competition for the medieval regulations that had controlled the production and distribution of wealth. In the century since Toynbee's esoteric commentaries, the expression *industrial revolution* has taken on great emotional and political freight and come to represent "a rapid change from the happy, bucolic life to a world dominated by dark, sweaty Dickensian factories and workshops." Historians argue that it was evolution, not revolution, and disagree about when it began and ended. Any large economic displacement is a landscape of a thousand brush strokes, and this is even truer of the Industrial Revolution. But given growing population, wider exploration, and more sophisticated credit and trade systems, a change in the concentration of capital and the scale of enterprises was inevitable. The only question was where and when it would happen first.

As it turned out, England between 1760 and 1830 was the revolution's birthplace, the textile industry its laboratory, and Richard Arkwright one of its leaders. Arkwright, the thirteenth child of a barber, was a member of one of the first generations in which individuals could be born poor and die rich. The money economy was chipping away steadily at the rigid stratification of society. In manufacturing and trade, a small amount of capital, combined with an enormous investment of resourcefulness and sweat, could result not only in a fortune but also in a title. When a patronizing lord told a London trader to "hold his tongue, for he was no gentleman," the trader retorted, "No, Sir, but I can buy a gentleman, and therefore I claim a liberty to speak among gentlemen."

The Industrial Revolution passed over many people, who left a trail of nostalgic lamentation in recorded history. Before the eighteenth century, many of England's agrarian families were largely self-sufficient. They grew, fished, hunted, built, and wove most of what they needed to survive. Although little money circulated, barter worked well enough for most items. After Arkwright's time, many members of the working class had few resources besides money and never quite enough of that. A similar change occurred on a national scale: Arkwright's factory system helped transform England from a nearly self-sufficient country, its economy built on agriculture and domestic manufacturing, into the workshop of the world.

In the eighteenth century, Britain was probably the wealthiest nation in the world. Its natural deposits of coal and iron provided fuel and raw material for tools. Turnpikes and "liquid roads"—canals—offered relatively cheap transport, and England's richly indented coastline made it possible for ships to reach many major cities. Overseas trade was Britain's lifeblood, so the country had a large and aggressive merchant marine and a navy that acted as both warrior and trader. Commerce with England's colonies was booming.

War had not ravaged the infrastructure of England as it had France and Germany. A minimum of internal customs barriers and feudal tolls made England the largest common market in Europe. The government bureaucracy was less obstructive than that in most states, and it largely ignored manufacturing, neither overregulating nor overtaxing it—indeed, the high tariffs it imposed on imports gave home industry some breathing space. Britain's enthusiasm for science and engineering helped make it a world leader in instruments and timepieces. Financial-exchange techniques were becoming faster, cheaper, and more reliable, and the paper-money economy was expanding. Interest rates were low because capital was plentiful. The Bank of England was sound.

The British population, like most of Europe, had been increasing for the past few centuries; under later Malthusian theory, food prices would be expected to start rising, a famine or plague would surface, and the population would thin out. But in the eighteenth century, food production was rising, too, as farmers experimented with new methods of rotating crops, fertilizing fields, and breeding livestock. For the first time, population and living standards rose together instead of canceling each other out. The flow of improvements was self-sustaining. "Until the industrial revolution, every burst of growth came up against a ceiling imposed by agricultural output, the available means of transport, sources of power or market demand," noted the historian David Landes. "Modern growth begins when that ceiling or limit recedes indefinitely into the distance—which isn't to say some kind of ceiling may not be reached in the future."

The enclosure movement, widely hated by romantic agrarians, had already begun remaking England's landscape by the time Arkwright was born. Enclosure involved transferring land that once had been held cooperatively by villages to individual owners. Some ten million acres of forests, meadows, and open fields were fenced and hedged and passed into private hands, either for raising sheep or to create commercial farms. Larger, more efficient farms could better feed England's growing cities.

Although enclosure was defended as a way to "rationalize" England's agriculture, it also removed a layer of insurance for the commoner and created a class of hired hands who had once been subsistence farmers. People could no longer survive by hunting and foraging. Now they had to buy the products they had once made or found. As a clergyman at the time noted, "an amazing number of people have been reduced from a comfortable state of partial independence to the precarious condition of mere hirelings." Indeed, enclosure introduced many people to the idea of working for wages. Others joined the new class called the "wandering poor."

But a greater social disruption than enclosure was the creation of machines, which, even if human powered like the spinning wheel, multiplied the output of a single person by three or four times. Before mechanization, a vast proportion of people were employed in pure drudgery. Wrote H. G. Wells, "Where a weight had to be lifted, men lifted it; where a rock had to be quarried, men chipped it out; where a field had to be ploughed, men and oxen plowed it. . . . But as time passed, human beings were less wanted as a source of mere indiscriminate power. The human being was needed now only where choice and intelligence had to be exercised. For the first time in history, the shackles were taken off the productive power of human societies."

Although farmers in Arkwright's England still relied on flails, sickles, and scythes as their main implements, other kinds of machines, such as spinning wheels and hand-powered looms, hummed in thousands of cottages. The British countryside was infused with manufacturing well before the Industrial Revolution. Home workers were making lace, nails, hosiery, paper, and, especially, textiles.

So-called cottage industry fit neatly into farmers' long periods of inactivity during the winter, and setting up a spinning and weaving operation required little capital. England had always had an abundant supply of raw wool. Every member of farm families, including young children, was expected to work, and there was usually a simple division of labor: The women and girls did the less strenuous spinning of wool or cotton (and so were spinsters), and the men and boys wove it.

In time, a "putting-out" system evolved, in which small entrepreneurs provided families with raw materials—and sometimes even looms or spinning wheels—and then bought the finished product from them at a piece rate. Even the most accomplished entrepreneurs, however, had a problem this system couldn't solve: It took the output of some five spinning wheels to produce enough yarn for just one loom. Their solution was a further division of labor: Some families got raw wool or cotton to spin into yarn; others got yarn to weave into cloth.

Over time, whole villages became centers of weaving or knitting, and artisans sometimes gathered in workshops. With some people starting to work exclusively in textiles, the first cracks in the foundation of agrarian self-sufficiency began to show. Little towns sprouted up; big towns became cities. In 1750, London had some 750,000 inhabitants, making it the largest city in the Christian world. There was a growing division of labor between city and countryside, but also frequent contact because rural cottages were still the most common source of labor for manufacturing.

The farmers like the putting-out system, but the small capitalists who bought and distributed the raw materials and collected and sold the finished products weren't as content. They spent days hauling and fetching material to and from dozens of workers. Their spinners often embezzled raw materials for their own use, and their weavers were notorious for dropping their work in the event of a farm emergency. Furthermore, most spinners and weavers were content to earn only enough for the bare necessities of life; beyond a certain well-defined standard of living, they preferred leisure to income. If their wages were high, they simply worked fewer days, celebrating the weekly holiday of "St. Monday" as well as many other festivals and holy days throughout the year. The worker "who can subsist on three days work will be idle and drunken the remainder of the week," declared a writer in 1747. Ironically, small capitalists sometimes found themselves wishing for higher food prices; low prices and high wages were said to breed laziness due to people's innate disinclination to work.

Another shortcoming of cottage industry was that once every family in the region was operating a loom or spinning wheel, there was no way to expand production to meet increased demand. During the second half of the eighteenth century, the growth of demand for textiles began to outstrip the supply of available labor. Domestic demand for textiles was strong, and the workers in Britain's expanding colonial empire—India, Australia, parts of the Caribbean and North America—wanted sturdy but inexpensive clothes. Whether necessity or greed is the mother of invention, both loomed large in eighteenth-century England. Somehow, the same number of people had to produce more cloth. The solution, of course, was machines.

Early machines were not usually invented by scientists, but the English people had a great appreciation for and curiosity about science. There was no split yet between superior "pure" and inferior "applied" scientists, so it was acceptable for a scientist to devote himself to solving productive problems. British science was empirical, experimental, and pragmatic. Communication between scientists, engineers, and entrepreneurs was strong, and they engaged in a common effort to solve technological problems. This partly explains why in eighteenth-century England it was possible to buy umbrellas, toothbrushes, bellpulls, and alarm clocks that would automatically light candles.

In Lancashire in northern England, tinkerers were trying to build machines that could spin and weave. They were not trained scientists in special laboratories—they were merchants, craftsmen, carpenters, blacksmiths, locksmiths, even barbers trying their hands at technical design. Dabbling in their spare time, they were attempting to create a way to exceed the limits of human productivity. Richard Arkwright was one of those men, and he and the machine he invented—or stole from an acquaintance—became the nucleus of the Industrial Revolution.

* * *

Born in 1732 in a small English town, Richard Arkwright received no formal education. Government-financed schools didn't yet exist, and the Arkwright family was poor. What minimal literacy he acquired came from the tutoring of an uncle. "I am tired with riteing so Long a Letter & think you can scairsly Reed it," Arkwright noted in a correspondence in 1772. When he was fifty years old, he took up the study of grammar again.

Almost nothing is recorded of Arkwright's childhood, and he next appears in the historical record at the age of eighteen, when he became apprenticed to a barber and wig maker. Wigs were fashionable then for both men and women, and selling them could provide a decent living. When Arkwright's master died, Arkwright established his own business, also selling shaves in a basement for a penny. He was also said to be "very capital in Bleeding and toothdrawing." He married twice (his first wife died in 1761, three years after giving birth to a son), and his second wife had enough money to capitalize a business in wig making. Arkwright traveled around the countryside buying the hair of young women—he was apparently a skilled negotiator—dyeing it, and turning it into wigs.

In the tiny village of Bolton, where Arkwright set up shop, many citizens made cotton in their thatched-roof cottages. As an industry, cotton was a distant third to wool and linen, but it had been growing. Raw cotton had to be imported rather than grown at home like wool, so the raw material was more costly. But cotton's tough vegetable fibers could withstand mechanical processes better than wool or linen could, and the finished product was lighter, cheaper, and easier to wash. For the first time in history, cotton fabric made it possible for ordinary people to wear underclothes. But as in the wool industry, spinners of cotton couldn't keep up with the weavers' demand. "It was no uncommon thing for a weaver to walk three or four miles in a morning, and call on five or six spinners, before he could collect weft to serve him for the remainder of the day," wrote a nineteenth-century historian. The imbalance had intensified after

1733, when a new kind of loom, using a flying shuttle, allowed wider material to be woven while speeding the process.

In theory, spinning is elementary. It simply turns loose fibers into thread by stretching and twisting them together. But spinning had always been performed by one of nature's most sophisticated inventions: the human finger and opposed thumb. To mimic the variable pressure applied almost instinctively by human digits was not a trivial problem. Furthermore, the inventors were working with crude metal, wooden parts and tools, no instructions, and few precedents. Several of Arkwright's neighbors had taken on the problem unsuccessfully, and Arkwright himself was ruminating on it when in 1767 he met a clock maker, John Kay, who claimed to have solved it. Arkwright took Kay to a tavern and questioned him closely. He asked Kay to make a model of his idea, and some weeks later Kay produced one, for which Arkwright paid him an unknown sum. Kay's machine stretched the cotton fibers through four pairs of rapidly spinning rollers.

The biggest controversy in the Richard Arkwright chronicles is over how much of his invention he invented and how much he stole from his partner. Arkwright had no technical experience—he was neither weaver nor mechanic. According to a historian writing in 1823, Arkwright's " 'great mechanical abilities' consisted solely in having cunning enough to pump a secret out of a silly, loquacious clockmaker, and in having sense enough to know when he saw a good invention." Karl Marx called Arkwright "the biggest thief of other people's inventions."

But many half-baked inventions sat in people's yards, barns, and parlors; it took a certain talent to recognize the one machine among many that would work on a large scale. All through history, the story has been the same: Inventors of new products rarely achieve great wealth unless they also set up their own companies. "Innovation, as opposed to invention, is the relating of individual genius to the economic and commercial context of the age," wrote the historian Peter Mathias. "Most innovations were the products of inspired amateurs." Arkwright adapted "by head-work the hand-work of others." He "personified the new type of great manufacturer, neither an engineer nor a merchant, but an organizer of production and a leader of men."

The only suggestion that Arkwright may have tinkered with machines was an allegation that Arkwright's second wife left him because she was so annoyed by his disorderly hobby. "Convinced that he would starve his family by scheming when he should have been shaving, she broke some of his experimental models of machinery." This story is considered dubious by most Arkwright scholars, but it's true that at some point the Arkwrights separated.

Little was recorded about Arkwright's personality or manners, but in what survives words such as *charming, kind,* or *generous* are notably absent. One historian described Arkwright as "hard, dull, misunderstood by those around him." A portrait that Arkwright commissioned of himself (then a popular diversion for the wealthy) showed him to be a "plain, almost gross, bag-cheeked, pot-bellied Lancashire man, with the air of painful reflection, yet also of copious free digestion," wrote the nineteenth-century English author Thomas Carlyle. Francis Espinasse thought the portrait revealed "a vulgar Lancashire man, successful over much."

The transition from inventor to industrialist was rarely made successfully, even in Arkwright's era, when England was awash in a "wave of gadgets." Without a record of success, it was difficult for entrepreneurs to raise the capital to test their ideas. The nation's banks generally offered only short-term credit for commercial transactions. There were no more than a handful of joint-stock companies. Indeed, the Bubble Act of 1720 had virtually outlawed the company form of enterprise in manufacturing. Most inventors either capitalized themselves with savings or turned to informal capital markets, such as friends, relatives, or partners. To expand their businesses, early industrialists typically plowed profits back into them.

In 1768, Arkwright decided to take the small wooden model of his and Kay's machine and seek investors in Nottingham, then the center of the cotton hosiery industry. Nottingham had a ready market for cotton yarn and plenty of mechanics accustomed to working on textile machines. In Nottingham, Arkwright persuaded two rich hosiers to underwrite his efforts to obtain a patent for the machine and to try to put it to use. Thirteen months after applying, Arkwright received a patent for his spinning frame.

Britain had a fully operational patent system in the eighteenth century, as did several other European countries, to more or less effect. Governments struggled to find the right balance between protecting inventors and diffusing new technology. In England, patents gave the holder an exclusive right to the machine for fourteen years. Although some inventors eventually found their patent brought them nothing but a bottomless pit of litigation, others believed a patent could guarantee a high return on a successful invention. That belief, however often wrong, probably enticed many would-be inventors to spend time and energy searching for technological improvements. Then, as now, patenting required full disclosure of technical details, so inventors had to choose between getting a patent and keeping their innovation secret from the competition.

Patent in hand, Arkwright set up a workshop in Nottingham, consisting of a few machines powered by three or four horses harnessed to a wheel fitted on a vertical shaft. But horsepower was inadequate for the scale of operation that Arkwright envisioned. Some primitive steam engines existed by this time, but they were enormous and couldn't sustain a steady flow of power. The most constant (and cheapest) source of power was water rushing over a wheel, particularly streams in narrow valleys that could be easily dammed to create waterfalls. Arkwright and his partners moved their shop to Cromford, a region of high hills in southern Lancashire described by one traveler as "so beautiful that a poet might pitch his tent in it." The flow of the mill's water was continuous year-round; it didn't dry up in summer or freeze in winter. And the climate around Lancashire—damp with moderate temperatures in all seasons—was helpful in making fine cotton thread. Finally, the region's marshes and moors made it less than ideal for farming.

However, the area was also poor, with few roads or towns. Its inhabitants lived in mud, turf, and straw huts, and occasionally even in underground dugouts. An iron pot might be their only piece of furniture. The area was largely lawless, but that had its benefits—no guilds were setting rules for new business enterprises. There were few blue-blooded families in the area, and virtually no temptations to stop making money for a life of enjoyment. Writing in 1823, Richard Guest described life in rural England as dull and repetitious. "The mind became contracted from general stagnation and its being so seldom roused to exertion," he wrote. "Men had not their understandings rubbed bright by contact. . . . They witnessed a monotonous scene of life."

Creating a factory from scratch in those days was no small endeavor. Machine production depended on the production of machines, so the earliest factory masters had to make their own. Fortunately, the country's abundant supply of cheap metal made available a wide range of construction materials, although iron is difficult to work with on a large scale. Britain's population included skilled mechanics and practical technicians, including shipbuilders, millwrights, mining engineers, and clock makers. But there was no standardization of parts—every screw had its own thread. Putting a machine together was an exacting process of adjusting hundreds of pieces, many of them wood, so they would fit together.

Arkwright's mill, built of local stone, was typical of early factory design—five stories of about 100 feet by 30 feet that borrowed architectural detail from surrounding houses. Some people saw the mills as romantic additions to the landscape, a symbol of humankind's sovereignty over nature. Others lamented the factories' hulking presence: "Speaking as a tourist," wrote Lord Torrington in 1790, "these vales have lost all their beauties. . . . Every rural sound is sunk in the clamours of the cotton works, and the simple peasant . . . is changed into the impudent mechanic." On many mill roofs, bells became the visible and audible symbols of the new factory discipline.

The first decades of industrialization involved a constant battle against machine breakdowns and human resistance to the new organization of labor. Because early mills were powered by waterfalls, they were often situated far from even small population centers. This meant factory masters had to find a way to entice laborers into an unfamiliar work environment in a remote corner of the country. Most professional spinners and weavers preferred working in their own homes on their own schedules and refused to leave them. To enter a mill meant to fall in status from a self-employed person to a servant of a machine. Most workers entered factory work not from choice but because there was no alternative. By 1779, Arkwright's spinning mill employed three hundred workers. (Although later mills didn't use water power, the term *mill* stuck).

Eventually, a big textile factory could generate profits of 100 percent or more, and over the next decade Richard Arkwright became one of the wealthiest men in the world. Indeed, in the first two generations of the Industrial Revolution, the rich accumulated income so fast and in such vast quantities "as to exceed all available possibilities of spending and investment." Moreover, they were virtually untaxed. They commissioned Chippendale and Hepplewhite furniture, bought Chelsea porcelain, filled orangeries with pineapples and camellias, and bred new kinds of dogs. People traveled not for religion or health, as they once had, but for pleasure. They flocked to Italy and France and at home turned Bath into one of Britain's biggest towns, as people pretended to "take the waters" but actually idled, drank, and gambled. Foxhunting became a ritualized pastime. Moralists deplored the "effeminate" urge for comforts that was sapping the nation's fiber.

Arkwright used his fortune to build a Gothic-style castle on the slopes of the river, overlooking his Cromford factory. This marked another way England's geography was transformed by the Industrial Revolution. In medieval days, the land inside the city walls was reserved for the wealthy, the land outside for the poor and destitute. Now the poor were gathering in cities, the wealthy fleeing them. Outside Manchester, other wealthy "cotton lords" were also building grand villas. Their gardens sprouted grottoes, follies, and hermits' caves.

Arkwright's castle included three ale and five wine cellars. A local critic who toured the interior called the house "an effort of inconvenient ill taste." Arkwright was one of the few home-owners of the day who could afford plate-glass windows—panes that were thicker than ordinary and had an even, lustrous finish. But like all houses, however fine, Arkwright's castle was lit by candle, and perhaps one of them ignited the fire that destroyed much of the house before Arkwright had even moved into it.

It was initially costlier for manufacturers to bring people to the machines than to leave them in their homes, where they paid their own overhead. If demand slackened, the cottage-industry manufacturer could simply stop giving them work. Demand, not supply, restricted industrial output then, and cottage work gave industry flexibility. Large shops or plants required capital investment for land, buildings, and machines, and manufacturers became prisoners of their investments. Three years passed before Arkwright's Cromford mill began to make a profit.

The great advantage of the factory system was that workers could be monitored, disciplined, and timed. Accustomed to stopping their tasks at whim, workers needed extensive retraining in laboring steadily and subordinating their wills to the machine. It was difficult to find effective penalties and incentives. Most

workers were unaccustomed to responding to monetary induce-
ments, and, living in rural areas, they had little use for money
anyway. Some mill owners found the only solution to this problem was to pay the workers so little and fine them so much for
transgressions that adapting to the system became a question of
survival. Gradually, the workers' task orientation gave way to
time orientation.

Richard Arkwright's factory proved that workers could be
retooled to the monotonous rhythm of mechanical processes. "I
made men give up the irregular habits to which they had been accustomed, and brought them into a condition of constant regularity, the regularity of automata," Arkwright himself said. In
less approving terms, workers became "hands," appendages of
machines, commodities. Increasingly, they were paid not by how
much they produced but by how long they spent in the factory.
But factories also created demand for another kind of worker,
with skills once needed only by military commanders and sea
captains: the person who could organize, coordinate, and manage people doing complex and interdependent tasks.

With their high fixed costs, manufacturers wanted to
keep their factories running at the highest possible capacity.
Arkwright's factory ran six days a week, and, after gas illumina-
tion became widespread, six nights, too, one set of workers occupying the bunks just vacated by another set. There was a
saying that in Lancashire the beds never got cold. There were almost no official holidays.

Early factories were usually managed by their owners; few
early manufacturers would trust their costly works to people
who weren't family members. "An industrialist risks his own
fortune and runs his own show." Arkwright himself appeared at
the mill every day, perfecting his system of discipline that became
praised so widely. He attended to his affairs from 5 A.M. to
9 P.M.; when he became more successful, he saved commuting
time by using a four-horse carriage. Early capitalism retained an
essentially individual character. Most managers wrote their own

correspondence and did their own clerical work. Constant attempts at industrial espionage gave manufacturers another reason to sequester their machines behind thick walls.

Early manufacturers also had to give "wage slaves" a reason to want to perform their jobs well. "To support life," wrote the British reformer and industrialist Robert Owen, "you must be tyrant or slave." When bad yarn made its appearance in any one of Arkwright's mills, "he swore a loud oath, according to the vile fashion of the time." Josiah Wedgwood, who founded his pottery company at about the same time, strode around his factories smashing bad vases and bowls with his wooden leg—but he imposed such standards that for the first time plates could be stacked and lids fitted. In his "Law Book" for the enormous ironworks he owned, Ambrose Crowley began each instruction with the words "I do order." There were foremen but rarely any other middle managers, although skilled workers sometimes subcontracted their own unskilled assistants, turning themselves into overseers.

To attract and control employees, early industrialists often built some facilities for their employees and families. At Cromford, Arkwright constructed cottages, a hotel, and a chapel. Other mill owners built schools and shops. With greater demands for money to pay wages and to buy supplies, the scarcity of coinage became more acute. Factory owners resorted to odd payroll techniques—paying less frequently ("long pay"), paying in goods ("truck"), or paying in credit slips. Some factory owners issued currency, and a few even established their own banks, giving them a greater hold over their workers. Like feudal lords, the so-called millocracy organized sports, feasts, bands, and choirs. Robert Owen tried to set up a utopian community at his spinning works in New Lanark to test whether social engineering could vanquish poverty and other human suffering.

Textile mills generally needed cheap, unskilled workers, which meant immigrants, women, and children. Unmarried women would work for very low wages—no other employment opportunities were available to them, and they were believed to be docile and dexterous. By 1833, some four fifths of Britain's textile workers were women and children, a few as young as four years old. Orphans in lots of fifty, eighty, or one hundred—the so-called pauper apprentices—were sent by their parishes in wagons to a factory, where they remained captive for many years. Children were more easily molded and disciplined into a state of passive dependence than older workers, and sometimes their only wages came as room and board. The savagery of some employers and the relentless labor led some to commit suicide. Accidents and mutilations were common, because children usually worked as the unguarded machines were operating. Children work well in cotton mills, wrote one observer, "their small fingers being more active and endowed with a quicker sensibility of feeling than those of grown persons."

Eventually, Arkwright's mills stopped hiring children younger than ten years old, the principal reason being "that they might learn to read before they came," Arkwright said. But he conceded that pressure from parents to get their children hired for mill work sometimes reduced the literacy standard to being able to read a few small words. Many factory owners hired whole families, who offered themselves as teams, and used the parents to enforce discipline. "Men, women and children are yoke-fellows with iron and steam," wrote a doctor in 1831. "The animal machine—fragile at best, subject to a thousand sources of suffering . . . hastening to decay—is matched with an iron machine insensible to suffering and fatigue."

The lives of eighteenth-century factory workers varied dramatically, according to the disposition of the factory owner. Some factory buildings were hastily or flimsily constructed and could be hot and poorly ventilated. They were always clamorous with the sound of looms. Dinner for the children working a twelve-hour shift in one Manchester mill was "Eight Cow Heads boiling in a pot," according to inspectors. Like many of Britain's cities, Manchester had no trade guilds, so employment conditions were almost totally unregulated. When the machinery broke down, the workers' pay was docked. The machinery didn't stop during mealtimes, so many workers, including children, ate while continuing their tasks. In some factories, workers were forbidden to bring watches, so they wouldn't know exactly when quitting time came. Turnover was high: One Manchester factory lost 100 percent of its workforce every year. When workers reached about the age of forty, many were no longer useful in factories, but there was no provision for illness or old age, and no small plot of land for them to fall back on.

Even those who believed mill work was no worse than trying to squeeze a living out of rocky ground could see that factories were overturning England's social values and traditions. Under the oppressive feudal system, a network of dependence insured some protection for even the lowest serf. In early factories, however, no human relationship existed between employer and employed. Wrote a clergyman about Manchester, "There is far less personal communication between the master cotton spinner and his workmen, between the master tailor and his apprentices, than there is between the Duke of Wellington and the humblest laborer on his estate." The payment of wages was considered to discharge any obligations to the labor force, and if workers lived in squalor, they had only their poor habits to blame. An able-bodied person who couldn't support himself reflected an individual moral failing, a personal responsibility.

Workers were forbidden by law to form unions for collective bargaining. Thwarted in their efforts to make their complaints heard, some workers turned to "collective bargaining by riot." Between 1765 and 1780, there were nine major riots against industrial targets. One mob destroyed a mill that Arkwright had recently built, which, with five hundred workers, was the largest factory in England. The angry swarm destroyed every machine in the mill driven by horse- or waterpower and then burned the structure to the ground. Early factories were extremely vulnerable to fire, since their floors, joists, and columns were normally made of wood. Even so, the scale of physical opposition to mechanization was trivial compared with the scale of the transformation taking place in business and society.

The ruling establishment vigorously suppressed the labor uprisings. Its members knew that resisting technological advances would lead to the flight of business from England. Furthermore, the British aristocracy and gentry were collecting rents on land they owned in cities and the countryside, and land values around coal mines and waterpower sites were rising. In 1769, destruction of machinery was made a capital crime.

While British factories were reconditioning domestic workers, they were also turning America into a land of owners and slaves. England needed U.S. slave labor to supply raw cotton—even if spinning and weaving could be mechanized, planting and picking cotton couldn't, and as demand for cotton rose, U.S. plantations switched to it. Without U.S. slavery, England would have run into another bottleneck. By 1776, English traders had carried three million slaves to America.

Aristotle once said that slavery would cease when the weaver's shuttle went through the warp without the guidance of a human hand. But it was another one hundred years after the shuttle was mechanized before slaves ceased to be casualties of the cotton industry.

The new machine at Arkwright's mill—the water frame, so named for its source of power—produced a stronger and more uniform thread than any human spinner could make with a wheel. Formerly, cotton cloth was woven of linen and cotton because cotton thread wasn't strong enough to be warp. Delicate goods—chintzes, tablecloths, silks, calicoes—had been imported from India until 1700, when Parliament banned them in Britain. Now, with sturdy cotton thread readily available, it became possible to weave pure cotton fabric. The pressure was now on weavers; with one link of the textile chain mechanized, all the other links had to be mechanized to restore balance. Invention followed invention in a process of "challenge and response."

Arkwright took out a second patent in 1775 that described several inventions and added token improvements to the water frame in an attempt to extend its patent protection. Meanwhile, Arkwright was erecting or acquiring control over eight factories, whose prototypes became the standard for thousands of mills in the next half century. By 1787, Britain had some 145 Arkwright-type mills. People who aspired to be textile manufacturers often approached Arkwright for money or help with technology.

One of England's first steam-power mills was built by Arkwright and his partners in Manchester. The steam engine, conceptually one of humanity's most radical inventions, was the motor of the Industrial Revolution. By converting heat into power, the steam engine provided humans who had a supply of coal with a constant source of power for the first time ever. James Watt, one of the steam engine's inventors, coined *horsepower* as a measure for his engines. The steam engine led to larger scales because it could power many machines simultaneously and had to recoup its high investment and operating costs. But because an engine has more geographical mobility than water, factories could move back to cities, where there were more workers.

Arkwright sold water frames and carding machines to other mill owners and enjoyed almost monopolistic control over cotton thread. "For several years, he fixed the price of cotton twist, no one venturing to vary from his prices." But some entrepreneurs balked at paying Arkwright's prices, and they launched competitive businesses based on his technology. Arkwright sued nine men for poaching on his territory, but only one case, that of a Colonel Mordaunt, came to trial. The colonel admitted he was using Arkwright's machine without permission, but he challenged the validity of the patent itself, saying it was obscure, misleading, and incomplete. Indeed, as one detractor noted, "There never was a greater practical attempt made to mystify a subject since the creation of the world."

Arkwright didn't deny that the patent was deliberately written to confuse others, but he claimed he had done so to prevent foreigners from stealing Britain's industrial secrets. A jury was not swayed by his patriotic defense, and Arkwright's patent claim was annulled. The other cases were dropped. Arkwright, said merchants who opposed his claim, had already "realized such a Fortune as every unprejudiced Person must allow to be an ample compensation for the most happy Efforts of Genius."

The patent decision threw open the cotton business. For the next four years, scores of new mills were built, and some thirty thousand workers hired. After another patent fight, which Arkwright also lost, more capital and labor rushed into cotton manufacturing. Sales of manufactured cotton goods soared. The cotton industry grew faster, and its costs declined faster, than any industry in recorded history. By the early nineteenth century, one spinner could generate what two hundred spinners had produced seventy years earlier. Arkwright's mills continued to thrive, employing some 1,800 workers.

In 1786, on the eve of his fifty-fourth birthday, Arkwright was knighted. The following year, he was appointed high sheriff of Derbyshire by George III, an unusual appointment for a man in trade. Despite these trappings of aristocracy, Arkwright was never embraced by the landed gentry. Once in the company of some other nobles, one of them asked Arkwright if he had been a barber. "Sir, I was once a barber," Arkwright responded, then continued, "I am apt to conclude, had your lordship been a barber, you must have continued a barber still."

Arkwright died of natural causes in 1792 at the age of fifty-nine.

Richard Arkwright is often referred to as a "self-made" man, and since the industrial era began, the notion of a person starting with nothing and becoming magnificently wealthy has become a beloved ideal. In the nineteenth century, the self-made man was any individual who had built a fortune rather than in- herited it. This didn't necessarily mean he had come from a working-class background, but because it proved that a person had "earned" his fortune, it suggested that great wealth could be "deserved." Although some people believe the idea of a self- made man is merely propaganda by the wealthy, rising from bar- ber to knight in four decades was an opportunity denied all previous generations—and now available to future ones.

EIGHT

Addicted to Trade

Howqua (1769–1843)

People have been smoking, swallowing, and injecting drugs for thousands of years, and speculation on the human appetite for respite or thrill has made many fortunes. Whether tobacco, coffee, alcohol, tea, or opium, the addiction business has proven to be indestructible, regardless of the determined opposition of many governments in many eras. Tea, coffee, chocolate, and tobacco, all of which contain addictive substances, have been deemed socially acceptable and legal. Opium, marijuana, heroin, and cocaine, however, are illegal in most of the world. Whether legal or illegal, the addiction business can be extraordinarily profitable. A reasonable estimate of the world drug trade today has been put at $400 billion—roughly 8 percent of total international trade and second in profitability and influence only to the arms trade.

For hundreds of years, the drug business has run parallel to the rest of business, a counterpoint to the doctrine of hard work, chin up, tough it out, grow up, face facts. Indeed, some historians believe stimulants became popular when human rhythm had to speed up to match that of machines, and then narcotics were needed to soothe the body during brief, artificial intervals of rest. Whatever the cause of people's hunger for escape or excitement, it has never been quashed by any force, human or otherwise. Taking advantage of people's determination to buy

171

addictive substances despite their governments' and other organizations' efforts to discourage them, many people have become wealthy. One of the wealthiest was a nineteenth-century Chinese trader known as Howqua.

Howqua's name at birth, in 1769, was Wu Ping-chien. Unlike westerners, most Chinese chose not to use their family names in business. In Howqua's case, the *qua* was an honorific, like mister or sir, and the *How* was likely a bastardization of *Wu.*

In early nineteenth century, only a few decades after Britain's factories began spinning and weaving, Howqua was known to just a few hundred people, all of them in China. He was not famous or powerful except in an area of a few square miles. He was so courteous and deferential that even his admirers thought him fainthearted and ineffectual. Yet in 1834, Howqua's wealth was estimated at $26 million—the equivalent of $3 billion or more today. At the time, it was probably the largest mercantile fortune in the world.

Seen with rigidly Confucian eyes, Howqua was of lowly status, little more than a glorified salesman. Like his father before him, Howqua was a merchant, and in China's stiffly stratified society merchants ranked below farmers and government bureaucrats. A merchant's job required little intellectual gift or training. Howqua merely tended his nation's gates like a clerk behind a counter, selling tea, silk, and porcelain to eager European traders with pockets full of silver. How difficult could that have been?

The job of a merchant in nineteenth-century Canton was terrible, life shortening, and extremely lucrative. To western traders, the Chinese looked like a nation of enthusiastic consumers. Great Britain, in particular, needed global outlets for its greatly expanded ability to produce surplus. Howqua's gates opened onto four hundred million people, many of whom had never seen anything produced outside their national borders. But the Chinese were xenophobic, and westerners were naively unprepared for a land whose horizons were inward.

Nineteenth-century China was as shuttered and self-reliant a nation as it had been a millennium earlier. Paranoid from centuries of attacks by Mongols and other marauders, Chinese leaders preached a gospel of national superiority. China was, after all, the biggest, oldest, strongest, and most advanced society in Asia. The emperor, who ruled by divine right, was second to no other human ruler, nor did his subjects have equals among other peoples. China was the source of true culture. Ideas of international law, long established in Europe, were unknown to the Chinese.

The Chinese wanted to be left alone. They didn't need foreign trade, as the industrialized British did. Their agrarian economy—"40 centuries of farmers"—was self-sufficient, and the country had enough internal trade in the few items manufactured in its cities. Foreigners were admitted to the Chinese port of Canton purely on sufferance. If the "sea barbarians" adhered to conditions, they were permitted to conduct a profitable, if highly controlled, business. But for the Chinese, this trade was just a concession to the disagreeable fact that they shared the globe with other people. The snobbishness of the mandarins—China's elite ruling class—toward merchants made it possible for them to pretend indifference to trade while skimming off fortunes from it.

After early encounters with western traders, the Chinese had concluded that they were uncouth and dishonest—not terribly different from land-based ruffians such as Genghis Khan. Characterizing westerners, one Chinese man wrote, "Their flesh is dazzling white, and their noses are lofty. . . . The men are violent and tyrannical and skilled in the use of weapons." The Chinese government encouraged a popular notion of westerners as an inferior species lacking higher thought processes. Indeed, a British translator remarked that the Chinese were "always surprised, not to say astonished, that we live otherwise than as a herd of cattle."

In Great Britain, meanwhile, steam-powered factories were

cranking out handkerchiefs and tablecloths so efficiently that supply was overtaking demand. Cotton prices fell because of a glut, while wealthy British manufacturers, such as Richard Arkwright's son, were becoming pillars of the empire. Wielding their new political power, manufacturers demanded the right to sell their goods wherever their ships could go. The British saw no reason to kowtow to the Chinese; they had conquered most of India—why not China?

Western aggression met Chinese isolationism in the harbor of Canton, and that's where Howqua made his millions. While enforcing bureaucratic and often corrupt regimens, Howqua developed cordial and profitable relationships with British and American traders. He was known to be honest, friendly, methodical, generous—and rich. The most stinging criticism of Howqua was that he was too tolerant—one of the very qualities for which he was so admired. The British praised his "great command of capital and superior intelligence" but added that "his natural timidity of character" made him the helpless victim of the exorbitant exactions of a "despotic and corrupt government." His other vulnerability was his great wealth, which was "always an object of attention to the government, eager to inculpate him whenever an opportunity presented itself, causing his entire submission to all their requisitions."

Canton was the first large port China opened to the western world. Once established in the mid-eighteenth century, the European settlement in Canton became so wealthy so quickly that both the British and Chinese became alarmed, though for different reasons. The tension between East and West grew, culminating late in Howqua's life in the first Opium War in 1839. Unlike most wars, the Opium War was fought over trade, not territory. China's restrictive policies, which helped enrich Howqua, were artifacts of a time when much of the world was still inaccessible to ships. In the end, the West's need for new markets overcame China's desire for isolation. The Opium War, noted John Quincy Adams in 1841, was as much about opium as the American Revolution had been about throwing tea into Boston harbor. "The cause of the war is the kowtow," he said.

The first Europeans to explore trade with China had been the Portuguese, who set up a trading base at Macao, a rocky peninsula sixty-five miles south of Canton. Early Portuguese and Spanish traders used plunder from the Americas—silver and gold—to buy Chinese goods. For years, Macao, with a resident population of some thirty thousand, was the Chinese base for trade with all nations. But the Chinese were steadfastly hostile, and only regular bribery maintained the flow of commerce. So determined were the Chinese to keep foreigners at bay that when a Chinese man was found to have helped foreigners explore China's interior, he was condemned to a death of one thousand cuts, his family was beheaded, and his native village was destroyed by fire.

In 1757, the Chinese moved their western trading base from Macao to Whampoa, the harbor twelve miles downriver from Canton. At the extreme southeast corner of the empire, Canton was sequestered geographically from the rest of the nation, which made it an ideal place, the Chinese believed, to contain relations between East and West. A seven-mile-long wall, forty feet high, already surrounded Canton, and foreigners were not allowed to pass through any of its twelve gates.

To assure that East and West didn't meet except under highly regulated circumstances, all foreign traders lived in a kind of quarantine in "factories" (so called because they were run by factors) at Whampoa. These thirteen enormous buildings on the banks of the Pearl River were divided into living quarters and commercial offices; outside was a small park where the residents—all men—could walk. The western traders were not permitted to leave this compound under any circumstances. Inside, their quarters were comfortable; the British East India Company's factory had a billiards room, a library with a full-time librarian, and an enormous dining room, the tables of which were set with silver plate. Obsequious staff attended their every need, making their quarters more like a gilded cage than a prison.

The Chinese called all visitors "Foreign Devils" and viewed them as "unruly children" who had never become acquainted with reason. Even in their factories, westerners were expected to conduct their personal lives according to Chinese regulations, lists of which were occasionally brought around and read aloud: Foreigners may not row around the river in their boats for "pleasure"; foreigners must not use sedan chairs—walking was good enough for them; foreign ships may not loiter and sell to "rascally natives" goods that were subject to duty. Women were not allowed even to visit the factories. Nor were foreign traders allowed to stay year-round; after the trading season, which was roughly October to March, foreigners were expected to leave China until the following autumn. Foreigners could plead no cause with the Chinese government personally—all communication had to pass through the hongs, even if the hongs were the source of complaint. In short, the governments of the two powerful nations of China and Britain spoke to each other only through a handful of merchants.

The hongs comprised a revolving group of between three and thirteen Chinese merchants who, in 1755, had been granted exclusive trading rights with foreigners. Together, the hongs formed the *cohong,* which until 1842 was the government's collection agency for its revenues from foreign trade. Like tax farmers, the hongs extracted as much as they could from foreign traders while withholding as much as possible from the Chinese government. The hong merchants were loosely organized and generally not monopolistic, but they conformed to the Chinese doctrine of responsibility, which meant the group was answerable for the actions of each member. This entailed each helping pay the others' bad debts. The hongs were also subject to frequent government "squeezes" to support public works, prevent starvation during rice shortages, or repair damage to the river.

Being a hong should have been a lucrative position, and in some cases, such as Howqua's, it was. But almost from the beginning, membership in the *cohong* was regarded as an ordeal as much as a privilege. Indeed, Howqua's father, who was also a hong merchant, had originally refused the "burdensome honor." The hong merchant traded on his own account for his own firm with his own capital for his own profit. Largely because China was so short of liquid capital, the hongs often had to borrow from foreign sources at high interest rates. Bankruptcies were frequent, and many hong members were eager to retire as soon as they could. Bankruptcy was a criminal offense, and bankrupt merchants might be exiled to Eli, on the frozen frontiers of central Asia. Such exile was called "visiting the cold country passage free."

The harbor of Whampoa was a world on water. Thousands of boats bobbed in the waves, from small sampans to large junks, many of them full-time residences. There were hotel boats, floating temples, and boats selling meat, charcoal, prepared food, clothes, and even toys. There were doctors' boats, fortune-teller boats, floating brothels—called flower boats—and boats of theatrical performers. Washerwomen collected laundry and returned it by boat, and a barber made weekly rounds to the anchored ships. There were even boats for the outcast lepers. "Imagine a city afloat," wrote an American merchant, William Hunter, "and it conveys a very correct idea of the incessant movement, the life and gaiety of the river."

When a western ship arrived in Canton with a load of cargo, the captain's first order of business was to establish a relationship with one of the hongs. The hong then collected all official, semiofficial, and unofficial customs charges from the captain and passed them along to the appropriate officials. The payments included the *cumsha*—literally, "golden sand"— which was a gift; the measurement, which was a duty based on the length and width of the ship; the pilotage fee; a fee to an interpreter; and a fee to the comprador, who had the sole right to provision the ship and its crew. All social and mercantile contact between westerners and the Chinese, from robbery to buying a basket of fruit, was mediated by the hongs, who were also known as "security merchants."

The hong provided western traders with offices, storage space, lodging, and servants. In return, the trader sold all his goods to his hong, who had the absolute power to fix prices. The foreign trader could not even walk through the nearby streets to see what was being bought and sold. Because there were no large docks at Whampoa, all the actual loading and unloading of goods took place on boats in the harbor. In the hong's warehouse, tea and silk from the interior were sorted, weighed, and repacked before being dispatched to the foreign ships. If tea or silk were returned because of bad quality, the hong would replace them without charge. The turnaround time for a ship in Canton was one to six months.

There were no banking facilities available to westerners except those of the hongs. Each hong had a strong room, which could contain thousands of silver coins, and a shroff (money dealer). Shroffs examined and weighed pieces of silver or other coins—like all metal, coins were valued by weight, not denomination. The Chinese themselves used only copper coins, and gold and silver were usually traded as bars or lumps. There was no government involvement in the manufacture of precious-metal bars or lumps; the shroff's stamp was the assurance of quality.

For sixty years, the hong applied the grease to the wheels of commerce between East and West. Very few Chinese in Canton could read or write English, and almost no westerners could speak or write Chinese—in fact, any Chinese caught teaching his language to a foreigner was subject to execution. Nevertheless, the hongs were expected to convey to their trading partners the capricious rules of Chinese trade. Canton's closed-door attitude, wrote one early trader, was the result of the "marvellous degree of imbecility and avarice, conceit and obstinancy" of the Chinese.

Since about 1715, pidgin English had become the commercial lingua franca of the hongs and foreign traders. Pidgin English (a term that derives from a corruption of "business" English) was an amalgam of Portuguese, Chinese, and English, with local additions. This international language amounted to a translation of Chinese into a restricted vocabulary, and its use probably explains why the Chinese and British misunderstood each other so often. Discussing a government squeeze, William Hunter asked Howqua, "You pay he how muchee?"

Howqua replied, "My pay he fitty, sikky tousand so."

Hunter: "But s'pose he no contentee?"

Howqua: "S'pose he, No. 1, no contentee, my pay he one lac."

Although Howqua's business dealings were recorded by some British and American diarists of his era, almost no westerners saw him at home or in any other setting outside the harbor. Little is known about how he spent his leisure time or what brought him the greatest happiness. But he did own a palatial home with five hundred servants and a pleasure garden of "ten thousand pines." He dressed in silks and satins of various rich colors. He presided over feasts with dozens of courses, among them bird's nest soup (the birds' nests imported from Java), shark fins, and roasted snails.

The hongs did most of their business with another monopoly—the British East India Company, which was the exclusive trading representative of the British Empire. Founded in 1600, the British East India Company was capitalized half by the government and half by private investors in one of the world's earliest joint-stock ventures. This pooling of risk was expedient in an industry beset by shipwreck, squalls, scurvy, and pirates—though the company's voyages frequently enjoyed armed escorts. In good times, everyone got a dividend; in bad times, no single investor lost everything.

The company's original mission was to buy pepper, nutmeg, cloves, and other eastern spices. But its horizons gradually widened to include other goods, routes, and roles. In India, for example, "the Honorable Company," as it was known, used its commercial power to become the country's de facto government. In 1715, the company decided to enter the China trade, and soon became the largest and most powerful foreign trader at Canton. To the Chinese, the East India Company was synonymous with Britain, even though its policy was dictated by commercial concerns. It had "the body of a government with the brain of a merchant." Both the hongs and the company traders being honorable men, and both making good money, relations between East and West were relatively smooth for several decades.

Indeed, despite their constant annoyance at Chinese discipline, foreign traders almost unanimously agreed that business in Canton could be done as easily as anywhere in the world. Buyers signed no contracts nor expected any receipts. Payments of even large amounts were made on simple scraps of paper signed with initials of the firm. The hongs—and Chinese traders generally—were said to be "able and reliable in their dealings, faithful to their contracts, and large-minded." Other foreign traders marveled at this "race of traders than whom there had not been in the world a shrewder and keener." When two hongs were on the verge of bankruptcy in 1809, the East India Company bought an unusually large amount of tea from them to prevent their financial ruin.

But a far larger conflict between East and West, dating back several centuries, sabotaged their mutual appreciation. From the earliest days of global trade, the West wanted to buy the East's goods, but the East didn't want to buy what the West produced. The Chinese shunned British wool, England's largest export, because it was unsuitable to their climate, and anyway they had silk. China accepted only silver in payment for tea and silk. In their first expedition to China, in 1637, the British brought no goods at all, just eighty thousand "pieces of eight." That pattern continued over the years so that one later ship heading for China carried a cargo that was 98 percent silver and 2 percent goods. "Once the silver gets into their hands, it never leaves them," complained a Florentine merchant at the end of the sixteenth century.

Since the West was always short of gold and silver, the East's demands caused a perpetual trade imbalance. Toward the end of the eighteenth century, the British were struggling to assemble enough metal money to take to China, and the gap between imports and exports was becoming a problem of national concern. Nor could the British simply refuse to trade anymore with China: Britain's population had developed a mass addiction to tea's caffeine charge, and at the time China was the only country in the world that grew tea. During the eighteenth century, per capita consumption of tea in Britain had increased fifteenfold. Tea was prescribed for medical conditions and drunk as a tonic for just about anything; some Britons sipped as many as fifty cups a day. Calvinists and Puritans welcomed tea as an emblem of sobriety and restraint, almost as a divine alternative to alcohol. Like other drug addictions, including opium smoking, tea drinking evolved into a formal ritual, complete with elaborate protocol and paraphernalia.

The East India Company, which had lost its right to import Indian textiles because of rising domestic production, began to concentrate on the tea import-export business. Tea was one of the few commodities that was consumed widely but did not compete against home manufacture. The company's charter even required it to have a year's supply of tea on reserve in London at all times, lest a trade crisis provoke epidemic withdrawal. In 1761, the East India Company's tea shipment from Canton amounted to 2.6 million pounds; forty years later, the company was dispatching 23.3 million pounds of tea to England. While tea with sugar became a cheap source of calories for the working class, the upper class gradually shifted to finer and more expensive teas. The Chinese were convinced that the British couldn't live without tea and would become blind and contract intestinal diseases if the supply line was cut.

As English thirst for tea increased, China developed no reciprocal appetite for anything English. For a brief period, the Chinese were captivated by what they called "singsongs"—British clocks, watches, and mechanical toys—but this was a small-scale business, and the fad passed. There seemed to be only one product for which there was a constant and robust demand among the Chinese that the English were in a position to supply: opium. "We bring the Chinese nothing that is really popular among them," noted a British official in the middle of the nineteenth century. "Opium is the only 'open sesame' to their stony hearts."

The charm of opium had been recognized centuries before Howqua's lifetime—the Sumerians called the poppy the plant of joy. Over the years, opium had been eaten, drunk (as laudanum), and smoked. In England, where so many women worked long hours in cotton mills, opium was a common pacifier for their infants. Druggists recommended it for a variety of medical conditions, including gout. It was easy to get and was used by all social classes. In the modern world, opium's derivatives are morphine and codeine.

Until relatively recently, opium was a global commodity. But opium can be dangerously addictive in two ways: A user needs increasingly higher doses to get the same effect, and withdrawal triggers terrible and sometimes fatal physical reactions. China in Howqua's time became the first nation to make a concerted effort to control the distribution of narcotic drugs. It found that the appetite was so strong and the business so profitable, that it was like trying to hold water in a net.

Opium had a loyal following in China going back at least one thousand years. It appealed first to the bored and the stressed: Eunuchs caught in the ritualized web of court protocol used opium, as did some members of the palace bureaucracy with pointless jobs. A well-to-do leisure class was living under regimes that stifled creativity—opium gave them an outlet. Concubines were given opium to keep them docile. Merchants preparing for business deals, students studying for state examinations, even nuns and monks found that opium helped them deal with anxiety or bitterness. Later, the drug filtered down to all classes of the population.

Opium was generally eaten in China until tobacco arrived from the New World in the early seventeenth century. Tobacco became so popular that the emperor prohibited it. By the time the prohibition was rescinded, however, the Chinese had figured out how to combine the pleasures of tobacco and opium by burning opium extract and inhaling its fumes through a pipe. By the 1830s, the opium trade to China, though no longer legal, was probably the largest commerce of the time in any single commodity. Europeans had not introduced "the foreign mud" to China, but they organized its production and distribution on a large scale for the first time.

The British East India Company had a virtual monopoly over opium production in India. Peasant tenants worked company land and received an advance from the government; in exchange, they sold their products only to a designated agency at a fixed price. Vast tracts of productive land in India were turned over to poppies. As cultivation rose, so did consumption by Indian laborers, leading the company's governor-general to proclaim that "opium is not a necessity of life but a pernicious article of luxury, which ought not to be permitted except for purposes of foreign commerce only."

Chinese officials repeatedly issued edicts outlawing the use or sale of the "edible demon," but after a brief lull the trade rebounded with vigor. In 1729, for example, an imperial edict prohibited the domestic sale and consumption of opium and fixed the penalty at one hundred strokes of a bamboo cane and possible exile. But local governments were rife with corruption, and if they didn't enforce the emperor's edicts, no one did.

Meanwhile, the foreign community treated Chinese prohibitions, warnings, and threats "as a rule, very cavalierly," noted William Hunter.

In Canton, opium was traded like any other commodity until 1800. It was subject to an excise duty and was handled and sold openly to the hongs. Opium was considered no more immoral than whiskey. A British trader who kept a journal wrote under one date, "Employed delivering [opium] briskly. No time to read my Bible." In 1800, China's emperor issued an edict that, for the first time, explicitly prohibited the importation of opium. Only then did the hongs and the East India Company formally cease buying and selling opium. Informally, however, they continued to encourage and profit from it. Opium was, after all, a superior cargo. It didn't deteriorate, and demand increased as addicts were created.

Indian opium was thenceforth sold at auction to private traders, who were licensed by the East India Company. The traders in turn shipped it to China in armed boats or sometimes ex–naval warships. Chinese buyers were always reassured when they saw the opium carried the mark of the East India Company. "The father of all smuggling and smugglers is the East India Company," proclaimed a private trader in 1839. The company tried to force its licensees to adhere to its tradition of profitable gentility, but the private traders were more interested in money than manners. The private traders became "a chink in the wall of monopoly" and soon turned Canton into a field of war.

The British trade, both company and private, was a triangle: British cotton to India; Indian opium to China; Chinese tea to England. The private traders deposited their silver proceeds into a company treasury in Canton and were issued bills of exchange in England. The British then used the silver to subsidize their enormous tea purchases. The process only worked in one direction, because the Chinese didn't want British cotton, and the English didn't want to bring home Indian opium. But for many years, the arrangement was so lucrative that the East India

Company could pay its stock dividends solely from its China profits.

For the first two decades after the edict of 1800 was issued, opium trading continued to expand, although in a more furtive atmosphere. China's enormous, ragged coastline was indefensible, and because Chinese military forces had usually fought continental enemies, not maritime ones, the country's navy was weak. Opium importers made alliances with Chinese merchants, and Chinese merchants bribed local officials with "tea money" to keep their eyes closed.

Officials of the British government knew their traders were flouting Chinese law, but they pretended not to know. Their consciences were assuaged by reports from traders in China that "smoking was a habit, as the use of wine was with us, in moderation." William Jardine, a prodigiously successful British opium trader in China, called the opium business "the safest and most gentleman-like speculation I am aware of." The opium trade troubled other consciences, however: Selling opium to China is not considered "vulgar" because it is a wholesale business, noted one opponent, where gentlemanly (large) amounts of money change hands; however, "that which, sold in chests, is commerce and to be applauded, becomes vulgar and mean when doled out in small lots." But Britain's treasury was addicted to opium: Around 1800, opium provided less than 3 percent of the company's revenue from India; by the 1850s, it represented more than 12 percent.

In the 1820s, enough opium was coming to China to sustain one million addicts. Opium-smoking paraphernalia was sold openly in Canton shops and on the street. A little more than a decade later, it was estimated that four million Chinese were opium addicts. Some poor people were spending half their annual income on opium. In certain coastal provinces, as much as 90 percent of the adult population was addicted. Many government soldiers were addicted to opium, resulting in a humiliating defeat when they tried to quash a rebellion in 1832. When an

English official, Hugh Hamilton Lindsay, took a boat north along the China coast to explore other trading opportunities, he found that everywhere he stopped local bureaucrats and merchants expected opium to be aboard his ship and could hardly be convinced otherwise.

In 1821, after a dispute brought the opium problem back to the surface, the government invoked new penalties against importing opium: Anyone found with it would be executed. Meanwhile, Chinese officials bore down on Canton, where the bulk of opium was still entering the country. They put tremendous pressure on Howqua, then the senior merchant, to control the traders in his bailiwick. He was deprived of his official rank until the opium traffic had been eliminated. The hong merchants finally refused to secure any more ships carrying opium.

But the drug trade was too firmly entrenched, and human nature too weak, to purge opium from China and Britain's economic and social systems. Ships receiving opium simply removed themselves farther from shore, to the island of Lintin, outside Chinese jurisdiction. Permanently anchored in the harbor—and known as the outer anchorages—these ships were exposed to typhoons but protected from Chinese authorities. Within a few years, as many as twenty-five receiving ships were anchored for months, sometimes even years, around Lintin. "Their guns were not removed, and they became floating fortified opium warehouses commanded by British officers." The opium trade also stimulated the development of a new breed of ship—clippers—whose long, narrow hulls, three slanting masts, and clouds of sails made it possible for British traders to get to China and back more than once a year. An American clipper could reach China in less than seven months, whereas earlier journeys had taken more than fourteen months.

At Lintin, ships carrying opium transferred it to a receiving ship and then took their legitimate cargo the rest of the way to Whampoa. Chinese opium dealers then approached the sides of the ships in armed, two-masted river craft with crews of sixty to seventy men and twenty or more oars on both sides. Known as "fast crabs" and "scrambling dragons," these swift and agile boats could usually elude the mandarin guards. But they rarely had to: Although the opium was transferred from boat to boat in broad daylight, and the oarsmen wore distinctive conical caps with red, white, and blue triangles, the guards and customs officials in the harbor usually studiously ignored them. By 1831, as many as two hundred of these boats roved the Canton waters, illustrating the vitality of the drug trade.

For the Chinese, halting the opium trade was imperative for more immediate reasons than arresting the moral degradation of their citizens. The opium business was teaching bad lessons in commerce: As a cash trade (paid in advance of delivery) on an open market, it offered far more attractive terms than negotiating with a hong, whose best deals still involved only credit. Opium commanded high prices, and the proceeds were available immediately. During the first few decades of the nineteenth century, semiannual net profit on India–China opium traffic was more than 15 percent of capital invested. No wonder opium traders were "unwilling to embark in any other branch of commerce or business."

Worst of all, the opium trade was causing a massive drain of silver, creating an unfavorable balance of trade for the first time in Chinese history. China had never produced much silver itself, and in the early nineteenth century, world production of silver began declining. In both East and West, hoarding was widespread, constantly threatening the government with short supply. The Chinese needed British silver and were getting British opium instead. When American traders arrived in the early nineteenth century, they brought a fresh source of silver, but as they became more involved in opium and began selling more cotton goods in China, they brought less silver to trade.

The Chinese people were required to pay their taxes in silver, so rising silver prices meant higher taxes and the social unrest that often ensues. The increasing value of silver affected other businesses, including salt merchants, whose monopoly of their trade was protected by a special fleet of government cruisers but was taxed at every stage. Their taxes, too, were due in silver, and a position that had once been a lucrative prize became a financial burden. Chinese officials worried that if silver kept flowing out of the country, people would be unable to pay any taxes at all.

Government prohibitions of drugs often have the effect of driving out the small operator in favor of bigger and more sophisticated criminal organizations. Canton's harbor area, a few hundred square miles, contained countless streams and channels. Other boats plied the same water, and it was often unclear which were fishermen and which were pirates. Indeed, if fishermen were unsuccessful with their nets, they often turned to plunder or smuggling. Corruption was so endemic in the enforcement system that the "smug boats" that delivered opium were sometimes mandarin boats whose function was to prevent smuggling. The official prohibition gave corrupt Chinese officials an excuse to demand higher bribes, which simply raised the price of opium.

The opium ban was ineffectual from the beginning, and the annulment of the East India Company's trading monopoly rights in 1833 struck another blow. Although China probably didn't know it at the time, private traders were about to pry open China's market like a tin can. They were delegates of the West's new capitalist philosophy: Trade should be limited only by the natural laws of supply and demand and the ability of people to transport goods. Government, diplomacy, tradition, protocol— what did these have to do with commercial transactions? Private traders typically began as agents for firms in London or India but then started speculating in rice and opium for their own accounts and eventually established their own houses. They also became bankers, profiting from the dearth of capital in Canton by lending money to the hongs at interest rates of 2 percent or more a month.

The private traders in Canton irritated both the British and Chinese with their unrestrained aggression, but in Britain they became the heroes of the manufacturing class. They pressured Parliament to let them compete against the increasingly active American traders. Meanwhile, Manchester cotton manufacturers and other British industrialists were condemning the British East India Company as an obstacle to their export business. With its monopoly gone, the company withdrew entirely from Canton, ending the stability of the old order. Many of the company's officials returned to London with colonial fortunes and earned the derisive nickname "nabobs" because of their financial excesses.

In Canton, however, hundreds of private traders now competed for business without any conventions except the love of laissez-faire. American ships streamed into the harbor, none having a government monopoly and asking only "a fair field and no favor." These American merchant-adventurers had one goal: to make as much money as they could in the shortest time. On the whole, trade with China was very profitable, wrote an American in 1857, running from $180,000 to $200,000 a year. The hong merchants liked the Americans because they paid for so much with silver dollars. Although Americans tried to sell ginseng, a root found in New England, and Hawaiian sandalwood to the Chinese, they were most successful with fur pelts and a sea slug called bêche-de-mer, which the Chinese considered a delicacy. Compared with the British, Americans were far less involved in the opium business, but not because of moral scruples. American traders had to obtain their opium from Turkey, whose supply was tiny compared with India's production. The Americans ran a distant second to Britain in opium, accounting for only about 10 percent of the market.

British and American private traders began to launch new campaigns to evade and overthrow the restrictive hong system at Canton. They refused to accept the hongs' seniority system and fixed prices. They dealt separately with each ship's cargo and threw their business to whichever hong merchant would give them the best price. The hongs were losing control over the harbor, and there was no way to turn back to isolationism.

In 1839, the emperor made his most concerted effort to check the opium trade. He appointed an educated and incorruptible commissioner named Lin—a corpulent man with a heavy black mustache and beard—to go to Canton and crush the opium industry. Lin left Peking in a sedan chair carried by twelve bearers and accompanied by six servants and three cooks. He and his entourage made the 1,200-mile journey to Canton in sixty days.

Lin knew a war with the British over opium would be a disaster for the Chinese. The Chinese navy couldn't prevail in any armed conflict with the foreigners. Militarily, many westerners viewed the Chinese as blustering wimps. It was always "a flourish of trumpets, and enter Tom Thumb."

Lin called the hongs together, and as the twelve men faced him on their knees, he denounced them for conspiring with westerners in the opium trade for the sake of commerce. "Truly I burn with shame for you," Lin told the hong merchants. Lin ordered all trade in "smoke" to stop immediately, and he demanded that the hongs make this position clear to foreign traders: They must surrender all the opium they held in storage in Canton and sign bonds agreeing not to import any more opium, under penalty of confiscation of property and death. The hongs had three days to accomplish this task; failure would confirm their inappropriate collaboration with the opium traders, and one or two would be decapitated. Howqua, according to an American merchant, was "crushed to the ground by his terrors."

The traders agreed to sacrifice a fraction of the $12 million of opium in their warehouses, for which Howqua himself would compensate them. Lin disdainfully refused the compromise. He threw Howqua's son in prison and demanded that one of the leading opium traders, Lancelot Dent, be brought before him for questioning. Lin said if Dent refused to comply, Howqua would be executed. Desperate, Howqua appeared at the factories, a chain around his neck, and pleaded with Dent to go. But Dent refused unless his safe return was guaranteed.

In retaliation, Lin forbade foreigners to leave the city, and a few days later all commerce and communication ceased. The 350 foreigners who remained became, for all practical purposes, house prisoners for the next seven weeks. All Chinese were ordered out of the area on penalty of decapitation. Soldiers surrounded the factories and assaulted the captives with the incessant sound of horns and gongs. Inside, the traders suffered the indignities of having to cook their own food, sweep their own floors, and wash their own dishes. Eventually, the foreign traders agreed to relinquish all their opium, and life began to return to normal.

But tensions between the Chinese and the westerners continued to simmer. The confiscation and destruction of so much opium drove up prices, making smuggling even more lucrative. The British and Chinese governments were unable to negotiate without one side offending the other. Before long, a British ship fired on a Chinese junk, and the first Opium War began.

The war was little more than a series of skirmishes and minor naval clashes. The Chinese army was unskilled, and thousands of soldiers and civilians ended up committing suicide rather than facing defeat. Many of the British casualties were from malaria or dysentery. In one battle, the shots of the Chinese ships were too high, and the only damage inflicted was to British sails and rigging. "Their wretched gunnery hurt no one," noted a witness. The Chinese had never seen steam-driven warships, which could go against the wind and navigate shallow water, and they were terrified.

The hongs were hit hard by the war. They were squeezed to finance the building of fortifications, war junks, and cannons, creating a heavy burden "of which not a small share falls upon my poor old shoulder," Howqua wrote to an American merchant. The Opium War, Howqua moaned to the same merchant in another letter, "has caused me the loss of a great deal of money"—some $2 million, as it turned out. In 1841, when Canton was under siege, the factories were damaged badly, and several of them burned.

War ended in August 1842 with the signing of the Treaty of Nanking, which the Chinese justifiably called the "Unequal Treaty." The treaty abolished the *cohong;* henceforth, foreign merchants would be free to buy and sell as they pleased at prices settled by mutual agreement. The treaty named five cities, including Canton, as "treaty ports" open to foreign trade; and it turned Hong Kong into a British colony. Opium wasn't mentioned. The Chinese would not legalize it, and the British would not suppress it. Opium imports rose sharply. In 1845, there were some eighty vessels based in Hong Kong that were running opium. China had been unable to dislodge either opium or foreigners. In 1858, the importation of opium was legalized by treaty, and a tariff rate was fixed. Howqua was not alive to see this milestone in the opium trade. He died in September 1843 at the age of seventy-four.

The Opium War arose from the first of many unsuccessful attempts by governments to prevent their citizens from using drugs. The drug industry has always been a high-profit, though high-risk, way to get rich. From a business perspective, drugs such as opium, cocaine, and heroin are ideal commodities. Relative to bulk and weight, they are quite valuable. Produced in countries where labor is cheap, they are sold easily in rich markets without development or advertising. They can sustain enormous price markups. They are usually paid for in cash. And the world's appetite for drugs appears limitless.

Today, the illegal drug industry is characterized by highly centralized management control, vertical integration, and inexpensive labor for menial tasks. Drug dealing has always demanded constant innovation, and today's top competitors are experimenting with fertilizers and preservatives; trying to differentiate their products; and using sophisticated communication and transportation devices. The Colombian cartels have even manufactured their own submarines to reach the U.S. market.

In contemporary America, drug trading is the largest source of illegally earned income. A mass market arose in the United States during the 1960s and 1970s and transformed the drug business into a global giant. In the 1980s, the boundaries between many financial markets dissolved, and a truly global capital market emerged. Profits are so high that drug traffickers (distribution is the most profitable stage of the business) find it difficult to hide their money, let alone spend it. Money laundering—transforming tainted cash into ordinary money—has become drug traffickers' top business problem and has spawned a professional class of money launderers who are ac-countants, lawyers, and bankers. Moving the cash can be more complicated than moving the drugs.

In the nineteenth century, Howqua watched the alien ships glide into his harbor, knowing they held the mysteries and wealth of other worlds, and he rejoiced at their arrival. What they carried was less important to him than that they had come at all. Trading was his life, and his mission was to facilitate the meeting of buyers and sellers from opposite sides of the earth. Whether they brought opium, sandalwood, or silver, Howqua bowed and welcomed his guests. He knew a man could get rich by helping people get what they wanted.

NINE

Outmanning the Men

Hetty Green (1834–1916)

For the first eight centuries of the second millennium, almost all the rich were men or their wives and daughters. Except when they were born royal, like Cleopatra or Elizabeth I, women had no way to make fortunes except for occasional under-the-table speculation. The ascendance of the money economy and industrialization pushed women farther from production and closer to consumption. In most countries throughout history, women couldn't even inherit businesses or land, let alone earn money from them. During the eighteenth and early nineteenth centuries, the cult of domesticity emphasized woman's primary role as keeper of the spiritual and moral flames. Much of women's work was hidden in the home. Before about 1880, running a brothel may have been the most lucrative kind of female proprietorship in the United States. In Helena, Montana, in the 1880s, for example, female brothel keepers provided most of the town's banking services, especially mortgage loans, and owned a substantial amount of local real estate.

By the end of the nineteenth century, however, the tidal wave of American capitalism had swept away some traditions of womanhood. Women's labor was needed to fuel the post–Civil War industrial boom. More women were becoming educated, and their social-reform movements were growing noisy and effectual. They were inheriting money. For the first time in history, women could become rich not just passively, by birth or beauty, but by using their brains. Early successful women were widely disliked, and their constant battles with scornful peers often gnarled their personalities. Such a woman was Hetty Green, known even in her lifetime by the nickname "the witch of Wall Street."

Green was a one-woman freak show. Disheveled and sometimes demented, she worked on the floor of her Wall Street office, surrounded by bags and piles of loose papers. Today, she would be diagnosed as paranoid, obsessive-compulsive, or borderline. While other women workers were being advised to be "gracious and pleasant and womanly," Hetty Green's financial blitzkriegs made grown men weep. "When I fight," she once said, "there is usually a funeral, and it isn't mine, either." At her death, Hetty Green was worth $100 million—well over $1 billion in today's dollars. If Hetty Green was crazy, she was crazy like a fox.

Historians snicker at mean, mad Hetty Green. Her biographies were written by priggish men who decried Green's repudiation of Victorian womanhood. Furthermore, no one could understand how a person as rich as Hetty Green could be so stingy. Here she was, living in the midst of America's first great era of excess, the so-called Gilded Age, when a new wealthy class indicated its status by smoking tobacco wrapped in hundred-dollar bills. Yet she lived in cheap boardinghouses and wore her clothes until they were paper-thin. At Green's death in 1916, the Boston *Transcript* sneered, "Hetty Green . . . was unable to take her immense fortune with her when she quit this world for the next"; the headline read, SHE, TOO, LEFT HERS BEHIND. Hetty Green wouldn't have given their words a passing thought. "I go my own way, take no partners, risk no one else's fortune," she once said, "therefore I am Madame Ishmael, set against every man."

* * *

To say that Hetty Green lived in a reckless, unrestrained era in American history is an understatement. Men were manlier then, and the manliest of all were the new class of cutthroat capitalists who munched little people for breakfast. An excessive temper was considered an important ingredient of success. Business was "regarded as a faro-game for giants, and only those with healthy nerves were expected to sit at the table." The womanly woman, on the other hand, was pure, tightly cosseted, and susceptible to nervous exhaustion. If Freud was right that money is a symbol for excrement, women shouldn't even think about it, let alone own it. Until the middle of the nineteenth century, a married woman's earnings in many parts of the country automatically belonged to her husband. If she could keep her wages, they were referred to as "pin money."

In theory, every man in America took off in the success race from the same starting line, and in theory the swiftest and smartest would win. America had no royalty, nobility, or aristocracy with head starts, just two million people who had been created equal (plus half a million slaves). In Hetty Green's era, the English philosopher Herbert Spencer popularized the phrase "survival of the fittest," which suited the new industrial capitalists perfectly. Among humans, as animals, the theory went, the strong triumphed over the weak according to a natural law of competition. If monopoly somehow ensued, that must also be a law of nature. In this context, *people* always meant *men*.

In late nineteenth-century America, the businessman became the epitome of masculinity and leadership. Books, editorials, and tracts described wealthy men as noble, just, courageous, and virtuous. "Business thinking" became synonymous with "sound thinking," and the height of praise for an idea was that it might be a "money-making proposition." Even in New York's high society, plutocracy triumphed over aristocracy. "The modern nobility springs from success in business," reported Henry Clews, a nineteenth-century stockbroker. It was not vulgar to speak of one's money, as it had been in the first world. With so few inborn marks of status, money became the most widely accepted way of ranking people. The price tags of possessions became a common topic of conversation. "Money-making having become a virtue, it was no longer controlled by the virtues, but ranked *with* them, and could be weighed against them when any conflict occurred," one historian noted.

Organized religion offered no resistance; church and state had long since separated in the United States. Furthermore, Protestantism was America's most popular faith, and Calvinism preached that dedication to business was itself a kind of holiness. To relax in contentment was depraved. Nor could government restrain the feverish competition in business. The federal government was weak, its officials frequently enriched by business titans. Congress imposed few restraints on commerce except for protective tariffs against foreign competition. Both federal and state judiciaries sympathized with private interests. People's consciences—their rationalizations—were the final moral authority. In the seventeenth century, Americans looked up to their divines, Robert Heilbroner wrote, in the eighteenth century to their soldiers and statesmen. In the nineteenth century, the nation worshiped its captains of industry.

America's wealthy had money to burn, but they had no conventions for spending big money in ways that didn't appear grotesque. They threw themselves into a frenzied contest of conspicuous consumption. They gave balls on horseback—the horses' shoes padded with rubber, their riders eating truffles and drinking champagne. They gave "poverty socials," where guests wore rags, sat on broken soapboxes, used newspapers as napkins, and drank beer from rusty tin cans. They ransacked Europe for art treasures, stripping medieval castles of their carvings, paintings, and tapestries, ripping out whole staircases and ceilings so their new houses, copies of Renaissance châteaus and palazzis, would look authentically regal. John Jacob Astor's wife's divan was known as "the throne."

One millionaire built a Tudor mansion in Newport and began sprinkling his conversation with Tudor-style words, frequently beginning sentences with "Prithee." A staff of servants was de rigueur for the parvenu: It took two domestics to serve a single cup of tea. E. L. Godkin, founder of *The Nation* magazine, described America's wealthy as a "gaudy stream of bespangled, belaced and beruffled barbarians." Such prodigality threw Henry Adams into despair: "The American wasted money more recklessly than anyone ever did before," he wrote. "He spent more to less purpose than any extravagant court aristocracy."

In their business life, too, the new wealthy often seemed more like primitive warriors than modern businessmen, except their weapons were railroads, oil fields, and telegraph lines. The industrial big feet—Jay Gould, Cornelius Vanderbilt, John D. Rockefeller—lurched around the country snatching up natural resources, fixing prices, cheating the government, and trying to destroy one another. If lesser men and women were destroyed in the process—and plenty were—this was simply the natural if regrettable result of social Darwinism. This philosophy bolstered the capitalist battle cry of "anything goes."

The ethic of the smart man was also born in this era. "He is a smart man" was the repeated defense of those who had grabbed the national infrastructure away from everyone else— what did society want him to do, *not be smart?* As for the small investors, they were like "marionettes dancing on an invisible wire." Unlike some of their European forebears, poor Americans didn't dream of overthrowing the rich, they dreamed of joining them, and at the turn of the century, it looked like the stock market was their best vehicle. Across the nation, farmers, widows, and wage earners threw their life savings into the market. But as Daniel Drew, a pitiless stock manipulator of the time, warned, "Anybody who plays the stock market not as an insider is like a man buying cows in the moonlight." There was no Securities and Exchange Commission and no restrictions on stock manipulation.

* * *

Nineteenth-century industrialists had at least one thing in common with plunderers like Machmud of Ghazni: They owned the country's resources not because they had produced or earned them "but because they owned them," as Thorstein Veblen wrote. The robber barons prevailed partly because they were good gamblers but also because they had no ethical scruples, and no person or agency was powerful enough to stop them. The new tactics "go by the names of business shrewdness and strategy, but they differ from ordinary cunning only by the degree of adroitness by which the victim is outwitted." Indeed, so engaged in ruinous competition were the new industrialists that their transportation and communication systems actually retarded the development of other industries. "We do not ride on the railroad," wrote Henry David Thoreau. "It rides upon us."

On the eve of the Civil War, 80 percent of Americans lived and worked in rural areas, and their wealth was still measured largely in land. Then, over the next few decades, America was drawn into an industrial revolution, and its economic center turned from small farms and local businesses to large-scale banking, insurance, manufacturing, and retailing.

As the population grew—mostly by immigration—and railroads and telegraphs spanned the continent, business advanced to a scale unimaginable only a few decades earlier. Moneyed interests began joining forces in gigantic corporations, which was the only way to raise enough capital for large-scale production. The joint-stock company, the cardinal invention of capitalism, reduced each investor's liability and provided more continuity than family partnerships. A whole new way to make money became possible for the common person: They could wager on the future prosperity of the country even if they had to borrow the money to put down the bet. As long as the economy continued to grow, those with a little money could make more, and those with a lot of money could make fortunes. In the hectic half century after the Civil War, mineral output tripled, railroad trackage quadrupled, telegraph lines quintupled, and the value of manufactured goods rose by a factor of fifteen. By 1900, America had the highest per-capita standard of living in the world. It was the heroic age of American capitalism.

Not coincidentally, Horatio Alger was the most popular writer. The heroes of Alger's more than one hundred books for boys (with such titles as *Strive and Succeed, Fame and Fortune*) told tales of boys who asked the world for nothing more than an even playing field, where intelligence and determination would win the day. The bootstraps sagas reinforced America's faith that an individual had the power to transform him- or herself. With inverted snobbery, it became fashionable to boast of the poverty rather than the wealth of one's forebears. Yet by the late nineteenth century, wealth was distributed more unequally than at any earlier period of American history. In 1840, there were fewer than twenty millionaires in the United States; indeed, there were so few millionaires that the word was frequently italicized when it was printed. Just fifty years later, in 1892, there were more than four thousand millionaires. One of the wealthiest of them was Hetty Green.

Hetty Robinson Green was born November 21, 1834, in New Bedford, Massachusetts, the only child in a family that today would be labeled grossly dysfunctional. Her mother was the former Abby Howland, one of whose ancestors rode the *Mayflower* to America. The Howland fortune had begun with one cow in Plymouth, but the family prospered over time by farming, trading with the Indians, and dealing in land and slaves. Then, in 1811, Isaac Howland, Hetty's grandfather, dipped his toe into the merchant-adventuring business. He soon built America's greatest whaling fleet in New Bedford. Although the Howlands were the wealthiest family in town, they were also devout Quakers, eschewing ostentation and self-indulgence.

Hetty's father, Edward Robinson, was also a Quaker, but

that was the only thing he and his neurasthenic wife shared. The energetic, domineering Robinson was nicknamed Black Hawk, and not for his mild manners. Around New Bedford, it was said that Robinson squeezed a dollar until the eagle screamed. Robinson worked for Abby's father, Gideon Howland, and took a well-trod path to promotion by marrying the boss's daughter. Abby and Edward had a girl, Hetty, and less than two years later a boy, who died in infancy. Abby took to her bed and stayed there for the rest of her life with a string of real and imagined illnesses. Little Hetty was dispatched to live with her grandparents and Aunt Sylvia Ann.

Growing up in New Bedford, the booming center of the whale-oil business, was useful training for Hetty Green's future warfare on Wall Street. If the whaling ships came back empty, the crew didn't get paid. If the ship was overflowing with barrels of oil, captains would haze crew members relentlessly, hoping they would desert ship and thereby forfeit their shares. Referring to the Quaker shipowners of New Bedford, Samuel Eliot Morison later wrote, "They were as tightfisted, cruel and ruthless a set of exploiters as you can find in American history."

Morison could have been describing Hetty Green's grandfather and father. As a girl, Hetty sat on their laps while they read the business news and stock-market reports to her. Later, when their eyesight began to fail, she did the same for them. She had few friends her age; her only intimate associates were members of her family. At the age of eight, before banks welcomed small customers, she insisted on opening her own account. Her only hobby seemed to be riding horses—sidesaddle, in one of her rare concessions to social convention. Whenever she could, Hetty accompanied her grandfather or father as they made their rounds of the whale business—to the office, warehouse, commissary, countinghouse, and wharf.

Educated first by a governess, Hetty then attended a boarding school for three years but never mastered even fundamental grammar or spelling. "I was sent to a Quaker school," she recalled. "There I learned to be thrifty and careful, not to waste, to be just, and to read the Bible." Since Quakers traditionally regarded women as men's equals, Hetty's natural assertiveness was encouraged rather than frowned upon.

Her final two years of formal education were spent at Miss Lowell's Boston finishing school, where she learned to dance and play the piano, the two accomplishments considered most important for genteel women. She was said to be reasonably attractive—tall and blue-eyed, with a pretty complexion. She also had, one historian wrote, "a bosom high and full." But all her life Hetty was careless with her personal appearance, occasionally waiting too long between baths. She never wore corsets, and in the winter she wore men's underwear because it was warmer. Once when Hetty went to New York for the winter social season, her father gave her $1,200 to buy clothes. She invested $1,000 of the allowance in bonds instead. All through her life, she held high society in utter contempt.

Hetty adored money from an early age. When she was thirteen years old, she got a terrible shock when her grandfather died and left her nothing in his will. His fortune was to be divided between his two daughters: Hetty's mother and her aunt, Sylvia Ann. Already, Hetty knew she wanted the Howland fortune for herself, and during the next several years she fretted about how much she might inherit when the remaining three members of her family died. Yet in 1860, Hetty's mother died at the age of fifty-one without having made a will. Hetty and her father both wanted Abby's money so badly that they agreed to arbitration by a mutually acceptable lawyer. In the end, her father received $120,000 in cash, while Hetty won only $8,000 in real estate.

Meanwhile, the combined forces of petroleum and the Civil War were driving business and wealth out of New Bedford. Seeing the handwriting on the wall, Hetty's father moved to New York, where he began investing in shipping. Shortly afterward, the Howland whaling company was liquidated.

Hetty stayed behind in New Bedford with her ailing aunt

but now worried she would lose control of her father's money, too. He was only fifty-nine and still handsome. He could marry again, even sire an heir to supersede her. Robinson didn't marry again, however, and when he died he left his estate of about $6 million to his daughter. Yet here again, Hetty's ambitions to control a fortune were thwarted: Her father had left his bequest in a trust to be administered by two male executors.

In the years Hetty lived with her aunt in New Bedford, the two bickered constantly over money. Whatever her aunt spent was that much less that Hetty would inherit. Hetty badgered Sylvia Ann about having too many servants and eating expensive food. Sylvia Ann taunted Hetty with threats to cut her out of her will. This intimidation carried more weight then than it does now, when tax laws have made lifetime transfers more advantageous than waiting for death.

In 1863, Hetty left New Bedford and moved to New York. She attended balls, parties, and concerts in high society. But when her aunt died in 1865, Hetty hurried back to New Bedford for the reading of the will. Once again, she was dismayed by what she heard: Sylvia Ann had left Hetty only half of her $2 million estate, and even that came in the form of a lifetime trust that would pay about $70,000 a year. Hetty immediately contested the will. She produced another document, complete with Sylvia Ann's signature, stating that Hetty and Sylvia Ann had made a pact to leave each other their entire estates. The legal wrangling lasted until 1870, consuming $150,000 of the estate in fees, lawyers, and expert witnesses. Dr. Oliver Wendell Holmes testified that he believed the signature of Sylvia Ann had been traced by someone else.

In the midst of this tortuous litigation, Hetty, then thirty-two years old, married Edward H. Green, forty-six, who had been an associate of Hetty's father in his clipper-ship business. Green came from an old, respectable, and modestly wealthy Vermont family. For twenty years, Green, a tall, elegant man who spoke several languages, including Chinese, had represented an American trading firm in China and Manila, dealing in tea, silk, and tobacco. When he married Hetty, Edward Green was worth some $1 million. Unlike Hetty, however, he enjoyed spending it. He was so extravagant that he owned more than thirty suits. Meanwhile, Hetty's income from her various holdings amounted to roughly $1,000 a day, yet she wore the same dress every day. It would be difficult to find a couple more poorly matched, at least in terms of financial habits, than Hetty and Edward.

The couple spent the first eight years of their marriage in London, where Edward continued trading and Hetty dabbled in the financial markets. They had two children—Edward, known as Ned, and Sylvia. Hetty eagerly bought up U.S. government bonds, which, in the years just after the Civil War, were being sold for as little as forty cents on the dollar. Most investors thought they would never be redeemed at full value. Hetty also began buying American railroad stocks and bonds. In one year in London, she made more than $1.25 million on her investments.

The family returned to America in 1874, not long after a Wall Street panic had decimated railroad stocks, of which Hetty Green was a large holder. The four Greens moved to Edward's hometown of Bellows Falls, Vermont. There, Hetty's eccentricities, particularly her miserliness, took root and spread. She haggled with servants, bickered with local tradesmen, and dressed her daughter in cast-off clothing. Edward began to spend more time away from home. Eventually, the two separated, and Hetty and her children moved to a cheap apartment in Brooklyn. Hetty set up headquarters at the Chemical National Bank in Manhattan, which gave her a free desk in return for her multi-million-dollar deposit.

Whether women had any business in business was a hotly debated topic of the late nineteenth century. The foundation of good business was clearheaded rationality, and women were seen as muzzy-headed crybabies. "One can easily imagine the effect produced by several hundred women interested in stocks, being present at a panic and giving way with feminine impulsiveness to the feelings of the hour. . . . A bevy of dames dissolved in tears, with hair disheveled, and giving way to hysterics," wrote a man of the time. In 1910, there were 13,729 stockbrokers, of whom 207 were women. Entry-level office positions were called "office boys" regardless of their gender, which explains this classified ad: "Wanted—a boy, either sex." But whereas a boy could grow up to be a clerk or even a manager, a girl was likely to remain a boy.

A working woman in Hetty Green's era was usually either prehusband or posthusband. A married woman who worked suggested a weak, incompetent spouse. Regardless of their marital status, middle- and upper-class women had few occupations open to them other than governess or companion. Conspicuous leisure was a way to convey status. Indeed, the ideal woman had small, delicate limbs and waist—such features, wrote Thorstein Veblen, demonstrated that the woman is incapable of doing anything useful and must therefore be supported in idleness by her owner.

What a remarkable use of affluence—turning women into luxuries. How far from the days when the basic unit of production was the family, and the man needed the berries woman gathered as much as the woman needed the meat man hunted. Later, the man needed the clothes, soap, and candles she made, the beer she brewed, and the chickens she kept. As production moved to offices and factories, women's lives were severed from the crucible of wealth, and money replaced the former satisfactions of labor. If they tried to enter offices and factories, they were perceived as competitors. Women were not admitted to graduate programs at business schools such as Harvard or Columbia.

Even the president of the Carnegie Foundation for the Advancement of Teaching, addressing the 1907 graduates of the all-women Simmons College, said, "I believe that the best job that may come to any woman is . . . as a sweetheart, as a wife, as a mother." Yet women's domestic workloads had already been falling, with the white birth rate declining from about seven children per married couple in 1800 to 4.24 children by 1880. As business outgrew the family in America, the family less often operated as a business partnership; unlike thrifty French and Dutch women, who could feel themselves to be part of their husbands' enterprises, American women often felt alienated from the source and meaning of money.

Raising capital had always been a problem for women—they had few resources to offer as collateral. The gradual shift to corporate capitalization exacerbated that situation as financial markets became more formal, restrictive, and conservative. Women who flouted social convention and entered business tended to gravitate toward areas related to household tasks, such as food preparation, textiles, and dressmaking. One 1895 advice book was titled *How to Make Money Although a Woman.* Another book, *100 New Money Making Plans for Untrained Women,* published in 1904, suggested such jobs as "bric-a-brac surgeon," giving "conversation classes," and "entertaining invalid children." If women earned money, they were advised to save it: "The first and most important rule, SAVE MONEY," advised *How,* an 1893 "Practical Business Guide for American Women." "To earn $10 each week and spend $10 is not to make any money." When women inherited money, it was usually as trust funds, which were typically managed conservatively.

As America expanded and prospered, there were new labor demands from large corporations, particularly banks, insurance companies, and government bureaucracies. Offices became more complex, requiring additional clerical and administrative assistance. In 1880, 6,600 women were engaged in clerical occupations; by 1900, that number had jumped to more than 200,000. Women were considered docile and acquiescent, and because they had no expectations based on tradition they were less likely to complain about low status and wages. A woman's earnings were adversely affected by her potential to marry. A single woman's wages were enough to keep her from starvation but not enough to make leaving home attractive.

Once they made it through the gates, women were advised to keep their heads bowed, their voices soft, and their egos in check. "The French have a saying that 'the clever man is he who conceals his cleverness,' " declaimed the Carnegie Foundation's Henry Smith Pritchett.

> And in many of the callings most accessible to the educated woman, she who conceals her cleverness, she who is willing to do a large and responsible work without figuring in the world's eye, who is willing to handle the reins without seeming to touch them, to do work that involves enormous power and influence without desiring to have that fact known, is the one who gets the greatest success. . . . Many a secretary carries in her hands a larger measure of power than falls to the lot of men whose names appear every week in the daily papers, but who is wise enough to do the work and say nothing about it.

This most emphatically does not describe Hetty Green, who was competing with unscrupulous men amid the anarchy of the nineteenth-century financial markets. The stock exchange was a volatile mix of traders, who took as much pleasure from injuring others as from enriching themselves. Without regulations, traders and investors were like children loosed from parents, grabbing at everything without moral qualms. No one dared to stop them because they owned the apparatus of prosperity. They destroyed one another by manipulating stock prices with the blind enthusiasm of barbarians: "A man is robbed on the Stock Exchange, just as he is killed in a war, by people whom he never sees." It was unnervingly easy for the corporations of the time to raise money by issuing ever more shares of stock, "hollowing themselves into husks that crumbled at the slightest pressure."

In the middle of the nineteenth century, "call" or "margin" loans—loans against the collateral of stock—started to dominate the New York stock market. Call loans increased the volatility of a market already subject to constant manipulation and cornerings. The aim of a "corner" was to acquire the entire stock of a commodity in order to resell it at a higher price; a perfect corner obliterated the bears who had sold stock short in anticipation of buying it back cheaper at a later date. Hetty Green herself once cornered a well-known stock operator named Addison Cammack. Cammack had received inside information that the Louisville and Nashville Railroad was going to cut its dividend; anticipating a drop in the price of the stock, he started selling it short. Sure enough, the dividend was cut, the stock price fell, and then Cammack discovered there were no shares of the stock anywhere with which he could cover his shorts. Hetty Green had it all. "I was in a slaughter house," he told a financial reporter. "Whichever way I looked I spurted blood." Cammack personally handed Hetty Green a check for her stock that represented a profit to her of $400,000.

With the help of a corrupt press, a shrewd stock manipulator such as Jay Gould might destroy entire banks, and sometimes a full-scale panic ensued. "A Wall Street panic comes suddenly like thunder from a blue sky. No shrewdness can see and no talent avert it."

Hetty Green thrived on market panics. She not only wouldn't sell, but because she never bought stock on margin, she usually had cash on hand. She went around buying whatever she could. In the panic of 1890, she waited until the market was at its lowest ebb and then began to invest heavily in railroad stocks. But she always kept herself in the background, trading as quietly as possible. "When I see a good thing going cheap because nobody wants it, I buy a lot of it and tuck it away," she explained later. "Then when the time comes, they have to hunt me up and pay me a good price for my holdings." In the panic of 1907, "some of the solidest men in Wall Street came to me," she said, "and tried to unload all sorts of things, from palatial residences to automobiles." Investors like Hetty Green were known as "panic birds," but as Andrew Carnegie once said, "The man who has money during a panic is a wise and valuable citizen."

Hetty Green's favorite investments were railroads and real estate—the two most popular areas for financial speculation in the nineteenth century. Money that had previously chased ocean shipping had shifted to railroads. Operating under the names Westminster Company and Windham Realization Company, Hetty Green invested conservatively and for the long term, never allowing herself to be enticed far from the security of 6 percent interest. In this, Hetty Green was typical of most women investors of her era—mortgages on real estate were their favorite investments, in the form of loan-and-building associations and insurance companies.

Green did most of her business sitting on the stone floor at Chemical National Bank, surrounded by trunks and suitcases. As she pored over financial news, a stream of bankers, brokers, and other supplicants called on her, asking for advice or, most often, money. She required only a few hours of sleep a night and had almost total recall. She rarely used her private office, preferring to roam around with her ears open. The bank tolerated her as any smart bank would have—her fortune on deposit meant hundreds of thousands of dollars in interest for them. She began keeping many of her clothes at the bank, and when she left town she stored other possessions there until she returned.

One of her earliest investments was in a fifty-eight-mile-long branch line of the Houston and Texas Central Railroad, which came with 277,000 acres of land. The price was $1.375 million. At the time, the American railroad system consisted of short stretches of track haphazardly linking towns all over the country. Connecting them to form a transcontinental passage would be one of the greatest business triumphs of the era. But Hetty Green's railroad became a bone of contention between her and

Collis P. Huntington, the rapacious monopolist who owned the Southern Pacific all around her. Their extended litigation cost both sides dearly, but Hetty Green enjoyed a good fight. In 1899, she learned that Huntington was borrowing heavily from a certain bank and was falling behind on some obligations. Green began making large deposits at the bank while Huntington continued to borrow. One day, she went to the bank and asked for her $1.6 million in deposits on the spot. Bank messengers rushed to Huntington's office to call in his notes. He narrowly escaped bankruptcy.

Green's real-estate portfolio consisted of hundreds of parcels of land in Cincinnati, Denver, Saint Louis, and especially Chicago, then the railroad center of the nation. Between 1885 and 1900, Green acquired more than $17 million of real estate in Chicago, including office buildings, stores, factories, and undeveloped land. After the Chicago World's Fair, she bought a number of properties that had been foreclosed on because of deflated real-estate values. The city was growing so quickly that wise investors did not have to either sell or improve their holdings. In 1830, a person could have bought a quarter acre of land in the heart of Chicago for $20. By 1894, that land was worth $1.25 million.

In one day in Cincinnati, Green foreclosed on two mortgages; sold a block of property for a large profit; bought eight hundred acres of suburban farmland; posed for a picture; and was interviewed for a newspaper story. "Two hundred thousand dollars is the largest sum I ever made in a day," she told a journalist in 1900. When she died, she was said to own more than seven thousand pieces of property.

In 1905, she lent the city of New York $4.5 million at 4 percent interest, undercutting the banks' rate by a fraction of a percent. Having no overhead expenses, she was nearly always willing to "shade" the prevailing price of money. "She had the best banking brain of anyone I ever knew," recalled a former

New York City comptroller. A conservative estimate of Hetty Green's income in 1900 was $7 million; the average annual income at the time was $490.

Yet Hetty Green never enjoyed spending her money, and that made her unusual among her gender. The typical generalization about money and gender is that women regard money in terms of things it can be converted into, while men regard it in terms of the power its possession implies. "A woman wants enough money to make herself and her family comfortable—enough, perhaps, to enable her to live in luxury. But once she reaches that level of wealth, she usually quits striving for more. Many men, on the other hand, go on furiously piling up wealth long after they've got more than they can possibly spend." In this framework, Hetty Green was more like men than women. But perhaps many other women were similarly like men. As Dorothea Dix, the nineteenth-century social reformer, wrote, "Stripped of all the chiffons of gallantry, poetry and romance, in which the matter has been shrouded for ages, the burning desire of every woman's heart is financial independence."

Whatever their gender, wealthy people who don't spend their money have always been regarded with suspicion by their contemporaries. They are criticized as cheapskates, penny-pinchers, skinflints, and tightwads. "In temperament," pronounced *Forbes* magazine in the late twentieth century, "tightwads tend to be an aggrieved and mirthless bunch, eternally peeved at the world."

Daniel Ludwig, a twentieth-century shipping magnate who was once known as the richest man in the world, was so discreet about his money that when he died in 1992, his next-door neighbors in Darien, Connecticut, could barely remember what he looked like. Ludwig walked to his office, traveled tourist class, and owned one aging car. A 1986 biography of him was called *The Invisible Billionaire*. Sam Walton, who had some $20 billion to his name, drove an old Ford pickup and dined out at Fred's Hickory Inn. Once when a waiter tried to pour an expensive glass of wine for investor Warren Buffett, he covered his glass and said, "No thanks, I'll take the cash." Cary Grant was known so widely as a miser around Hollywood that his nickname was "El Squeako." And Fiorello La Guardia called the famously thrifty industrialist Russell Sage "one of the meanest skinflints who ever lived."

In every other sphere of her life besides business, Hetty Green was largely unsuccessful. Although she and Edward never divorced, they never lived together after separating. Edward Green liked to play the stock market, and after he lost his own fortune he accepted credit on the strength of Hetty's fortune. She bailed him out several times, but he disobeyed her once too often, and she finally limited him to a small allowance. He died in 1902. The Boston *Herald* reported, "Edward H. Green, husband of Hetty Green, richest woman in the world, died at the old Green homestead this morning."

When her son, Ned, was fourteen, he dislocated his knee while sledding. Hetty Green treated it with a poultice and sympathy. Four years later, Ned reinjured his knee severely and required medical help. Dressed in secondhand clothes, Hetty and Ned made the rounds of free clinics in Manhattan and Brooklyn, hoping to be accepted as charity cases. But Hetty was widely recognized, and a few days later she consulted a neighborhood physician who recommended an above-the-knee amputation. Both Ned and Hetty ignored the advice until the leg showed traces of gangrene. Finally, Ned's leg was amputated in 1887 and buried in the Green family plot in Bellows Falls; Ned was fitted with a cork leg in Pittsburgh, where a high accident rate in mills and mines had made the city a manufacturing center for artificial limbs and eyes. Ned eventually graduated from Fordham University and, at the request of his mother, pledged that he would not marry for twenty years. He joined the family business, supervising some of his mother's investments. But once when he got into debt and asked for his mother's help, she wired back,

"Not a cent." Green's daughter, Sylvia, was once asked in court where her brother was living at a certain time. "With my mother," Sylvia answered. "If you call that living."

In Hetty Green's day, wealthy women often took a "grand tour" of Europe, where they sucked up the culture of the mother continent and brought home titled men to marry their daughters. It was a simple exchange of wealth for status, the social equivalent of a corporate merger. The linking of the daughter of a rail magnate or meat packer with a duke or count guaranteed social acceptance. Between 1874 and 1909, approximately five hundred young American women married titled Europeans, and some $220 million changed hands as a result of these vows. Gladys Vanderbilt's marriage to a Hungarian count set the family back $12 million; Jay Gould's daughter, Anna, conferred several million dollars on an Italian count before the union dissolved. When asked how he spent so much money in ten years, the count replied, "My general existence, my chateaux, my palaces, my bibelots, my race horses, my yachts, my traveling expenses, my political career, my charities, my fetes, my wife's jewels and loans to my friends."

At one time or another, Sylvia Green was fixed up with a Spanish duke, an English earl, and a German count ("I call him discount," Hetty Green said). Eventually, Sylvia developed a relationship with Matthew Astor Wilks, a grandson of John Jacob Astor, who was twenty-five years older than she and lived on his dividends. Knowing that Wilks had his own fortune, Hetty encouraged this alliance, although she once described Wilks as a "gouty old man." Sylvia and Wilks married in 1909, after he signed a prenuptial agreement relinquishing all claims to his wife's family's fortune.

Hetty Green moved from boardinghouse to residential hotel to cheap apartment on either side of the Hudson River, never staying in one place long enough to call it home. Sometimes her

Skye terrier, Dewey, held title to real estate or was named as the lessor on residential leases. Not even her closest relatives were always aware of her current address. She lived this peripatetic lifestyle partly because she was paranoid and partly because she didn't want to pay taxes to New York State. Appearing before New York's tax commissioners in 1895, she brought two lawyers and two stenographers to contest an assessment of $1.5 million of personal property, which would have cost her about $30,000 in taxes. Hetty Green had checked out of the hotel where she had spent the previous night and said, "I don't know where I shall go tonight." One lawyer who represented her in a tax dispute noted, "She was always entertaining, even when she was irritating."

Just three years before she died, the Sixteenth Amendment to the Constitution was ratified, allowing the federal government to tax individuals and corporations. Indeed, William Jennings Bryan once named Hetty Green as an argument for why there should be a federal income tax, saying that on her $3 million income she contributed less to the community than a working man making $500 a year.

Compliance with the new tax system was less than perfect, to put it mildly. Great merchants, men known to own vast interests in real estate, banks, and insurance companies, would coolly swear that they possessed no personal wealth whatever. If it was necessary to perjure themselves to evade taxation, they committed perjury. There were no mechanisms for tracking down and assessing their holdings. In September 1925, *The New York Times* published the names of many rich people and the amount of income tax they had paid the year before. The legislation that had made these statistics public was repealed before a second year of figures was released. Ferdinand Lundberg wrote, "Public opinion would be greatly embittered, to be sure, if the monotonous yearly recurrence of stupendous individual revenues would be observed."

*   *   *

In Hetty Green's later years, she became convinced that her father and aunt had been murdered and that her relatives were plotting to murder her, too. Her paranoia had increased after her friend, the skinflint millionaire Russell Sage, had been shot by a robber in 1891. Green claimed she was afraid of robbery, too, and was granted permission to carry firearms, after which a small-caliber revolver was usually among the contents of her handbag. But when asked later why she carried a gun, she replied, "Mostly to protect myself against lawyers."

Where there is wealth, there are lawsuits, and Hetty Green was deeply involved in litigation, as plaintiff or defendant, in several states. One action reached the Supreme Court, involved five states, and established a legal precedent. Yet she despised those in the legal profession and never missed an opportunity to insult lawyers publicly. "Every time a lawyer gets near me," she said, "I want to throw up." After another lawsuit, she declared, "I had rather that my daughter should be burned at the stake than to have her suffer what I have gone through with lawyers." The lawyers who represented her frequently had to hire other lawyers to help them collect their fees. "No!" she declared to a lawyer's collector who appeared at her house one day. "Haldane has charged me for every time he tipped his hat to me when we met on the street." Nor did she have any affection for judges: "My dear young judge," she addressed the man adjudicating one lawsuit, "you don't understand this case. Let me explain it to you."

Once, an insurance company accidentally paid a tax bill on a piece of property that actually belonged to Hetty Green. When insurance-company officials realized their error, they asked Green to reimburse them for their $1,105. She refused, and they sued her. After several days of hearings, the judge ruled that Hetty Green had no legal obligation to refund the tax money. Whatever obligation existed, the judge said, was moral. "I'll take the moral responsibility of not paying," she told her lawyer.

Green's one concession to luxury was her willingness to travel in a private railway car. Starting in the 1870s, the private railroad car became a symbol of wealth, as the private jet is today. Jay Gould, who suffered from ulcers and had to drink a lot of milk, traveled with a pedigreed cow. Green's son, Ned, commissioned his own private car, designed by George Pullman himself, with three staterooms, four bathrooms, a dining room, a kitchen, and an office, at a cost of about $75,000.

Green drew up her will in 1908, and in the words of her attorney, "It was tight." Her holdings included blue-chip stocks, railroad bonds, and some $20 million in cash, among other assets. She left nothing to charity. Although most people considered this a scandal, Andrew Carnegie believed that charitable gifts at death were unwise because they "created the unseemly impression that the givers would not have left the money at all had they been able to take it with them." Green left all her money to her two children.

In early 1916, Green was living as a guest of a wealthy socialite friend when she became embroiled in a quarrel with the cook and had a stroke. Over the next few months, she suffered five or six additional strokes, and she died on July 3 at her apartment on West Ninetieth Street in Manhattan.

The states of New York, New Jersey, and Vermont immediately staked claims against her estate, but in suits that went all the way to the Supreme Court, her son and daughter were victorious in claiming that Green had been a resident of Vermont. With his mother's grip on him finally loosened, Ned went berserk with his new fortune, buying, among other things, a $50,000 diamond-studded chastity belt for his mistress of twenty-four years.

If Hetty Green could walk down Wall Street at the turn of the third millennium, she would likely be amazed by how many women are making millions of dollars trading and investing in the financial markets. But she might also be struck by the tenacious stereotype that her gender doesn't have the mental agility and toughness to beat men at this high-stakes game. Hetty Green would disagree. "There is no secret in fortune making," she once said. "All you have to do is buy cheap and sell dear, act with thrift and shrewdness and be persistent."

TEN

The $100 Billion Man

Bill Gates (b. 1955)

A very rich man consulted a psychiatrist for the first time. "I have everything a man could want," the man complained. "Great wife, kids, health, four homes, servants, my own vineyard, a young girlfriend who used to be an acrobat—"

"My dear man," interrupted the doctor, "you should be very happy."

"Happiness, happiness," the patient moaned. "What is happiness? Can it buy money?"

In twentieth-century America, wealth replaced gods, armies, and the family as the altar around which society determined and exalted its values. Bill Gates became this society's divinity. Neither war hero nor king, neither athlete nor president, Gates became known and revered for having made more money than anyone else in the world.

It's fitting that Gates is the poster boy for western prosperity at the turn of the third millennium. His business is technology, and technology has infiltrated virtually every business on earth. Products and information are moving around the globe with breathtaking speed. A steadily increasing and better-educated population is working, investing, and spending. American shops import bread from Paris daily; "fresh" tomatoes come from Holland; and you can send an instant message to

New Zealand for the price of a local telephone call. By the end of the twentieth century, the world had become the global village that Marshall McLuhan had foreseen decades earlier. Never has it been so easy to buy and sell to so many people. With the help of increased productivity, a benign government, and scientific advances, the wealth of America has been mushrooming.

In America's first one hundred years, there were few routes to wealth, and they centered on the ownership of land. But after the Industrial Revolution in the late nineteenth century, many new ways of becoming rich were born—in the embryonic steel, railroad, telegraph, oil, and chemical industries, for example. By the second half of the twentieth century, the number of ways that people could become wealthy seemed almost infinite. People made fortunes selling real estate, insurance, entertainment, cars, clothes, food, furniture, appliances, cosmetics, and art, just to name a few businesses that boomed in the twentieth century. The cost of food and fuel declined steadily as technology and economies of scale increased supply. Transporting goods became less expensive and more efficient. The population multiplied, but in most of the western world, productivity more than kept pace. In America, borrowing for consumption, once considered morally wrong, became commonplace. With so much money in so many hands, it wasn't necessary to capture all of any one person's or community's wealth—a small part of everyone's wealth was enough. A meal at McDonald's cost just a few dollars, but selling millions of those meals made some people very rich.

In America's increasingly diverse and mobile culture, people increasingly appraised their—and their neighbors'—value differently than they had in the days when families were rooted in a fourth- or fifth-generation community. Then, their surnames, family sagas, and social connections established hierarchical claims. But as ideals of democracy and capitalism reinforced the notion of America as an impartial meritocracy, a person's social standing increasingly became pegged to his or her monetary value. Net worth *was* worth. In science, technology, and brains,

Americans prefer to talk of quantities rather than qualities, noted the philosopher George Santayana.

Indeed, America's wealthy have demonstrated their status primarily by consuming many products and services: enormous houses, dozens of cars, yachts as big as ocean liners, extreme vacations, $18-a-pound ostrich salami, and $1,500 bottles of balsamic vinegar. And despite a standard of living unmatched in world history, the battle cry of many political campaigns has been lower taxes. It wasn't enough to have everything; one must have more. Ironically, Americans' sense of possession is weaker than Europeans', Santayana argued, because Americans' wealth usually takes the form of money, and money is mobile and indifferent to its holder.

Furthermore, wealthy Americans were in the unprecedented position of seeing the emblems of wealth replicated so widely and quickly that they lost any value as status symbols. In earlier centuries, the distinction that accrued from owning precious things was a natural consequence of rarity. But in the twentieth century, the number of the rich had multiplied so explosively that they themselves had become a debased currency. In eighteenth-century England, when people were testing ever-greater extremes of fashion, a few gentlemen began to concern themselves with "cut." Now, everybody can afford cut. The only easy way to tell a cheap garment from an expensive one is to look at the label. In the twentieth century, wrote the historian Ray Ginger, "America became a country of people in flight, running over unmarked fields without traditions to guide them or visions to serve as beacons, with no havens for rest and no end but the grave, with no goal but wealth, and of wealth there was never enough."

No twentieth-century figure better personifies this era than William Henry Gates III, cofounder and chief executive of Microsoft, the world's largest maker of personal-computer software. Indeed, Bill Gates may very well be the wealthiest person of all time, although it's impossible to say with certainty, since earlier wealth was often hidden or unquantifiable by today's terms. Even so, in the late 1990s, Gates's individual fortune was calculated as second only to that of Napoleon Bonaparte, who, among other conquests, looted most of the great art treasures of the western world. But the value of Microsoft stock has continued to rise since that assessment, possibly propelling Bill Gates ahead of Napoleon in wealth, if not power or charisma. Yet, as an economist noted, "Napoleon might have had lots of money, but he couldn't fly the Atlantic."

Bill Gates became wealthy the way many people did in the twentieth century: He understood that it was necessary to capture only a tiny slice of any one person's money to become magnificently wealthy. By the end of the twentieth century, there were six billion potential consumers in the world marketplace, most of whom could be reached quickly and efficiently. China's doors opened in the late twentieth century, as did those of many parts of the former Soviet Union. Even in poor regions of the world, such as parts of Africa, South America, and India, people could buy Coca-Cola or a tube of toothpaste. America led the world in affluence, and it sold the world its appetites and tastes. Only one hundred years earlier, the east and west coasts of America were separated by weeks of difficult travel. Today, Federal Express promises quick delivery to just about any person on earth.

Naming the richest person in history, in the millennium, or even in the century is an entertaining but hopeless exercise. Quantifying people's assets has always been difficult, and comparing them across the millennia impossible. How do Genghis Khan's five million square miles of land compare with Bill Gates's stock in Microsoft? A single commodity—Mansa Musa's rooms full of gold—will be worth different amounts at different times. If a person's fortune is bound up in the stock market—or in oil fields or pork bellies, for that matter—its value fluctuates from day to day, even minute to minute. Furthermore, the wealthy don't always forthrightly disclose their holdings. Even if they did, how can art, jewelry, or property be valued if it hasn't been on the market for several decades? Even *Forbes* magazine, which compiles numerous lists of the wealthy, concedes that when comparing individual fortunes over long periods, "you can make the numbers support just about any conclusion you want to reach."

Indeed, a review of books, videos, and websites about the wealthiest people in America suggests that wealth cannot be measured reliably and is often in the eye of the beholder. For example, there are *Andrew Carnegie, The Richest Man in the World*; *The Du Ponts: America's Richest Family*; *J. Paul Getty: The Richest American*; *The Mellons: The Chronicle of America's Richest Family*; *Sam Walton: The Inside Story of America's Richest Man*; and *Bill Gates, the Richest Mortal in the World*.

Although the mere mention of the Consumer Price Index puts most people to sleep, its usefulness as a gauge of wealth over time deserves a brief explanation. America's federal government has been compiling the Consumer Price Index, or CPI, since 1800. Comparing buying power for basic goods across time, the CPI shows what one dollar in the early nineteenth century would be worth today. For example, an annual income of $3,000 in the nineteenth century is the equivalent of about $50,000 today. As John Steele Gordon pointed out, such an income could at that time maintain a family of six plus five servants in a spacious house, whereas today it would barely buy a down payment on a modest house in many parts of America. Only a century ago, food could command more than half a person's annual income. Laundresses were once cheaper than washing machines. In the past two and a half centuries, daily life has changed more than it did in the 750 years before—and so has the portrait of the wealthy. Such social and economic changes now occur ever faster: A typical computer today is quite different from its counterpart of just five years earlier.

Another way of comparing old and new fortunes is to put

them alongside the gross national product, or GNP, of the time. Figures for America's GNP go back to the mid-nineteenth century, but before 1929 they are educated guesses. Nor would this or any other similar method work globally; after all, Machmud of Ghazni and Genghis Khan owned their kingdoms' entire output.

But for the argument, using percentage of GNP, John D. Rockefeller, the oil monopolist who died in 1937, was the richest man in American history; his net worth at its peak was some 2 percent of America's annual income. Andrew Carnegie, the philanthropic steelmaker who died in 1919, may have been the second wealthiest American, with a similar slice of the GNP. Bill Gates's net worth amounts to less than 1 percent of current national income. An economy that has grown into the trillions of dollars makes it less likely that any individual can own a substantial part of it. That fact alone means Bill Gates will probably never enjoy the political power that Rockefeller and Carnegie wielded at the peaks of their careers.

A third way to compare wealth across time is to look at the ratio between the earnings of the richest people and the earnings of the average citizen. By that calculation, the gap between Bill Gates and the Main Street man or woman is wider than at any time in history. In fact, in 1997 it was calculated that for Bill Gates to buy a $250,000 Lamborghini would be the same as the average American buying something for 63 cents. But whether the gap was greater or less for Machmud or Genghis Khan and their subjects is impossible to say. How does one count elephants or kingfisher feathers in such a calculation? How can income or buying power be measured in moneyless societies?

In 1999, Bill Gates's net worth passed the $100 billion mark. Even with the nearly infinite number of ways a person can spend money in the twentieth century, Bill Gates is hitting the limits of modern consumption—he can't get rid of his money as fast as it comes in. He built a 45,000-square-foot mansion near Seattle that is filled with technological wonders—the master bathtub, for example, can be programmed to fill to the right temperature and depth by Gates from his car. He takes vacations on a private railroad train. He owns his own jet and a fleet of sports cars. What does Bill Gates want that he doesn't have? It's difficult to imagine what the Gates fortune will buy in one hundred years that it can't buy right now—a city? An ocean? The moon? "In an economy, such as that of the United States of America, where leisure is barely moral," wrote the economist Wilfred Beckerman, "the problem of creating sufficient wants . . . to absorb productive capacity may become chronic in the not too distant future."

More proof of Bill Gates's status as the cultural hero of late twentieth-century America is that the country's working class doesn't seem to hate him as they did so many earlier multimillionaires. That may be explained by their own standard of living, which, though not constantly rising, greatly exceeds that of their immigrant great-grandparents, who lived in tenements, worked six-day weeks, and buried many of their own children. Earlier millionaires worried about labor upheavals or even a working-class revolution with good reason. Bill Gates, by contrast, is much beloved on his corporate campus near Seattle and ferociously defended by purveyors and adherents of the American dream.

The infant Bill Gates arrived in the world just after the middle of the twentieth century, when some terrifying economic disasters were still fresh in most Americans' minds. Ferdinand Lundberg estimated there were 7,500 millionaires in 1914 and more than five times that number (38,889) by 1929. But then, almost overnight, $30 billion of wealth was erased when the stock market crashed. It was a crushing blow to America's business, which quickly became the nation's goat. The Depression ushered in a period of discretion in personal expenditures. The rich worried that ostentation might drive the masses into a revolutionary fury. Gradually, the wealthy took on the protective coloration of the average businessman, flaunting their hours in the office rather than their weekends in Palm Beach. The wealthy wanted to be seen as producers, not slackers, working hard just like everyone else. Where display and elaborate expenditure had been a source of distinction, now prestige and power were more identified with those who administered productive activity. The captain of industry was admired for much the same reason that primitive man stood in awe of the warrior: He was "gifted with ferocity," wrote John Patrick Diggins.

Bill Gates was one of tens of thousands of Americans who made their first millions when a private company went public—what Lester Thurow calls instant wealth. Sam Walton, Michael Dell, Ross Perot, William Hewlett, and David Packard—whatever their original idea, all became millionaires or billionaires by owning corporate stock. Global conglomerates pushed wealth accumulation onto a new scale—in 1999, *Forbes* magazine estimated there were 465 billionaires in the world.

The growth of large companies also created a new class of corporate wealth, whose members, while not in Bill Gates's league, are nevertheless among the top 1 percent of the wealthy in America. In the late twentieth century, the average chief executive officer had an annual compensation package of almost $6 million, while the nation's median household income was about $30,000. The corporate executive and his or her family enjoy all the trappings of great wealth, often by leveraging their income with debt. But because the income is earned and therefore can be curtailed, it is often accompanied by a nagging anxiety about the future.

Many members of the corporate rich try to hide their affluence; Bill Gates consistently refuses to disclose or discuss his fortune except in connection with his philanthropy. Indeed, many of the members of the richest families in America are unknown to the public. Why hide? Partly because they are sitting ducks for professional fund-raisers, kidnappers, and slick entrepreneurs looking for investors. About 70 percent of J. Paul Getty's mail, he said, was "made up of letters written by people who ask me to send them money. . . . Some plead. Others demand. A few even threaten." Bill Gates, too, is inundated with requests for money. Privacy, a precious good that money can still buy, is often the cheapest and most effective form of security. When Gates married Melinda French in 1994, he reserved every hotel room, car, and camping site on the Hawaiian island of Lanai, as well as every helicopter on nearby Maui.

Getting rich, even if not on Bill Gates's scale, is a largely unquestioned goal in modern America, where the last vestiges of money guilt were sloughed off after World War II. The new creed, widely embraced by the burgeoning middle- and upper-middle classes, was that acquisitiveness was a rational striving for economic growth and a better life for all. Now that it was established that wealth was not a zero-sum game, in which one person's wealth was another's poverty, why not become rich if possible? Wealth was a reward for pluck and luck. With people in an increasingly quantitative frame of mind—"what kind?" turning into "how much?"—the rewards of labor were increasingly defined in terms of salaries and benefits. Before the nineteenth century, the concept of "income" had little importance—people were assessed by variables such as the size of their land, robustness of their herds, or the yield of their fields. In twentieth-century America, people were required to know their incomes, and income consciousness became a civic obligation. People learned how to translate their possessions into numbers—a single bottom line—and then compare their result to other people's results. "How Do You Stack Up?" asked a cover of *Money* magazine in 1999.

The stock-market run-up of the 1990s created so many rich people so quickly that some of those who worked for a living began to feel like chumps and losers, further widening the gap between production and consumption. Why wasn't everyone a millionaire? The monthly *Millionaire* magazine—"The Very

Best the World Has to Offer"—offered a Millionaire Kit ("You say you're not a millionaire yet?"). Pitches for moneymaking ventures spread like weeds. At some point, "How to Become a Millionaire in Just 15 Years" must have sounded like a get-rich-quick scheme. But as America's wealth soared, fifteen years started seeming like a long time to wait. Hence: "Become a Millionaire in 12 Months," "The Five-Day Millionaire," and, finally, "Become an Instant Millionaire." In fact, these days it appears to be actually more difficult to sit at home doing nothing than to become a millionaire: "Can You Afford Not to Be a Millionaire?" asked one promotion. Barry Kaye's enormous advertisements in national newspapers screamed, "Make millions. Save millions. Leave millions for your heirs!" Kaye's best-known book, *Die Rich and Tax Free,* could be ordered by calling 1-800-DIE-RICH.

Yet even in the late twentieth century, wealth was neither as random nor as democratic as the stock-market millionaires seemed to suggest. Of the four hundred wealthiest Americans named by *Forbes* magazine in 1989, 40 percent had inherited their way to richness. One hundred years earlier, only 18 percent of the four thousand millionaires who were analyzed had inherited money. "Your Plucky Dicks of Horatio Alger's old business romances, your ragged farm boy or newsboy filled with the 'pure' entrepreneurial spirit, has become a rare bird in the executive suites of today," wrote Matthew Josephson. Yet Americans still cherish the idea that economic opportunity is available to anyone with a determined glint in his or her eye. In 1996, a CBS News poll asked, "Do you think it's possible to start out poor in this country, work hard and become rich?" A full 78 percent said yes; only 18 percent said no.

For those who do attain quick and serendipitous wealth, such as lottery winners, a brief period of giddy celebration may be succeeded by a drifting back to their former level of happiness. "Eventually, the thrill of winning the lottery will itself wear off," theorized Philip Brickman, who studied the relative happiness of lottery winners and accident victims. "If all things are judged by the extent to which they depart from a baseline of past experience, gradually even the most positive events will cease to have impact as they themselves are absorbed into the new baseline against which further events are judged." Other researchers have gone further, hypothesizing that winning the lottery may actually be more painful than pleasurable because sudden changes cause so much stress.

Other economic observers worry that America's relativistic sense of happiness puts everyone on a hedonistic treadmill, acting on the assumption that getting more money will bring more happiness. But more money may bring greater happiness only if others don't also get more. When all incomes generally increase, no one, on average, feels better off. Yesterday's luxuries become today's necessities, and definitions of poverty change. While economic growth appears to be producing an ever-more-affluent society, to those involved in the process affluence may remain a distant, urgently sought, but never attained goal.

Where there is affluence, there is consumption, and the world has never seen a spending spree like America's in the late twentieth century. There seems no end of ways, exotic and ordinary, that people can convert their money into something else. In fact, some people say throwing money around has become a new sort of performance art, which economists have labeled "hyperconsumption." A high level of consumption disturbs some people, especially if there is obvious poverty or inequality of opportunity nearby. The acquisitive society, wrote R. H. Tawney, assures people there are no ends other than their ends, no law other than their desires, no limit other than what they think advisable. It makes the individual the center of his or her own universe. In the past, feudal lords spent their money hiring warriors for protection and display of power. Now that the state has assumed protection and security duties, the rich can avoid the appearance of open power. They can spend riches on themselves.

Indeed, without the institutional struts of church, school, military, and family, modern society has increasingly become individualistic, buttressed chiefly by science. The white-collar world, wrote C. Wright Mills, has become a "personality market," in which each person "sells himself" to get ahead. The cult of rugged individualism can be ideal for making money, of course, but it is neutral on the subject of spending. Spending has become not only more secularized and private but, as never before, planless.

Yet there is also a school of thought that believes that moralizing about consumption is just so much puritanical nonsense. "Goods are neutral, their uses are social," wrote the anthropologist Mary Douglas. "They can be used as fences or bridges." In a similar vein, the historian Peter Burke noted that consumption is a natural way for people to try to present themselves in a favorable light. In fact, he pointed out, it is not only conspicuous consumption that helps present the self—inconspicuous consumption transmits its own message and so does conspicuous nonconsumption. In other words, we should avoid identifying conspicuous consumption with magnificence.

One of the first moves from poverty to wealth is away from death. Americans' life expectancies doubled in the twentieth century. Part of that can be attributed to the conquest of diseases such as typhoid and smallpox, but part is the result of increased safety and security—accident prevention. In Bill Gates's house, for example, there are hidden cameras embedded in walls and ceilings, and sensors in the floor can track a person to within six inches. Ironically, this ties in with the modern brand of optimism, which offers a dream of perpetually avoiding crises by interventions of one kind or another. The unexpected is gradually phased out, except for the occasional drought or hurricane. But men who live daintily, wrote Alexis de Tocqueville in the nineteenth century, soon forget the charms of action and overemphasize its risk, finding it ever harder to rouse themselves from their smothering ease. A high-tech society exacerbates that tendency, because less human life is connected to natural systems such as seasonal or regional patterns, and people become, by and large, "present minded."

So much has been written about Bill Gates that the details of his childhood and career trajectory are nearly as well known as his name. Born in Seattle in 1955, Gates grew up in Protestant and Republican affluence. His father was a well-connected senior partner at a white-shoe law firm; his mother was a teacher who also served on the boards of several charitable organizations. Young Gates, who had two sisters, was so shy in primary school that his parents sent him to a psychiatrist. ("He was a cool guy," Gates remembered.) They also took him out of public school and put him in an all-male prep school, where he was widely known as smart and arrogant. He hung out in the school's computer room, combining his aptitude for technology with his entrepreneurial streak to start a small business. "I'm easier to get along with if I'm in charge," he once told an older friend.

In 1973, Gates entered Harvard College, where he played high-stakes poker while developing a computer programming language called BASIC for the first microcomputer—the MITS Altair 8800—with an old friend from Seattle named Paul Allen. In his sophomore year, he dropped out of Harvard, and in 1975 he and Allen founded Microsoft. The two already knew the smart money in computing would be in software, not hardware. At a time when there were fewer than one hundred microcomputers in the world, Gates vowed to put "a computer on every desk and in every home running Microsoft software."

He was the classic brilliant, slightly otherworldly entrepreneur—careless about his personal appearance and often rocking, pacing, jumping, or fidgeting as he talked, as though his thoughts were too deep to be disturbed by such trivia as social graces. His girlfriends were industry grown. In modern terms, Gates was "uber-nerd," as *Time* magazine put it. He lived in his own world, by his own set of rules. On one drive Gates made between Albuquerque and Seattle in his twenties, he got three speeding tickets, two from the same cop.

Whether Gates was a superior programmer or just a mediocre opportunist, he soon owned the souls of America's machines. And what everyone soon learned about Bill Gates was that like most wealthy people of the millennium, he wouldn't stop working no matter how rich he became. His job was his passion, his cause, and his first baby (although he also has two human children). In his first six years at Microsoft, Gates once calculated, he averaged just two vacation days a year. As C. Wright Mills noted decades ago, the very rich in America are not dominantly an idle rich and never have been. "In this business," Bill Gates once said, "by the time you realize you're in trouble, it's too late to save yourself. Unless you're running scared all the time, you're gone. . . . People underestimate how effective capitalism is at keeping even the most successful companies on edge."

Gates is neither ostentatious nor outrageous with his wealth. For years, he flew coach class on domestic flights, splurging for business class only for international trips. He declined to ride in limousines. "I wouldn't want to get used to being waited on or driven around," he once said. "Living in a way that is unique would be strange." Even Gates's hobbies are relatively modest: golf and bridge.

His definition of intelligence reflects the pace of contemporary life, the prejudice that a quick mind is a smart mind, and that a contemplative, reflective, or just unhurried personal style is ill suited to the business world: "Smartness is an ability to absorb new facts," Bill Gates told *Playboy* magazine. "To walk into a situation, have something explained to you, and immediately say, 'Well, what about this?' To ask an insightful question. To absorb it in real time. A capacity to remember. To relate to domains that may not seem connected at first."

Perhaps it is inevitable that a person who becomes very wealthy must then build an enormous domicile. The early rich built themselves castles or palaces, but for most of the millennium they lived at some distance from one another, and so their estates could be appreciated by only a few neighbors or passing travelers. The vast majority of peasants or artisans lived in modest quarters with little furniture or ornamentation. Today, the simplest clerk in a business office would be miserably unhappy and probably fall mortally ill of a croup were he to spend a winter month in the gilded halls of unheated, unwashed Versailles.

The first big wave of mansion building in America came in the late nineteenth and early twentieth centuries. The new rich wanted their homes to look like European palaces; to assemble enough land for such estates, they might buy up a dozen working farms. In 1910, two Long Island magnates bought four hundred acres of land and destroyed sixty structures to build their homes. "We destroyed the village of Lattingham to get the view we wanted," one of them told a local newspaper. The early wealthy in America wanted their houses on high ground for all to see and admire. Bill Gates tucked his house into a hillside for the sake of privacy.

The climax of domiciliary ostentation was San Simeon, the Hearst castle in California that was so big (165 rooms in more than 90,000 square feet) that the family couldn't give it away. The biggest private house in America remains the George Vanderbilt mansion near Asheville, North Carolina, which was designed to suggest a sixteenth-century French chateau. It has 175,000 square feet, including thirty-four bedrooms and forty-three bathrooms—although the bathrooms had no sinks. Wealthy people weren't supposed to draw their own water. During the 1920s, many famous American chateaus were closed down because of taxes and the costs of upkeep. Not since then has mansion building been as widespread as it is today.

Bill Gates's compound just east of Seattle ended up costing somewhere between $80 million and $100 million, including $6.5 million for the swimming pool. In the past, $200 a square foot has been considered a typical price for luxury building; the Gates mansion came in at something less than $2,000 per square foot.

Gates's house, which took seven years to build, has been described as a high-tech lodge. Guests wear an electronic pin that registers their preferences in art, music, lighting, and heating. As the guest moves around the house, each room responds to his or her presence by playing the appropriate music and showing the appropriate art. A movie or the news could also follow the guest. When two or more pins are in the same room, the house responds with a mix of styles, unless one of those pins belongs to Bill Gates. The telephone nearest the guest will ring for his or her incoming calls. Gates's wife's clothes hang on a rack that operates like a dry cleaner's. There were so many workers on the construction site that, to reduce traffic, some of them were bused to work. Gates bought another house next door to his property and tore it down to increase the size of his estate.

But even Bill Gates's house looks small compared with the mansion under construction by Ira Rennert in eastern Long Island, planned at 100,000 square feet with twenty-nine bedrooms, thirty-nine bathrooms, a 164-seat theater, two bowling alleys, and a restaurant-size kitchen with five refrigerators. "The change now is from the rich to the incredibly rich," said one historian, "and from huge houses to incredibly huge houses."

Another status investment of the corporate rich is art and rare objects. Buying art has always been a way to look like old money fast, but in places like Silicon Valley today, there's no tarnish on new money, nor any tradition of amassing great art collections as the Fricks, Morgans, and Mellons once did. There are some 250,000 millionaires in Silicon Valley, or the Valley of the Dollars as David A. Kaplan nicknamed it. The technology fortunes were made by relatively young men and women who never learned the finer points of being rich. A San Francisco gallery owner described a conversation she had with a wealthy computer executive whom she was trying to interest in collecting. " 'Hey, you can collect anything you want,' I told the man. 'Old Master paintings.' He didn't respond. 'Chippendale furniture.' Nothing. 'Mickey Mouse lunch pails.' Only then did he show a flicker of interest."

Gates paid more than $30 million for one of Leonardo da Vinci's scientific notebooks, outbidding some of the world's great museums and libraries. "Buying priceless and desirable art objects was the classic Renaissance way of transforming yourself from successful entrepreneur into respected toff," wrote Lisa Jardine. But most of Gates's art is virtual—computer images reproduced from originals to which he has bought the electronic reproduction rights.

For several years, Bill Gates was both extremely wealthy and relatively uncharitable, a combination that gave rise to a low-level buzz of public criticism. In 1994, he created the William H. Gates Foundation with $210 million in assets and began making large gifts, primarily to regional institutions in the Northwest. Gates responded to pressure to increase his giving by arguing that anybody can give money away, but he wanted to give it away intelligently. Furthermore, the amounts Gates could give would present daunting administrative challenges to most established charities. Since 1994, Gates has created two other philanthropic organizations under the umbrella of the Bill and Melinda Gates Foundation. The foundation's total assets at the turn of the millennium amounted to some $17 billion.

Philanthropy has always been a concomitant of wealth, from the days when the ancients made offerings to the gods to thank them for good harvests and military victories. Both

Christianity and Judaism urge wealthy believers to help those less fortunate than themselves. In Europe, the charitable tradition was personal giving—dispensing food and clothing to the poor of their village or estate. That practice continued in America, as did the central role of the church in administering the wealthy's noblesse oblige. But as the world gradually became more complex and less personal, it wasn't as obvious which social causes were worthiest of support. "How properly to alleviate the troubles of the poor is one of the greatest troubles of the rich," wrote O. Henry.

In America, the tradition of personal giving began to erode between 1885 and 1915, when the new class of industrial wealth had to find ways to dispose of unprecedented amounts of money. The rich wanted to reinforce bootstrap notions of self-reliance while discouraging the lazy dependence that might come from people being on the dole.

People began to donate to educational and religious institutions that would help the poor help themselves while simultaneously disseminating values justifying the existence of the moneyed elite. The rich soon learned that grandiose acts of charity could proclaim great wealth as efficiently as grandiose manifestations of luxury.

In 1911, Andrew Carnegie established his foundation, the world's largest philanthropic organization, signaling an end to the era of the individual philanthropist. He funded more than two thousand public libraries. Two years later, in 1913, the year the federal income tax amendment was ratified, John D. Rockefeller created his own foundation. During the rest of the century, many other wealthy people did the same thing. In millennial America, there are some 45,000 grant-making foundations, and philanthropic giving has become more activist. A popular catchphrase is "strategic investing," which means using philanthropy to advance personal goals, not just handing out a check to the opera, orchestra, or United Way every year. Such donors are "very results oriented," commented one foundation executive, and try to make the projects self-sustaining rather than de-pendent on annual grants. It's philanthropy as venture capital.

John D. Rockefeller would be interested to see that his foun-dation actually teaches a course on how to donate shrewdly, as do a few other organizations. But such an approach brings to mind Ambrose Bierce's disdain for "philanthropists who deem it more blessed to allot than to bestow." As a result of this kind of sanitized giving, the rich today have almost no personal charita-ble relation with the poor, or in fact little contact of any kind.

Like most wealthy men and women throughout history, Andrew Carnegie preferred philanthropy to paying his workers higher wages because it gave him more control over the ultimate use of the money. Yet unlike that modern apostle of dying rich, Barry Kaye, Carnegie believed the wealthy should divest them-selves of their entire fortunes before they died. ("The man who dies . . . rich dies disgraced.") Or as Godfrey Lowell Cabot said, "You ought to give money away when you're alive, when it costs you something."

In 1997, Ted Turner, then vice chairman of Time Warner, pledged $1 billion to the United Nations after denigrating the lack of generosity among his fellow billionaires, whom he de-scribed as "old skinflints." Aside from religious organizations, the bulk of philanthropic giving in the late twentieth century went to institutions of higher education, which were not only usually socially and politically innocuous but also frequently provided what's known as a "naming opportunity." Bill Gates gave $20 million to the Massachusetts Institute of Technology, with the understanding that its new computer-science build-ing would be named after him. In just a single year, sixteen of the forty largest philanthropic donors identified by *Fortune* magazine had university buildings named after them. At the University of Iowa, donor Henry B. Tippie will be acknowledged with the Henry B. Tippie College of Business; at Boston College, Peter and Carolyn Lynch will be remembered with the Peter S. and Carol A. Lynch School of Education; Sierra Nevada College's new library will be named the William W. Zink Library and Learning Resource Center in honor of Zink.

Religious institutions have always been popular places for people to donate money, although in the 1960s and 1970s, there was a fad of supporting religious groups to purify oneself—Hare Krishnas, and the Mahara Ji, for example. "They [wealthy donors] feel that they are—quote—cleansing themselves, doing something responsible with their money," commented Sarah Pillsbury of the Minneapolis grain family. "I think that there's a way that they're wounded—and their wounded spirits are in tune with this feeling that our society is sort of sick. So they get involved a lot of times well beyond self-improvement—hoping to change the world, make it an entirely new world."

But gurus of the 1980s and 1990s were more likely to preach to people on the subject of accumulating wealth than of purifying themselves by giving it away. Deepak Chopra exhorted his followers to think wealthy, meditate on wealth, and let their spirits become infused with wealth consciousness. Wealth was a state of mind, an openness to becoming rich; it took *The Courage to Be Rich,* as Suze Orman wrote. Other authors produced books with titles such as *Think and Grow Rich; The Complete Idiot's Guide to Getting Rich; God Wants You to Be Rich; Play and Grow Rich;* and, yes, *Pray and Grow Rich*—all conveying the idea that wealth is nothing more than being in the right place at the right time with the right attitude.

Each of the nine men and one woman profiled in this book was exactly that—in the right place at the right time with the right attitude. That was only the beginning, however. Each of them also embodied other qualities that turned those circumstances into fortune. Some of those qualities were admirable— courage, fortitude, creativity, wit, and confidence. Some were less commendable—ruthlessness, egotism, elitism, and crassness, to name a few. The rich can show the way to money but not to happiness.

The rich are different from everyone else, but not as different as it might appear from lower down on the wealth scale. Except for Bill Gates, no matter how rich a person is, there will always be someone richer. And if the past millennium is a guide to the next one, before long even Gates will be displaced as the world's richest person by a creative, ambitious, and lucky person who can see the future.

NOTES

Introduction: The Wealthy, Then and Now

xvii "A rich man": Georg Simmel, *The Philosophy of Money* (London: Routledge, 1990).

xvii hypothetical man: Herb Goldberg and Robert T. Lewis, *Money Madness: The Psychology of Saving, Spending, Loving, and Hating Money* (New York: New American Library, 1978).

xx "a blip on your computer screen": Peter Applebome, *The New York Times,* Feb. 28, 1999, Week in Review section, p. 5.

xxi "In mobilizing wishes": James Buchan, *Frozen Desire* (New York: Farrar, Straus and Giroux, 1997), p. 19.

xxi–ii Yet the barstools: Robert H. Frank, *Luxury Fever* (New York: Free Press, 1999), pp. 5–25.

xxii "Leisure, like money": Tibor Scitovsky, *The Joyless Economy* (New York: Oxford University Press, 1976), p. 113.

xxiii made a typist: Philip Elliot Slater, *Wealth Addiction* (New York: Dutton, 1980).

xxiii Indian maharaja: David Frost, *David Frost's Book of Millionaires, Multimillionaires, and Really Rich People* (New York: Crown, 1984), p. 31.

xxiii John D. Rockefeller: Slater, *Wealth Addiction.*

xxv "The best way to make money": Herbert Inhaber, *How Rich Is Too Rich* (New York: Praeger, 1992), citing Fernand Braudel, *The Wheels of Commerce* (New York: Harper and Row, 1982), p. 122.

xxvi important business leaders: G. William Domhoff, *The Higher Circles: The Governing Class in America* (New York: Random House, 1970).

xxvi a lord's family: Inhaber, *How Rich Is Too Rich,* p. 124.

xxvii "The less limited": quoted in George G. Kirstein, *The Rich: Are They Different?* (Boston: Houghton Mifflin, 1968), p. 212.

xxix "The typical self-made man": Alfred Messer, quoted in Max
Gunther, *The Very, Very Rich and How They Got That Way* (New
York: Playboy Press, 1972), p. 233.

xxx "We are all slaves": Jay Gould, quoted in Frederic Cople Jaher, ed.,
*The Rich, the Well Born, and the Powerful: Elites and Upper Classes
in History* (Urbana, Ill.: University of Illinois Press, 1973), cited in
W. D. Rubinstein, *Wealth and the Wealthy in the Modern World*
(London: Croom Helm, 1980), p. 262.

xxxi money prices belong in their times: Buchan, *Frozen Desire.*

xxxii "Who is rich?" Kirstein, *The Rich,* p. 26.

Chapter One: When Thieves Were Kings:
Machmud of Ghazni

4 war and wealth: V. G. Kiernan in Jack Goody, et al., eds., *Family and
Inheritance: Rural Society in Western Europe, 1200–1800.*
(Cambridge: Cambridge University Press, 1976), p. 366.

5 a change of clothes: Carlo M. Cipolla, *Before the Industrial
Revolution* (New York: W. W. Norton, 1993), p. 25.

6 heaping platters of meat: Ibid., p. 25.

7 products of the soil: Henri Pirenne, *Economic and Social History of
Medieval Europe,* trans. I. E. Clegg (New York: Harcourt, Brace, and
Company, 1936), p. 7.

7 betrayed the sin of avarice: Ibid., p. 13.

9 a serious national danger: Mohommad Habib, *Sultan Mahmud of
Ghazni* (Delhi: S. Chand and Company, 1967), p. 83.

9 devouring the land: Stanley Lane-Pool, *Mediaeval India* (New York:
Kraus, 1970), p. 15.

11 the chimps quit: Robert L. Heilbroner, *The Quest for Wealth: A
Study of Acquisitive Man* (New York: Simon and Schuster, 1966),
p. 22.

11 possible future scarcity: Helga Dittmar, *The Social Psychology of
Material Possessions: To Have Is to Be* (New York: St. Martin's
Press, 1992).

11 fat seagulls: Kirstein, *The Rich,* p. xvii.

11 people often took their tools: Kiernan in Goody, et al., *Family and
Inheritance,* p. 368.

12 "wealth is a burden": Marshall David Sahlins, *Stone Age Economics*
(New York: Aldine, 1972), p. 11.

12 Among foragers: Robert J. Wenke, *Patterns in Prehistory* (New York:
Oxford University Press, 1990), p. 283.

12   no class differences: James Russell, *Modes of Production in World History,* (New York, Routledge, 1989), p. 24.

12   trusting surrender to nature: Robert L. Heilbroner, *Behind the Veil of Economics: Essays in the Worldly Philosophy* (New York: W. W. Norton, 1988).

12   "nomad took a wider view": H. G. Wells, *A Short History of the World* (London: Penguin Books, 1922), p. 56.

12–13   "Zen road to affluence": Sahlins, *Stone Age Economics,* p. 2.

13   "neither free nor secure": John Wade, *History of the Middle and Working Classes* (London: Augustus M. Kelley, 1966).

14   Living in one place: Wenke, *Patterns in Prehistory,* p. 287.

14   shelter is worth: Ibid.

15   "your slashing horseman": D. H. Gordon, quoted in Lynn White, *Medieval Technology and Social Change* (London: Oxford University Press, 1962), p. 1.

15   factionalism was endemic: William D. Phillips, *Slavery from Roman Times to the Early Transatlantic Trade* (Minneapolis: University of Minnesota Press, 1985).

16   fatalistic religious attitudes: C. E. Bosworth, *The Medieval History of Iran, Afghanistan, and Central Asia.* (London: Variorum Reprints, 1977), p. 85.

16   "The mountaineers": Lane-Poole, *Mediaeval India,* p. 15.

19   objects in a collection: Russell Belk, "Attachment to Possessions," in *Place Attachment,* ed. Irwin Altman and Setha M. Low (New York: Plenum Press, 1992), p. 41.

20   "adaptation and learned helplessness": Adrian Furnham and Michael Argyle, *The Psychology of Money* (New York: Routledge, 1988).

20   "Things are our ballast.": Grant McCracken, *Culture and Consumption: New Approaches to the Symbolic Character of Consumer Goods* (Bloomington, Ind.: Indiana University Press, 1991), p. 124.

20–21   social communication system: Simmel, *Philosophy of Money,* p. 78.

21   "pets, wedding rings": Belk, "Attachment to Possessions," p. 46.

22   "To rob and to give": Ibid., quoted in Cipolla, *Before the Industrial Revolution,* p. 21.

23   "Affluence makes": W. D. Rubinstein, *Wealth and the Wealthy in the Modern World.*

23   "love of wealth": Quoted in Heilbroner, *The Quest for Wealth,* pp. 43–44.

24   "steeped and saturated": Ibid., p. 44.

24 "Money was young": Quoted in Jack Weatherford, *The History of Money* (New York: Three Rivers Press, 1997), p. 50.

25 molten gold was poured: Ray Vicker, *The Realms of Gold* (New York: Charles Scribner's Sons, 1975).

25 "walked like courtesans": Will Durant, *Caesar and Christ* (New York: Simon and Schuster, 1944), p. 132.

26 a huge agglomeration: Habib, *Sultan Mahmud of Ghazni*, p. 74.

Chapter Two: The Raider Who Came to Stay: Genghis Khan

30 growth of trade: Rondo E. Cameron, *A Concise Economic History of the World: From Paleolithic Times to the Present* (New York: Oxford University Press, 1989), p. 39.

30 Mongol cavalry: Robert Leonard Reynolds, *Europe Emerges: Transition Toward an Industrial World-wide Society, 600–1750* (Madison, Wis.: University of Wisconsin Press, 1961), p. 193.

30 major routes: M. G. Lay, *Ways of the World: A History of the World's Roads and of the Vehicles That Used Them* (New Brunswick, N.J.: Rutgers University Press, 1992).

31 ears boxed: John P. Powelson, *The Story of Land: A World History of Land Tenure and Agrarian Reform* (Cambridge, Mass.: Lincoln Institute of Land Policy, 1989).

32 Land was seen: Patricia Crone, *Pre-Industrial Societies* (New York: Basil Blackwell, 1989).

32 Defensive walls: Robert L. O'Connell, *Of Arms and Men: A History of War, Weapons, and Aggression* (Oxford: Oxford University Press, 1990).

33 taxpayer's point of view: William H. McNeill, *The Pursuit of Power: Technology, Armed Force, and Society since A.D. 1000* (Chicago: University of Chicago Press, 1982), pp. 16–17.

33 balancing act: David Morgan, *The Mongols* (Cambridge, Mass.: Blackwell, 1986), p. 102.

33 canny and cautious: B. Vladimirtsov, *The Life of Chingis-Khan*, trans. Prince D. S. Mirsky (New York: Benjamin Blom, 1930), pp. 165–68.

34 "medieval real-estate operator": Norman J. G. Pounds, *An Economic History of Medieval Europe* (London: Longman, 1994).

34 "horrified romanticism": Owen Lattimore, *The Mongols of Manchuria* (New York: H. Fertig, 1969).

35 command society: McNeill, *Pursuit of Power*, pp. 21–22.

35 totally lacked egos: Cameron, *Concise Economic History of the World*, p. 30.

35   largely indifferent to privacy: William Manchester, *A World Lit Only by Fire* (Boston: Little, Brown, 1992), p. 21.

35   "A cult of poverty": Kiernan, in Goody, et al., eds., *Family and Inheritance*, p. 395.

38   "extreme improvidence": Vladimirtsov, *Life of Chingis-Khan.*

38   a medieval peasant: Manchester, *World Lit Only by Fire,* p. 57.

38   "no margin for error": O'Connell, *Of Arms and Men.*

39   most lethal weapon: Morgan, *Mongols,* p. 91.

39   "Mongol and horse": Peter Brent, *The Mongol Empire* (London: Weidenfeld and Nicholson, 1976), p. 30.

39   the archers could fire arrows: Robert Marshall, *Storm from the East: From Genghis Khan to Khubilai Khan* (Berkeley, Calif.: University of California Press, 1993), p. 18.

39   no such natural barriers: Thomas Sowell, *Conquests and Cultures* (New York: Basic Books, 1998), p. 11.

40   beautiful captives: Vladimirtsov, *Life of Chingis-Khan.*

40   death penalty: Marshall, *Storm from the East,* p. 36.

42   "cruelty or his bloodthirstiness": Vladimirtsov, *Life of Chingis-Khan,* p. 165.

42   worked on their knees: Marshall, *Storm from the East,* p. 20.

42   preindustrial elites: Crone, *Pre-Industrial Societies.*

43   made a mistake: Paul Ratchnevsky, *Genghis Khan: His Life and Legacy,* trans. Thomas Nivison Haining (Cambridge, Mass.: Blackwell, 1991).

44   one group paid taxes: Russell, *Modes of Production,* p. 51.

44   exploited the workers: Crone, *Pre-Industrial Societies.*

45   Riders wore bells: Marshall, *Storm from the East,* p. 86.

45   Emperor Basil II: Sowell, *Conquests and Cultures,* p. 5.

46   Their tolerance: Morgan, *Mongols,* p. 41.

47   turned into an occupation: Marshall, *Storm from the East,* p. 42.

48   "Mongols in flight": Ibid.

49   "My descendants": Ibid. p. 61.

49   comforts of civilization: McNeill, *Pursuit of Power,* p. 59.

50   As William Blackstone wrote: quoted in Nelson W. Aldrich, *Old Money: The Mythology of America's Upper Class* (New York: Alfred A. Knopf, 1988).

Chapter Three: The Man in the Middle: Mansa Musa

52   "as remarkable for its size": E. W. Bovill, *The Golden Trade of the Moors* (London: Oxford University Press, 1958), p. 90.

54   enlarging their kingdom: Ross E. Dunn, *The Adventures of Ibn Battuta* (Berkeley, Calif.: University of California Press, 1989), pp. 290–307.

54   exchange rate: Jennifer Marx, *The Magic of Gold* (Garden City, N.Y.: Doubleday, 1978), p. 252.

54   people crave salt: Bovill, *Golden Trade of the Moors,* p. 236.

55   "big man" redistributors: Marvin Harris, *Cannibals and Kings* (New York: Vintage Books, 1993), pp. 104–8.

55   Shallow coastal waters: Sowell, *Conquests and Cultures,* p. 12.

55   malaria and yellow fever: Reynolds, *Europe Emerges,* p. 313.

56   beating their drums: Irene M. Franck and David M. Brownstone, *To the Ends of the Earth* (New York: Hudson Group, 1984), pp. 341–42.

56   Robin Hood's gang: Janet L. Abu-Lughod, *Before European Hegemony* (Oxford: Oxford University Press, 1991), p. 54.

57   shipment of coins: Weatherford, *History of Money,* p. 75.

58   flash flooding: Franck and Brownstone, *To the Ends of the Earth,* p. 338.

59   mules' ears: Ibid.

59   "trip across the wasteland": Ibid., p. 342.

61   wider trousers: Nehemia Levtzion, *Ancient Ghana and Mali* (New York: Africana, 1980).

61   "staple rights": Pounds, *Economic History of Medieval Europe.*

62   young Etruscan girls accumulated: Vicker, *Realms of Gold.*

63   a transitional stage: David S. Landes, *The Unbound Prometheus* (Cambridge: Cambridge University Press, 1969), p. 27.

63   the craving for gold: Weatherford, *History of Money,* p. 105.

64   "iron curtain": Bovill, *Golden Trade of the Moors,* p. 91.

66   Romans gathered: Milton Meltzer, *Slavery: A World History* (New York: Da Capo Press, 1993), pp. 161–71.

67   bones and shackles: David S. Landes, *The Wealth and Poverty of Nations* (New York: W. W. Norton, 1998), p. 117.

67   Merchant captains: John T. Flynn, *Men of Wealth: The Story of Twelve Significant Fortunes from the Renaissance to the Present Day* (New York: Simon and Schuster, 1941).

67   little more than a vehicle: Wolfgang Schivelbusch, *Tastes of Paradise: A Social History of Spices, Stimulants, and Intoxicants,* trans. David Jacobson (New York: Pantheon Books, 1992), p. 5.

67   a Portuguese king: Lisa Jardine, *Worldly Goods: A New History of the Renaissance* (New York: Doubleday, 1996), p. 54.

68   people "balled" together: White, *Medieval Technology and Social Change,* p. 67.

68   "margin of subsistence": David Hackett Fischer, *The Great Wave:*

Price Revolutions and the Rhythm of History (New York: Oxford University Press, 1996).

68 the khan undertook: Marshall, *Storm from the East.*
69 "Flee in haste": Howard Haggard, *Devils, Drugs, and Doctors* (New York: Harper and Brothers, 1929), p. 210.
70 galley oarsmen: Cipolla, *Before the Industrial Revolution.*
71 Overseas trade: Ibid., p. 227.

Chapter Four: Ungodly Rich: Pope Alexander VI

74 "To be 'magnificent' ": Jardine, *Worldly Goods,* p. 93.
75 "ploughs its profits": J. R. Hale, *The Civilization of Europe in the Renaissance* (New York: Atheneum, 1994), p. 225.
75 illegitimate son: Clemente Fusero, *The Borgias* (New York: Praeger, 1972).
75 Convicted criminals: Hale, *Civilization of Europe in the Renaissance,* p. 28.
76 alum profits: Eamon Duffy, *Saints and Sinners: A History of the Popes* (New Haven: Yale University Press, 1997), p. 149.
76 "loaded with costly rings": quoted in Hale, *Civilization of Europe in the Renaissance,* p. 224.
77 "serving God": Georges Duby, *A History of Private Life,* vol 2: *Revelations of the Medieval World,* trans. Arthur Goldhammer (Cambridge, Mass.: Belknap Press, Harvard University Press, 1993).
79 luxuries and wars: Jardine, *Worldly Goods,* p. 96.
80 "oldish men": Wells, *Short History of the World.*
82 "reputation for splendor": Jardine, *Worldly Goods,* p. 72.
82 "cloaked and booted": Fusero, *Borgias,* p. 118.
82 sacks of gold coins: Barbara Tuchman, *The March of Folly: From Troy to Vietnam* (New York: Ballantine Books, 1984), p. 76.
82 "visible expense": Jardine, *Worldly Goods,* p. 120.
83 More books were published: Steven E. Ozment, *The Age of Reform (1250–1550)* (New Haven: Yale University Press, 1980), p. 199.
83 Belief in institutions: Margaret Aston, *The Fifteenth Century: The Prospect of Europe* (New York: W. W. Norton, 1969), p. 149.
85 "gold-crazed Men": Marx, *Magic of Gold,* p. 287.
85 moneymaking impulse: Heilbroner, *The Quest for Wealth,* p. 77.
86 extensive plotting: Duffy, *Saints and Sinners,* p. 148.
86 garlands of flowers: Tuchman, *March of Folly,* p. 77.
90 bookkeeping techniques: James Gollin, *Worldly Goods* (New York: Random House, 1971), p. 428.

91   "religious and moral feeling": Tuchman, *March of Folly,* p. 60.

92   precious dynastic property: Jardine, *Worldly Goods,* p. 408.

93   as dowry prices rose: Ibid., p. 409.

Chapter Five: Money Begets Money: Jacob Fugger

98   "Debt was as much a feature": Jardine, *Worldly Goods,* p. 93.

98   "extremely occasional": John Gage, *Life in Italy at the Time of the Medici* (New York: Putnam, 1968).

98   lucrative franchises: Jardine, *Worldly Goods,* p. 128.

98   For the aristocracy: Pirenne, *Economic and Social History of Medieval Europe,* p. 125.

98   To admire something: Jardine, *Worldly Goods,* p. 124.

98   "Nowadays the rage": quoted in Hale, *Civilization of Europe in the Renaissance,* p. 146.

98   Price quantified everything: Alfred W. Crosby, *The Measure of Reality: Quantification and Western Society, 1250–1600* (New York: Cambridge University Press, 1997), p. 71.

99   "Money allows humans": Weatherford, *History of Money,* p. 43.

100   double-entry bookkeeping: Buchan, *Frozen Desire,* p. 68.

100   The notion of sin: Georges Duby, ed. *A History of Private Life,* vol. 2: *Revelations of the Medieval World,* trans. Arthur Goldhammer (Cambridge, Mass.: Belknap Press, Harvard University Press, 1993), p. 513.

100   "edgy religiousity": Hale, *Civilization of Europe in the Renaissance,* p. 149.

101   perpetuation, not progress: Robert L. Heilbroner, *The Making of Economic Society,* 10th ed. (Upper Saddle River, N.J.: Prentice Hall, 1998).

101   "economic revolutionists": Flynn, *Men of Wealth,* p. 14.

101   long-range trade: Cipolla, *Before the Industrial Revolution,* p. 226.

102   "interplay of politics": Miriam Beard, *A History of Business* (Ann Arbor, Mich.: University of Michigan Press, 1963), p. 239.

102   "The castle": Duby, *A History of Private Life.*

103   "cocky meritocracy": Crosby, *Measure of Reality,* p. 200.

104   "The secret of this great leap": Harris, *Cannibals and Kings,* p. 265.

105   the costume included: Duby, *A History of Private Life.*

105   "Among the upper levels": Hale, *Civilization of Europe in the Renaissance,* p. 210.

106   "When you have blown": Frank Swetz, *Capitalism and Arithmetic:*

The New Math of the Fifteenth Century (La Salle, Ill.: Open Court, 1987).

106   A common meal: Hale, *Civilization of Europe in the Renaissance,* p. 19.

106   A frivolity: Chandra Mukerji, *From Graven Images: Patterns of Modern Materialism* (New York: Columbia University Press, 1985).

106–7   German engravings: Braudel, *Wheels of Commerce,* p. 234.

107   Responding to epidemics: Hale, *Civilization of Europe in the Renaissance,* p. 24.

107   "Certain things": Cipolla, *Before the Industrial Revolution.*

107   5 percent of the cost: Hale, *Civilization of Europe in the Renaissance,* p. 140.

107   Foreign hosts: Sidney Homer and Richard Sylla, *A History of Interest Rates* (New Brunswick, N.J.: Rutgers University Press, 1991), pp. 92–93.

109   "damages" in the broad sense: Ibid., p. 73.

109   Florence's beautiful churches: Michael Veseth, *Mountains of Debt: Crisis and Change in Renaissance Florence, Victorian Britain, and Postwar America* (New York: Oxford University Press, 1990).

110   Extracting metal: Hale, *Civilization of Europe in the Renaissance.*

110   "having become bankers": Ozment, *Age of Reform,* p. 193.

112   a transfer from Poland: Raymond de Roover, *The Rise and Fall of the Medici Bank* (New York: W. W. Norton, 1966).

113   only a tiny number: Hale, *Civilization of Europe in the Renaissance,* p. 52.

113   late fifteenth century: Ibid., p. 47.

113   from king to peasant: Robert S. Lopez and Irving W. Raymond, *Medieval Trade in the Mediterranean World: Illustrative Documents* (New York: Columbia University Press, 1990).

114   his passion for hunting: Jardine, *Worldly Goods,* p. 98.

118   the power to regulate: Beard, *A History of Business,* p. 261.

118   "like polygamy": Ibid.

120   philosophical evangelist: Flynn, *Men of Wealth,* pp. 19–20.

120   a whole costume: Beard, *A History of Business,* p. 257.

Chapter Six: Dreamers, Gamblers, and Suckers: John Law

123   modern understanding of statistics: Cipolla, *Before the Industrial Revolution,* p. 229.

124   sack of guilders: Flynn, *Men of Wealth,* p. 54.

125 "the medieval dream": Buchan, *Frozen Desire,* p. 99.

127 "watchdog of capitalism": Simon Schama, *The Embarrassment of Riches* (Berkeley: University of California Press, 1988), p. 346.

128 Collect vast pools: Flynn, *Men of Wealth,* p. 56.

129 "heroic materialism": Schama, *The Embarrassment of Riches,* p. 346.

129 "like flies": Charles Mackay, *Extraordinary Popular Delusions and the Madness of Crowds* (New York: Three Rivers Press, 1980), p. 97.

130 sellers sold bulbs: Buchan, *Frozen Desire,* p. 111.

131 The mistress of a rich nobleman: Heilbroner, *The Quest for Wealth,* p. 129.

131 A man named Beaujean: Ibid., p. 132.

132 the amount of silver: Flynn, *Men of Wealth,* p. 67.

132 One study found: Ibid., p. 62.

133 Between 1702 and 1718: Ibid., p. 67.

134 He was educated: Beard, *A History of Business.*

135 gamblers often come: Furnham and Argyle, *Psychology of Money,* p. 119.

135 gambling becomes self-expression: Ibid., p. 120.

135 Freud believed: Ibid., p. 117.

135 gambling provides thrills: Ibid., p. 119.

138 rosy optimism: Heilbroner, *The Quest for Wealth,* p. 124.

138 an English clerk: Antoin E. Murphy, *John Law: Economic Theorist and Policy-Maker* (Oxford: Clarendon Press, 1997), p. 206.

139 prosperity shone: Mackay, *Extraordinary Popular Delusions,* p. 25.

139 overturn the carriage: Ibid., p. 18.

140 England's answer: Edward Chancellor, *Devil Take the Hindmost: A History of Financial Speculation* (New York: Farrar, Straus and Giroux, 1999), p. 61.

140 diverted money: Buchan, *Frozen Desire,* p. 143.

141 People shifted: Murphy, *John Law,* p. 222.

141 Informers on hoarders: A. W. Wiston-Glynn, *John Law of Lauriston* (Edinburgh: E. Saunders, 1907).

142 "most notorious cheat": Murphy, *John Law.*

142 a 44 percent plunge: Ibid., p. 251.

Chapter Seven: Men and Machines: Richard Arkwright

147 Sporadic fairs: M. J. Daunton, *Progress and Poverty: An Economic and Social History of Britain, 1700–1850* (Oxford: Oxford University Press, 1995), p. 270.

147 a greater proportion: Neil McKendrick, *The Birth of a Consumer*

Society: The Commercialization of Eighteenth-Century England (London: Europa, 1982).

148   ceramic tableware: Roy Porter, *English Society in the Eighteenth Century* (New York: Penguin Books, 1990), p. 318.

148   hats replaced shawls: Neil J. Smelser, *Social Change in the Industrial Revolution* (Chicago: University of Chicago Press, 1959) p. 346

148   "necessity of arousing": Kirkpatrick Sale, *Rebels Against the Future: The Luddites and Their War on the Industrial Revolution* (Reading, Mass.: Addison-Wesley, 1995), p. 38.

149   vices of avarice: Chancellor, *Devil Take the Hindmost*, p. 33.

149   "happy, bucolic life": Veseth, *Mountains of Debt*, p. 77.

150   patronizing lord: Beard, *A History of the Business Man*, p. 447.

150   internal customs barriers: Landes, *The Unbound Prometheus*, p. 46.

151   high tariffs: Porter, *English Society in the Eighteenth Century*, p. 187.

151   capital was plentiful: Ibid., p. 322.

151   flow of improvements: Landes, *The Wealth and Poverty of Nations*, pp. 186–87.

151   "every burst of growth": Fernand Braudel, *The Wheels of Commerce*.

152   hunting and foraging: Sale, *Rebels Against the Future*, p. 39.

152   "an amazing number": Porter, *English Society in the Eighteenth Century*, p. 211.

152   "Where a weight": Wells, *A Short History of the World*, p. 260.

153–4   low prices and high wages: Hans Wantoch, *Magnificent Money-Makers*, trans. J. H. S. Moore (London: Desmond Harmsworth, 1932), p. 112.

154   There was no split: E. J. Hobsbawm, *Industry and Empire: From 1750 to the Present Day* (London: Penguin Books, 1968), p. 60.

155   "no uncommon thing": Richard Guest, *Compendious History of the Cotton-Manufacture; with a Disproval of the Claim of Sir Richard Arkwright to the Invention of Its Ingenious Machinery* (Manchester: Joseph Pratt, 1823), p. 12.

156   Inventors of new products: Michael Patrick Allen, *The Founding Fortunes* (New York: E. P. Dutton, 1987), p. 221.

156   "Innovation . . . is the relating": Peter Mathias, *The First Industrial Nation* (London: Methuen, 1969).

157   "by head-work": Francis Espinasse, *Lancashire Worthies* (London: Simpkin, Marshall, and Company, 1874).

157   "personified the new type": Wantoch, *Magnificent Money-Makers*.

157   "starve his family": R. S. Fitton, *The Arkwrights: Spinners of Fortune* (Manchester: Manchester University Press, 1989), p. 209.

157 "hard, dull, misunderstood": Wantoch, *Magnificent Money-Makers,* p. 114.

157 Bubble Act of 1720: Mathias, *The First Industrial Nation,* p. 145.

158 the right balance: Daunton, *Progress and Poverty,* pp. 189–190.

158 patenting required: Joel Mokyr, ed., *The British Industrial Revolution* (Boulder: Westview Press, 1993), p. 41.

159 earliest factory masters: R. S. Fitton, *The Arkwrights,* p. 31.

159 no standardization: Landes, *The Unbound Prometheus,* pp. 190–92.

160 "Speaking as a tourist": Barrie Trinder, *The Making of the Industrial Landscape* (London: Phoenix Giant, 1982), pp. 64–65, 66.

160 "spending and investment": Hobsbawm, *Industry and Empire.*

160 new kinds of dogs: McKendrick, *Birth of a Consumer Society.*

161 "effeminate" urge: Porter, *English Society in the Eighteenth Century,* p. 223.

161 extensive retraining: Mathias, *The First Industrial Nation,* p. 138.

162 military commanders: Mokyr, *The British Industrial Revolution.*

162 "An industrialist risks": François Crouzet, *The First Industrialists: The Problem of Origins* (Cambridge: Cambridge University Press, 1985).

163 "he swore a loud oath": R. S. Fitton, *The Arkwrights,* p. 206

163 plates could be stacked: Beard, *A History of the Business Man,* p. 35.

163 In his "Law Book": Porter, *English Society in the Eighteenth Century,* p. 195.

163 scarcity of coinage: Mathias, *The First Industrial Nation,* pp. 139–40.

164 "their small fingers": Espinasse, *Lancashire Worthies,* p. 402.

164 hired whole families: Mokyr, ed., *The British Industrial Revolution.*

164 "yoke-fellows with iron": Sale, *Rebels Against the Future,* p. 31.

165 forbidden to bring watches: Paul Mantoux, *The Industrial Revolution in the Eighteenth Century,* trans. Marjorie Vernon (New York: Harcourt, Brace, and Company, 1927).

165 a clergyman about Manchester: Hobsbawm, *Industry and Empire,* p. 87.

165 an individual moral failing: Mathias, *The First Industrial Nation,* p. 189.

165 vulnerable to fire: Trinder, *Making of the Industrial Landscape,* p. 105.

166 scale of physical opposition: Porter, *English Society in the Eighteenth Century,* pp. 315–16.

166 collecting rents: Joel Mokyr, *The Lever of Riches: Technological Creativity and Economic Progress* (New York: Oxford University Press, 1990).

167   steam engine: Ibid.

167   coined *horsepower*: Porter, *English Society in the Eighteenth Century,* p. 272.

167   led to larger scales: Sale, *Rebels Against the Future,* p. 28.

167   "he fixed the price": Smelser, *Social Change,* p. 92.

Chapter Eight: Addicted to Trade: Howqua

171   rhythm had to speed up: Mandy Bentham, *The Politics of Drug Control* (New York: St. Martin's Press, 1998).

173   purely on sufferance: Harley Farnsworth MacNair, *Modern Chinese History: Selected Readings,* vol. 1 (Shanghai: Commercial Press, 1927), p. 45.

173   skimming off fortunes: John King Fairbank, *Trade and Diplomacy on the China Coast.* (Cambridge: Harvard University Press, 1953), p. 52.

173   "a herd of cattle": Ibid., p. 19.

174   "great command of capital": Hosea Ballou Morse, *The International Relations of the Chinese Empire: The Period of Conflict, 1834–1860* (New York: Longmans, Green, 1910).

174   "eager to inculpate him": Ibid.

175   he was condemned: Hallett Abend, *Treaty Ports* (Garden City, N.Y.: Doubleday, Doran, and Company, 1944), p. 9.

175   seven-mile-long wall: Ibid., p. 8.

176   gilded cage: Morse, *International Relations of the Chinese Empire,* p. 72.

176   "Foreign Devils": MacNair, *Modern Chinese History,* p. 44.

176   "burdensome honor": Morse, *International Relations of the Chinese Empire,* p. 86.

179   pidgin English: Yen-p'ing Hao, *The Commercial Revolution in Nineteenth-Century China* (Berkeley, Calif.: University of California Press, 1986), pp. 11–31.

179   bird's nest soup: MacNair, *Modern Chinese History,* p. 33.

179   pooling of risk: Philip Lawson, *The East India Company: A History* (London: Longman, 1993).

180   "brain of a merchant": Fairbank, *Trade and Diplomacy,* p. 58.

180   "able and reliable": Michael Greenberg, *British Trade and the Opening of China, 1800–42* (Cambridge: University Press, 1951).

180   "race of traders": Morse, *International Relations of the Chinese Empire,* p. 81.

180   verge of bankruptcy: Hao, *Commercial Revolution.*

181   consumption of tea: McKendrick, *Birth of a Consumer Society.*

181 Tea was prescribed: Lawson, *East India Company,* p. 60.

181 emblem of sobriety: Roy Porter and Mikulas Teich, eds., *Drugs and Narcotics in History* (Cambridge: Cambridge University Press, 1995), p. 35.

182 would become blind: Hao, *Commercial Revolution,* cited in Ernest May, *America's China Trade in Historical Perspective* (Cambridge: Harvard University Press, 1986), p. 15.

182 no reciprocal appetite: Greenberg, *British Trade.*

182 "their stony hearts": Hao, *Commercial Revolution.*

183 keep them docile: Martin Booth, *Opium: A History* (New York: Simon and Schuster, 1996), pp. 104–5.

183 students studying: Jonathan D. Spence, *The Search for Modern China* (New York: W. W. Norton, 1990), p. 131.

183 on a large scale: Greenberg, *British Trade.*

183 Vast tracts: Booth, *Opium,* p. 116.

183 "a pernicious article": Ibid., pp. 111–12.

184 "read my Bible": Fairbank, *Trade and Diplomacy,* p. 69.

184 "wall of monopoly": Greenberg, *British Trade.*

184 in one direction: Hao, *Commercial Revolution.*

185 flouting Chinese law: Ibid.

185 "the use of wine": MacNair, *Modern Chinese History,* p. 123.

185 "gentleman-like speculation": Booth, *Opium,* p. 114.

185 in Canton shops: Hao, *Commercial Revolution.*

186 local bureaucrats: Fairbank, *Trade and Diplomacy,* pp. 66–67.

186 ships carrying opium: Hsin-pao Chang, *Commissioner Lin, and the Opium War* (Cambridge: Harvard University Press, 1964) p. 20.

186 "fortified opium warehouses": Booth, *Opium,* p. 119.

186–7 two-masted river craft: Hao, *Commercial Revolution.*

187 "unwilling to embark": Ibid.

187 drain of silver: Chang, *Commissioner Lin,* pp. 40–46.

187 rising silver prices: Spence, *Search for Modern China,* p. 149.

188 a financial burden: Hao, *Commercial Revolution.*

188 which were fishermen: Fairbank, *Trade and Diplomacy,* p. 49.

188 "smug boats": Greenberg, *British Trade.*

189 as an obstacle: Hao, *Commercial Revolution.*

189 derisive nickname: Lawson, *East India Company,* p. 98.

189 "a fair field": Morse, *International Relations of the Chinese Empire,* p. 87.

189 merchant-adventurers: Hao, *Commercial Revolution,* cited in May, ed., *America's China Trade,* pp. 11–31.

189   trade with China: Ibid.

189–90   each ship's cargo: Hao, *Commercial Revolution.*

190   in a sedan chair: Chang, *Commissioner Lin.*

190   "a flourish of trumpets": Peter Ward Fay, *The Opium War: 1840–1842* (Chapel Hill, N.C.: University of North Carolina Press, 1975).

191   incessant sound: Spence, *The Search for Modern China,* p. 152.

191   series of skirmishes: Booth, *Opium,* p. 135.

191   "wretched gunnery": MacNair, *Modern Chinese History,* p. 132.

191   Howqua moaned: Hao, *Commercial Revolution.*

192   "Unequal Treaty": Booth, *Opium,* p. 135.

192   some eighty vessels: Ibid., p. 141.

192   appetite for drugs: Kathryn Meyer and Terry Parssinen, *Webs of Smoke: Smugglers, Warlords, Spies, and the History of the International Drug Trade* (New York: Rowman and Littlefield, 1998), p. 1.

193   their own submarines: United Nations *World Drug Report* (Oxford: Oxford University Press, 1997), p. 136.

193   global capital market: Bentham, *Politics of Drug Control.*

193   Profits are so high: Ronald Chepesiuk, *Hard Target: The United States War Against International Drug Trafficking* (Jefferson, N.C.: McFarland and Company, 1999).

Chapter Nine: Outmanning the Men: Hetty Green

195   cult of domesticity: Angel Kwolek-Folland, *Incorporating Women: A History of Women and Business in the United States* (New York: Twayne Publishers, 1998), p. 54.

195   In Helena, Montana: Ibid., pp. 65–66.

196   "I go my own way": Boyden Sparkes and Samuel T. Moore, *The Witch of Wall Street* (New York: Doubleday, Doran, and Company, 1935), p. 182.

197   the strong triumphed: Patricia O'Toole, *Money and Morals in America: A History* (New York: Random House, 1998), p. 149.

197   epitome of masculinity: Angel Kwolek-Folland, *Engendering Business: Men and Women in the Corporate Office, 1870–1930* (Baltimore: Johns Hopkins University Press, 1994), pp. 48–54.

198   "Money-making": James Truslow Adams, quoted in Heilbroner, *The Quest for Wealth,* p. 200.

198   In the seventeenth century: Heilbroner, *The Quest for Wealth.*

198   They gave "poverty socials": Matthew Josephson, *The Money Lords: The Great Finance Capitalists, 1925–1950* (New York: Weybright and Talley, 1972), pp. 339–40.

199   a Tudor mansion: Beard, *A History of the Business Man,* pp. 190–91.

199   a single cup of tea: Josephson, *Money Lords,* p. 334.

199   "The American wasted": quoted in Buchan, *Frozen Desire,* p. 233.

199   "anything goes": O'Toole, *Money and Morals,* p. 149.

199   ethic of the smart man: Heilbroner, *The Quest for Wealth,* pp. 171–203.

199   "marionettes dancing": Buchan, *Frozen Desire.*

199   dreamed of joining them: O'Toole, *Money and Morals,* p. 152.

199   "a man buying cows": Chancellor, *Devil Take the Hindmost,* p. 167.

200   "shrewdness and strategy": Josephson, *Money Lords.*

200   ruinous competition: Ibid.

200   from small farms: Kwolek-Folland, *Incorporating Women,* pp. 62–78.

201   highest per-capita: Jaher, *The Rich, the Well Born, and the Powerful,* cited in Rubinstein, *Wealth and the Wealthy,* pp. 192, 193.

201   heroic age: Ibid., p. 193.

201   bootstraps sagas: O'Toole, *Money and Morals,* p. 164.

201   boast of the poverty: Heilbroner, *The Quest for Wealth,* p. 186.

201   frequently italicized: Gustavus Myers, *History of the Great American Fortunes* (New York: Modern Library, 1936).

202   haze crew members: Ladbroke Black, *Some Queer People* (London: Sampson Low, Marston, and Company, 1931), p. 207.

203   "a bosom": Arthur H. Lewis, *The Day They Shook the Plum Tree* (New York: Harcourt, Brace, 1963), p. 20.

206   "A bevy of dames": William Worthington Fowler, *Twenty Years of Inside Life in Wall Street; or, Revelations of the Personal Experiences of a Speculator* (New York: Greenwood Press, 1968 [1880]).

206   stockbrokers: Kwolek-Folland, *Engendering Business,* p. 5.

206   a girl was likely: Ibid., pp. 30–31.

207   white birth rate: Kwolek-Folland, *Incorporating Women,* p. 55.

207   clerical occupations: Kwolek-Folland, *Engendering Business,* p. 4.

207–8   A woman's earnings: Anne E. Morris and Susan Nott, *All My Worldly Goods: A Feminist Perspective on the Legal Regulation of Wealth* (Brookfield, Vt.: Dartmouth Publishing Company, 1995).

208   "hollowing themselves": O'Toole, *Money and Morals,* p. 144.

209   Call loans: Chancellor, *Devil Take the Hindmost,* p. 158.

209   obliterated the bears: Ibid., p. 156.

209 "A Wall Street panic": Josephson, *Money Lords.*

211 the heart of Chicago: Dana L. Thomas, *The Money Crowd* (New York: G. P. Putnam's Sons, 1972).

211 "best banking brain": Sparkes and Moore, *Witch of Wall Street,* p. 274.

212 Hetty Green's income: Lewis, *Plum Tree,* p. 125.

212 "quits striving for more": Gunther, *The Very, Very Rich,* p. 230.

213 high accident rate: Lewis, *Plum Tree,* p. 80.

214 "Not a cent": Black, *Some Queer People,* p. 217.

214 "grand tour" of Europe: Josephson, *Money Lords,* p. 340.

214 Jay Gould's daughter: Jaher, *The Rich, the Well Born, and the Powerful,* cited in Rubinstein, *Wealth and the Wealthy,* p. 200.

214 "My general existence": Goldberg and Lewis, *Money Madness.*

215 checked out of the hotel: Sparkes and Moore, *Witch of Wall Street,* p. 219.

215 no mechanisms for tracking: Rubinstein, *Wealth and the Wealthy,* p. 179.

215 "stupendous individual revenues": quoted in Inhaber, *How Rich Is Too Rich,* p. 131.

216 plotting to murder: Flynn, *Men of Wealth,* p. 223.

216 "Haldane has charged me": Sparkes and Moore, *Witch of Wall Street,* p. 174.

216 "My dear young judge": Ibid.

216 "moral responsibility": Ibid., p. 223.

217 charitable gifts at death: O'Toole, *Money and Morals,* p. 148.

218 "buy cheap and sell dear": Sparkes and Moore, *Witch of Wall Street,* p. 139.

Chapter Ten: The $100 Billion Man: Bill Gates

221 a few gentlemen: McKendrick, *Birth of a Consumer Society.*

221 "people in flight": Ray Ginger, *The Age of Excess* (New York: Macmillan, 1965).

223 Even *Forbes* magazine: *Forbes,* October 19, 1992.

223 daily life has changed: Mokyr, *The Lever of Riches.*

224 Bill Gates's net worth: Frank, *Luxury Fever,* p. 15.

225 "creating sufficient wants": Wilfred Beckerman quoted in Galbraith, *Money, Whence It Came, Where It Went* (Boston: Houghton Mifflin, 1975).

225 7,500 millionaires: Jaher, *The Rich, the Well Born, and the Powerful,* cited in Rubinstein, *Wealth and the Wealthy,* p. 195.

226 productive activity: Galbraith, *Money.*

227 Privacy, a precious good: Allen, *Founding Fortunes,* p. 3.

227 income consciousness: Daniel J. Boorstin, *The Americans: The Democratic Experience* (New York: Random House, 1973).

228 "winning the lottery": Philip Brickman and Dan Coates, "Lottery Winners and Accident Victims: Is Happiness Relative?," *Journal of Personal and Social Psychology,* (Vol. 36, No. 8).

229 affluence may remain: Richard Easterlin, "Does Money Buy Happiness?," *The Public Interest* 20, p. 10.

229 "hyperconsumption": *New York* magazine, June 14, 1999.

229 feudal lords: Beard, *A History of the Business Man,* p. 230.

230 "personality market": quoted in Daniel Bell, *The Coming of the Post-Industrial Society: A Venture in Social Forecasting* (New York: Basic Books, 1976).

230 Spending has become: Beard, *A History of the Business Man,* p. 232.

230–31 men who live daintily: Ibid., p. 237.

231 Gates vowed: Robert X. Cringely, *Accidental Empires* (Reading, Mass.: Addison-Wesley, 1992), p. 99.

232 His girlfriends: Gary Rivlin, *The Plot to Get Bill Gates* (New York: Times Business, 1999), p. 65.

233 the simplest clerk: Beard, *A History of the Business Man,* p. 236.

233 "destroyed the village": *The Washington Post,* August 28, 1997.

233 The early wealthy: *The Atlanta Journal,* March 22, 1998.

234 $2,000 per square foot: Frank, *Luxury Fever,* p. 22.

236 help the poor: Jaher, *The Rich, the Well Born, and the Powerful,* cited in Rubinstein, *Wealth and the Wealthy,* p. 211.

236 "very results oriented": *Christian Science Monitor,* September 15, 1998.

237 paying his workers: O'Toole, *Money and Morals,* p. 154.

238 "their wounded spirits": quoted in Kit Konolige, *The Richest Women in the World* (New York: Macmillan, 1985), p. 329.

BIBLIOGRAPHY

Abend, Hallett. *Treaty Ports*. Garden City, N.Y.: Doubleday, Doran, and Company, 1944.

Abu-Lughod, Janet L. *Before European Hegemony*. Oxford: Oxford University Press, 1991.

Aldrich, Nelson W. *Old Money: The Mythology of America's Upper Class*. New York: Alfred A. Knopf, 1988.

Allen, Michael Patrick. *The Founding Fortunes*. New York: E. P. Dutton, 1987.

Argyle, Michael. *The Psychology of Happiness*. London: Methuen, 1987.

Aristophanes. *Works*. Trans. Palmer Bovie. Philadelphia: University of Pennsylvania Press, 1998.

Aston, Margaret. *The Fifteenth Century: The Prospect of Europe*. New York: W. W. Norton, 1969.

Baltzell, E. Digby. *Philadelphia Gentlemen: The Making of a National Upper Class*. Glencoe, Ill.: Free Press, 1958.

Bazelon, David T. *The Paper Economy*. New York: Vintage Books, 1963.

Beard, Miriam. *A History of Business*. Ann Arbor, Mich.: University of Michigan Press, 1963.

———. *A History of the Business Man*. New York: Macmillan, 1938.

Belk, Russell. "Attachment to Possessions." In *Place Attachment*. Ed. Irwin Altman and Setha M. Low. New York: Plenum Press, 1992.

Bell, Daniel. *The Coming of Post-Industrial Society: A Venture in Social Forecasting*. New York: Basic Books, 1976.

Bell, Daniel, ed. *Toward the Year 2000: Work in Progress*. Boston: Houghton Mifflin, 1968.

Bennett, Judith, et al. *Sisters and Workers in the Middle Ages*. Chicago: University of Chicago Press, 1989.

Bentham, Mandy. *The Politics of Drug Control*. New York: St. Martin's Press, 1998.

Bertelli, Sergio. *Italian Renaissance Courts*. London: Sidgwick and Jackson, 1986.

Bhakari, Major S. K. *Indian Warfare: An Appraisal of Strategy and Tactics of War in Early Medieval Period*. New Delhi: Munshiram Manoharlal Publishers, 1980.

Black, Ladbroke. *Some Queer People*. London: Sampson Low, Marston and Company, 1931.

Boorstin, Daniel J. *The Americans: The Democratic Experience*. New York: Random House, 1973.

Booth, Martin. *Opium: A History*. New York: Simon and Schuster, 1996.

Bosworth, C. E. *The Medieval History of Iran, Afghanistan, and Central Asia*. London: Variorum Reprints, 1977.

Bovill, E. W. *The Golden Trade of the Moors*. London: Oxford University Press, 1958.

Brandeis, Louis D. *Other People's Money and How the Bankers Use It*. New York: Frederick A. Stokes, 1932.

Braudel, Fernand. *The Wheels of Commerce*. New York: Harper and Row, 1982.

Bremner, Robert Hamlett. *Giving: Charity and Philanthropy in History*. New Brunswick, N.J.: Transaction Books, 1994.

Brent, Peter. *Genghis Khan*. New York: McGraw-Hill, 1976.

———. *The Mongol Empire*. London: Weidenfeld and Nicholson, 1976.

Brickman, Philip, and Dan Coates, "Lottery Winners and Accident Victims: Is Happiness Relative?" *Journal of Personality and Social Psychology* (Vol. 36, No. 8).

Buchan, James. *Frozen Desire*. New York: Farrar, Straus and Giroux, 1997.

Burckhardt, Jacob. *The Civilization of the Renaissance in Italy*. New York: Phaidon Publishers, 1951.

Cameron, Rondo E. *A Concise Economic History of the World: From Paleolithic Times to the Present*. New York: Oxford University Press, 1989.

Canfield, Cass. *Outrageous Fortunes*. New York: Harcourt Brace Jovanovich, 1981.

Cawelti, John G. *Apostles of the Self-Made Man*. Chicago: University of Chicago Press, 1965.

Chamberlin, E. R. *The World of the Italian Renaissance*. Boston: Allen and Unwin, 1982.

Chancellor, Edward. *Devil Take the Hindmost: A History of Financial Speculation.* New York: Farrar, Straus and Giroux, 1999.

Chang, Hsin-pao. *Commissioner Lin and the Opium War.* Cambridge, Mass.: Harvard University Press, 1964.

Chepesiuk, Ronald. *Hard Target: The United States War Against International Drug Trafficking.* Jefferson, N.C.: McFarland and Company, 1999.

Chesler, Phyllis, and Emily Jane Goodman. *Women, Money, and Power.* New York: William Morrow, 1976.

Cipolla, Carlo M. *Before the Industrial Revolution.* New York: W. W. Norton, 1993.

Clark, Alice. *Working Life of Women in the Seventeenth Century.* New York: Routledge, Chapman, and Hall, 1982 [1919].

Clarke, Ignatius Frederick. *Tale of the Future: From the Beginning to the Present Day.* London: Library Association, 1978.

Cloulas, Ivan. *The Borgias.* Trans. Gilda Roberts. New York: Franklin Watts, 1989.

Crawford, Tad. *The Secret Life of Money: Teaching Tales of Spending, Receiving, Saving, and Owing.* New York: Putnam, 1994.

Cringely, Robert X. *Accidental Empires.* Reading, Mass.: Addison-Wesley, 1992.

Crone, Patricia. *Pre-Industrial Societies.* New York: Basil Blackwell, 1989.

Crosby, Alfred W. *The Measure of Reality: Quantification and Western Society, 1250–1600.* New York: Cambridge University Press, 1997.

Crouzet, François. *The First Industrialists: The Problem of Origins.* Cambridge: Cambridge University Press, 1985.

Curtin, Philip D. *Cross-cultural Trade in World History.* Cambridge: Cambridge University Press, 1984.

Daunton, M. J. *Progress and Poverty: An Economic and Social History of Britain, 1700–1850.* Oxford: Oxford University Press, 1995.

Davis, William. *Children of the Rich.* London: Sidgwick and Jackson, 1989.

———. *It's No Sin to Be Rich: A Defense of Capitalism.* Nashville: Nelson, 1976.

De Quincey, Thomas. *Confessions of an English Opium-Eater.* New York: Oxford University Press, 1960.

de Roover, Raymond. *The Rise and Fall of the Medici Bank.* New York: W. W. Norton, 1966.

Dittmar, Helga. *The Social Psychology of Material Possessions: To Have Is to Be.* New York: St. Martin's Press, 1992.

Domhoff, G. William. *The Higher Circles: The Governing Class in America*. New York: Random House, 1970.

Duby, Georges. *The Early Growth of the European Economy*. Ithaca, N.Y.: Cornell University Press, 1974.

Duby, Georges, ed. *A History of Private Life*. Vol. 2: *Revelations of the Medieval World*. Trans. Arthur Goldhammer. Cambridge, Mass.: Belknap Press, Harvard University Press, 1993.

Duffy, Eamon. *Saints and Sinners: A History of the Popes*. New Haven: Yale University Press, 1997.

Dunn, Ross E. *The Adventures of Ibn Battuta*. Berkeley, Calif.: University of California Press, 1989.

Durant, Will. *Caesar and Christ*. New York: Simon and Schuster, 1944.

———. *The Renaissance: A History of Civilization in Italy from 1304–1576*. New York: Simon and Schuster, 1953.

Dvornik, Francis. *Origins of Intelligence Services*. New Brunswick, N.J.: Rutgers University Press, 1974.

Easterlin, Richard, "Does Money Buy Happiness?" *The Public Interest* 20 (winter 1973).

Ehrenberg, Richard. *Capital and Finance in the Age of the Renaissance*. London: Jonathan Cape, 1928.

Espinasse, Francis. *Lancashire Worthies*. London: Simpkin, Marshall, and Company, 1874.

Fairbank, John King. *Trade and Diplomacy on the China Coast*. Cambridge: Harvard University Press, 1953.

Fay, Peter Ward. *The Opium War: 1840–1842*. Chapel Hill, N.C.: University of North Carolina Press, 1975.

Fischer, David Hackett. *The Great Wave: Price Revolutions and the Rhythm of History*. New York: Oxford University Press, 1996.

Fitton, R. S. *The Arkwrights: Spinners of Fortune*. Manchester: Manchester University Press, 1989.

Floud, Roderick, and Donald McCloskey. *The Economic History of Britain since 1700*. Vol. 1, *1700–1860*. Cambridge: Cambridge University Press, 1994.

Flynn, John T. *Men of Wealth: The Story of Twelve Significant Fortunes from the Renaissance to the Present Day*. New York: Simon and Schuster, 1941.

Fourastie, Jean. *The Causes of Wealth*. Glencoe, Ill.: Free Press, 1960.

Fowler, William Worthington. *Twenty Years of Inside Life in Wall Street; or,*

Revelations of the Personal Experiences of a Speculator. New York: Greenwood Press, 1968 [1880].

Fox, Richard Wightman, and T. J. Jackson Lears, eds. *The Culture of Consumption.* New York: Pantheon Books, 1983.

Franck, Irene M., and David M. Brownstone. *To the Ends of the Earth.* New York: Hudson Group, 1984.

Frank, Robert H. *Luxury Fever.* New York: Free Press, 1999.

Frost, David. *David Frost's Book of Millionaires, Multimillionaires, and Really Rich People.* New York: Crown, 1984.

Furnham, Adrian, and Michael Argyle. *The Psychology of Money.* New York: Routledge, 1998.

Fusero, Clemente. *The Borgias.* New York: Praeger, 1972.

Gage, John. *Life in Italy at the Time of the Medici.* New York: Putnam, 1968.

Galbraith, John Kenneth. *Money, Whence It Came, Where It Went.* Boston: Houghton Mifflin, 1975.

Ginger, Ray. *The Age of Excess.* New York: Macmillan, 1965.

Goldberg, Herb, and Robert T. Lewis. *Money Madness: The Psychology of Saving, Spending, Loving, and Hating Money.* New York: New American Library, 1978.

Gollin, James. *Worldly Goods.* New York: Random House, 1971.

Goody, Jack, et al., eds. *Family and Inheritance: Rural Society in Western Europe, 1200–1800.* Cambridge: Cambridge University Press, 1976.

Green, F. C. *Eighteenth-Century France: Six Essays.* New York: D. Appleton and Company, 1931.

Greenberg, Michael. *British Trade and the Opening of China, 1800–42.* Cambridge: Cambridge University Press, 1951.

Greene, Bert, and Phillip Schulz. *Pity the Poor Rich.* Chicago: Contemporary Books, 1978.

Groseclose, Elgin Earl. *Money and Man.* Norman, Okla.: University of Oklahoma Press, 1976 [1934].

Guest, Richard. *Compendious History of the Cotton-Manufacture; with a Disproval of the Claim of Sir Richard Arkwright to the Invention of Its Ingenious Machinery.* Manchester: Joseph Pratt, 1823.

Gunther, Max. *The Very, Very Rich and How They Got That Way.* New York: Playboy Press, 1972.

Habib, Mohommad. *Sultan Mahmud of Ghazni.* Delhi: S. Chand and Company, 1967.

Hacker, Louis Norton. *The Triumph of American Capitalism*. New York: Simon and Schuster, 1940.

Haggard, Howard. *Devils, Drugs, and Doctors*. New York: Harper and Brothers, 1929.

Hale, J. R. *The Civilization of Europe in the Renaissance*. New York: Atheneum, 1994.

Handlin, Oscar, and Mary F. Handlin. *The Wealth of the American People: A History of American Affluence*. New York: McGraw-Hill, 1975.

Hao, Yen-p'ing. *The Commercial Revolution in Nineteenth-Century China*. Berkeley, Calif.: University of California Press, 1986.

Harris, Marvin. *Cannibals and Kings*. New York: Vintage Books, 1993.

Haswell, Jock. *Spies and Spymasters: A Concise History of Intelligence*. London: Thames and Hudson, 1977.

Heilbroner, Robert L. *Behind the Veil of Economics: Essays in the Worldly Philosophy*. New York: W. W. Norton, 1988.

———. *The Making of Economic Society*. 10th ed. Upper Saddle River, N.J.: Prentice Hall, 1998.

———. *The Quest for Wealth: A Study of Acquisitive Man*. New York: Simon and Schuster, 1956.

———. *Twenty-first Century Capitalism*. New York: W. W. Norton, 1993.

Herlihy, David. *Opera Muliebria: Women and Work in Medieval Europe*. New York: McGraw-Hill, 1990.

Herman, Andrew. *The Better Angels of Capitalism: Rhetoric, Narrative, and Moral Identity among Men of the American Upper Class*. Boulder, Colo.: Westview Press, 1999.

Hobsbawm, E. J. *Industry and Empire: From 1750 to the Present Day*. London: Penguin Books, 1968.

Homer, Sidney, and Richard Sylla. *A History of Interest Rates*. New Brunswick, N.J.: Rutgers University Press, 1991.

Hudson, Pat, and W. R. Lee. *Women's Work and the Family Economy in Historical Perspective*. Manchester: Manchester University Press, 1990.

Hunt, E. K. *Property and Prophets: The Evolution of Economic Institutions and Ideologies*. New York: Harper and Row, 1981.

Hunt, Edwin S., and James M. Murray. *A History of Business in Medieval Europe*. Cambridge: Cambridge University Press, 1999.

Hunter, W. C. *Bits of Old China*. London: Kegan Paul, Trench and Company, 1885.

———. *The 'Fan Kwae' at Canton Before Treaty Days, 1825–1844*. London: Kegan Paul, Trench, and Company, 1882.

Hyde, H. Montgomery. *John Law: The History of an Honest Adventurer.* Denver: Alan Swallow, 1948.

Inhaber, Herbert. *How Rich Is Too Rich.* New York: Praeger, 1992.

Jaher, Frederic Cople, ed. *The Rich, the Well Born, and the Powerful: Elites and Upper Classes in History.* Urbana, Ill.: University of Illinois Press, 1973.

Jardine, Lisa. *Worldly Goods: A New History of the Renaissance.* New York: Doubleday, 1996.

Jensen, De Lamar. *Renaissance Europe: Age of Recovery and Reconciliation.* Lexington, Mass.: D.C. Heath, 1981.

Josephson, Matthew. *The Money Lords: The Great Finance Capitalists, 1925–1950.* New York: Weybright and Talley, 1972.

Kathrens, Richard D. *Who Will Answer for Mr. Schwab?* Kansas City, Mo.: Burton, 1920.

Kirstein, George G. *The Rich: Are They Different?* Boston: Houghton Mifflin, 1968.

Konolige, Kit. *The Richest Women in the World.* New York: Macmillan, 1985.

Kwolek-Folland, Angel. *Engendering Business: Men and Women in the Corporate Office, 1870–1930.* Baltimore: Johns Hopkins University Press, 1994.

———. *Incorporating Women: A History of Women and Business in the United States.* New York: Twayne Publishers, 1998.

Landes, David S. *The Unbound Prometheus.* Cambridge: Cambridge University Press, 1969.

———. *The Wealth and Poverty of Nations.* New York: W. W. Norton, 1998.

Lane, Frederic C., and Reinhold C. Mueller. *Money and Banking in Medieval and Renaissance Venice.* Vol. 1, *Coins and Money of Account.* Baltimore: Johns Hopkins University Press, 1985.

Lane-Pool, Stanley. *Mediaeval India.* New York: Kraus, 1970.

Lasch, Christopher. *The Revolt of the Elites and the Betrayal of Democracy.* New York: W. W. Norton, 1995.

Latour, Anny. *The Borgias.* Trans. Neil Mann. New York: Abelard-Schuman, 1963.

Lattimore, Owen. *The Mongols of Manchuria.* New York: H. Fertig, 1969.

Lawson, Philip. *The East India Company: A History*. London: Longman, 1993.

Lay, M. G. *Ways of the World: A History of the World's Roads and of the Vehicles That Used Them*. New Brunswick, N.J.: Rutgers University Press, 1992.

Lebergott, Stanley. *Pursuing Happiness: American Consumers in the Twentieth Century*. Princeton, N.J.: Princeton University Press, 1993.

Leon, Vicki. *Uppity Women of the Renaissance*. Berkeley, Calif.: Conari Press, 1999.

Levtzion, Nehemia. *Ancient Ghana and Mali*. New York: Africana, 1980.

Lewenhak, Sheila. *Women and Work*. London: Macmillan, 1980.

Lewis, Arthur H. *The Day They Shook the Plum Tree*. New York: Harcourt, Brace, and World, 1963.

Lewis, Bernard. *Race and Slavery in the Middle East: An Historical Enquiry*. New York: Oxford University Press, 1990.

Lopez, Robert S., and Irving W. Raymond. *Medieval Trade in the Mediterranean World: Illustrative Documents*. New York: Columbia University Press, 1990.

McConnell, Donald. *Economic Virtues in the United States: A History and an Interpretation*. New York: Arno Press, 1973 [1930].

McCracken, Grant. *Culture and Consumption: New Approaches to the Symbolic Character of Consumer Goods*. Bloomington, Ind.: Indiana University Press, 1991.

Mackay, Charles. *Extraordinary Popular Delusions and the Madness of Crowds*. New York: Three Rivers Press, 1980.

McKendrick, Neil. *The Birth of a Consumer Society: The Commercialization of Eighteenth-Century England*. London: Europa, 1982.

MacNair, Harley Farnsworth. *Modern Chinese History: Selected Readings*. Vol. 1, Shanghai: Commercial Press, 1927.

McNeill, William H. *The Pursuit of Power: Technology, Armed Force, and Society since A.D. 1000*. Chicago: University of Chicago Press, 1982.

Mallett, Michael. *The Borgias*. Chicago: Academy Chicago Publishers, 1987.

Malone, John. *Predicting the Future: From Jules Verne to Bill Gates*. New York: M. Evans and Company, 1997.

Manchester, William. *A World Lit Only by Fire*. Boston: Little, Brown, 1992.

Mantoux, Paul. *The Industrial Revolution in the Eighteenth Century*. Trans. Marjorie Vernon. New York: Harcourt, Brace, and Company, 1927.

Marcus, George E. *Lives in Trust: The Fortunes of Dynastic Families in Late Twentieth-Century America*. Boulder, Colo.: Westview Press, 1992.

Marshall, Robert. *Storm from the East: From Genghis Khan to Khubilai Khan*. Berkeley, Calif.: University of California Press, 1993.

Martin, Frederick Townsend. *The Passing of the Idle Rich*. London: Hodder and Stoughton, 1911.

Martin, H. Desmond. *The Rise of Chingis Khan and His Conquest of North China*. Baltimore: Johns Hopkins University Press, 1950.

Marx, Jennifer. *The Magic of Gold*. Garden City, N.Y.: Doubleday, 1978.

Mathias, Peter. *The First Industrial Nation*. London: Metheun, 1969.

May, Ernest. *America's China Trade in Historical Perspective*. Cambridge: Harvard University Press, 1986.

Meltzer, Milton. *Slavery: A World History*. New York: Da Capo Press, 1993.

Meyer, Kathryn, and Terry Parssinen. *Webs of Smoke: Smugglers, Warlords, Spies, and the History of the International Drug Trade*. New York: Rowman and Littlefield, 1998.

Mills, C. Wright. *The Power Elite*. New York: Oxford University Press, 1956.

Miskimin, Harry A. *The Economy of Early Renaissance Europe*. New York: Cambridge University Press, 1975.

Mokyr, Joel. *The Lever of Riches: Technological Creativity and Economic Progress*. New York: Oxford University Press, 1990.

Mokyr, Joel, ed. *The British Industrial Revolution: An Economic Perspective*. Boulder, Colo.: Westview Press, 1993.

Molho, Anthony, ed. *Social and Economic Foundations of the Italian Renaissance*. New York: John Wiley and Sons, 1965.

Morgan, David. *The Mongols*. Cambridge, Mass.: Blackwell, 1986.

Morris, Anne E., and Susan Nott. *All My Worldly Goods: A Feminist Perspective on the Legal Regulation of Wealth*. Brookfield, Vt.: Dartmouth Publishing Company, 1995.

Morse, Hosea Ballou. *The International Relations of the Chinese Empire: The Period of Conflict, 1834–1860*. New York: Longmans, Green, 1910.

Mukerji, Chandra. *From Graven Images: Patterns of Modern Materialism*. New York: Columbia University Press, 1985.

Murphy, Antoin E. *John Law: Economic Theorist and Policy-Maker*. Oxford: Clarendon Press, 1997.

Murray, Gordon. *Slavery in the Arab World*. New York: New Amsterdam Books, 1989.

Myers, Gustavus. *History of the Great American Fortunes*. New York: Modern Library, 1936.

O'Connell, Robert L. *Of Arms and Men: A History of War, Weapons, and Aggression*. Oxford: Oxford University Press, 1990.

O'Toole, Patricia. *Money and Morals in America: A History*. New York: Random House, 1998.

Ozment, Steven E. *The Age of Reform (1250–1550)*. New Haven: Yale University Press, 1980.

Packard, Vance. *The Status Seekers*. New York: D. McKay, 1959.

Phillips, Kevin P. *The Politics of Rich and Poor: Wealth and the American Electorate in the Reagan Aftermath*. New York: Random House, 1990.

Phillips, William D. *Slavery from Roman Times to the Early Transatlantic Trade*. Minneapolis: University of Minnesota Press, 1985.

Pirenne, Henri. *Economic and Social History of Medieval Europe*. Trans. I. E. Clegg. New York: Harcourt, Brace, and Company, 1936.

Polachek, James M. *The Inner Opium War*. Cambridge, Mass.: Harvard University Press, 1992.

Pollard, Sidney, ed. *Wealth and Poverty: An Economic History of the Twentieth Century*. London: Harrap Books, 1990.

Porter, Roy. *English Society in the Eighteenth Century*. New York: Penguin Books, 1990.

Porter, Roy, and Mikulas Teich, eds. *Drugs and Narcotics in History*. Cambridge: Cambridge University Press, 1995.

Pounds, Norman J. G. *An Economic History of Medieval Europe*. London: Longman, 1994.

Powelson, John P. *The Story of Land: A World History of Land Tenure and Agrarian Reform*. Cambridge, Mass.: Lincoln Institute of Land Policy, 1989.

Ratchnevsky, Paul. *Genghis Khan: His Life and Legacy*. Trans. Thomas Nivison Haining. Cambridge, Mass.: Blackwell, 1991.

Reynolds, Robert Leonard. *Europe Emerges: Transition Toward an Industrial World-wide Society, 600–1750*. Madison, Wisc.: University of Wisconsin Press, 1961.

Richards, J. F., ed. *Precious Metals in the Later Medieval and Early Modern Worlds*. Durham, N.C.: Carolina Academic Press, 1983.

Rist, Charles. *History of Monetary and Credit Theory: From John Law to the Present Day*. Trans. Jane Degras. New York: Macmillan, 1940.

Rivlin, Gary. *The Plot to Get Bill Gates.* New York: Times Business, 1999.

Roberts, Edwin A., Jr., ed. *The Busy Rich.* Silver Spring, Md.: Dow Jones, 1967.

Rosenberg, Nathan L. E. Birdzell, Jr. *How the West Grew Rich: The Economic Transformation of the Industrial World.* New York: Basic Books, 1986.

Rosenblatt, Roger, ed. *Consuming Desires: Consumption, Culture, and the Pursuit of Happiness.* Washington, D.C.: Island Press, 1999.

Rostow, W. W. *How It All Began: Origins of the Modern Economy.* New York: McGraw-Hill, 1975.

Rubinstein, W. D. *Wealth and the Wealthy in the Modern World.* London: Croom Helm, 1980.

Rudgley, Richard. *The Alchemy of Culture: Intoxicants in Society.* London: British Museum Press, 1993.

Rush, Richard H. *The Techniques of Becoming Wealthy.* Englewood Cliffs, N.J.: Prentice-Hall, 1963.

Russell, James. *Modes of Production in World History.* New York: Routledge, 1989.

Sachs, Hannelore. *The Renaissance Woman.* Trans. Marianne Herzfeld. New York: McGraw-Hill, 1971.

Sahlins, Marshall David. *Stone Age Economics.* New York: Aldine, 1972.

Sale, Kirkpatrick. *Rebels Against the Future: The Luddites and Their War on the Industrial Revolution.* Reading, Mass.: Addison-Wesley, 1995.

Samuelson, Robert J. *The Good Life and Its Discontents.* New York: Times Books, 1995.

Schama, Simon. *The Embarrassment of Riches.* Berkeley: University of California Press, 1988.

Scheuermann, Mona. *Her Bread to Earn: Women, Money, and Society from Defoe to Austen.* Lexington, Ky.: University Press of Kentucky, 1993.

Schivelbusch, Wolfgang. *Tastes of Paradise: A Social History of Spices, Stimulants, and Intoxicants.* Trans. David Jacobson. New York: Pantheon Books, 1992.

Schneewind, J. B., ed. *Giving: Western Ideas of Philanthropy.* Bloomington, Ind.: Indiana University Press, 1996.

Schor, Juliet B. *The Overspent American: Upscaling, Downscaling, and the New Consumer.* New York: Basic Books, 1998.

Scitovsky, Tibor. *The Joyless Economy.* New York: Oxford University Press, 1976.

Sekora, John. *Luxury: The Concept in Western Thought, Eden to Smollett.* Baltimore: Johns Hopkins University Press, 1977.

Seligman, Ben B. *The Potentates: Business and Businessmen in American History.* New York: Dial Press, 1971.

Simmel, Georg. *The Philosophy of Money.* London: Routledge, 1990.

Simonton, Deborah. *A History of Women's Work: 1700 to the Present.* New York: Routledge, 1998.

Slater, Philip Elliot. *Wealth Addiction.* New York: Dutton, 1980.

Smelser, Neil J. *Social Change in the Industrial Revolution.* Chicago: University of Chicago Press, 1959.

Sowell, Thomas. *Conquests and Cultures.* New York: Basic Books, 1998.

Sparkes, Boyden, and Samuel T. Moore. *The Witch of Wall Street.* New York: Doubleday, Doran, and Company, 1935.

Spence, Jonathan D. *The Search for Modern China.* New York: W.W. Norton, 1990.

Stanley, Thomas J., and William D. Danko. *The Millionaire Next Door.* New York: Pocket Books, 1996.

Stares, Paul. *Global Habit: The Drug Problem in a Borderless World.* Washington, D.C.: Brookings Institution, 1996.

Stearns, Peter N. *The Industrial Revolution in World History.* Boulder, Colo.: Westview Press, 1993.

Swetz, Frank. *Capitalism and Arithmetic: The New Math of the Fifteenth Century.* La Salle, Ill.: Open Court, 1987.

Tawney, R. H. *The Acquisitive Society.* New York: Harcourt, Brace, and Company, 1920.

Thomas, Dana L. *The Money Crowd.* New York: G. P. Putnam's Sons, 1972.

Thompson, Jacqueline. *Future Rich: The People, Companies, and Industries Creating America's Next Fortunes.* New York: William Morrow, 1985.

Titton, R. S. and A. P. Wadsworth. *The Strutts and the Arkwrights.* Manchester: Manchester University Press, 1958.

Trachtenberg, Alan. *The Incorporation of America: Culture and Society in the Gilded Age.* New York: Hill and Wang, 1982.

Trinder, Barrie. *The Making of the Industrial Landscape.* London: Phoenix Giant, 1982.

Tuchman, Barbara. *The March of Folly: From Troy to Vietnam.* New York: Ballantine Books, 1984.

Twitchell, James B. *Lead Us Into Temptation: The Triumph of American Materialism.* New York: Columbia University Press, 1999.

United Nations *World Drug Report.* Oxford, Oxford University Press, 1997.

Veblen, Thorstein. *The Theory of the Leisure Class.* New York: Viking Press, 1945 [1899].

Veseth, Michael. *Mountains of Debt: Crisis and Change in Renaissance Florence, Victorian Britain, and Postwar America.* New York: Oxford University Press, 1990.

Vicker, Ray. *The Realms of Gold.* New York: Charles Scribner's Sons, 1975.

Vilar, Pierre. *A History of Gold and Money, 1450–1920.* London: NLB, 1976.

Vladimirtsov, B. *The Life of Chingis-Khan.* Trans. Prince D. S. Mirsky. New York: Benjamin Blom, 1930.

Wade, John. *History of the Middle and Working Classes.* London: Augustus M. Kelley, 1966.

Wall Street Journal, the editors of *The. American Dynasties Today.* Homewood, Ill.: Dow Jones–Irwin, 1980.

Wallerstein, Immanuel. *Capitalist Agriculture and the Origins of the European World-Economy in the Sixteenth Century.* New York: Academic Press, 1974.

———. *Mercantilism and the Consolidation of the European World-Economy, 1600–1750.* New York: Academic Press, 1980.

Walvin, James. *Slavery and the Slave Trade: A Short Illustrated History.* London: Macmillan, 1983.

Wantoch, Hans. *Magnificent Money-Makers.* Trans. J. H. S. Moore. London: Desmond Harmsworth, 1932.

Weatherford, Jack. *The History of Money.* New York: Three Rivers Press, 1997.

Weber, Max. *General Economic History.* New Brunswick, N.J.: Transaction Books, 1981 [1927].

Wells, H. G. *A Short History of the World.* London: Penguin Books, 1922.

Wenke, Robert J. *Patterns in Prehistory.* New York: Oxford University Press, 1990.

White, Lynn. *Medieval Technology and Social Change.* London: Oxford University Press, 1962.

Wiedemann, Thomas. *Greek and Roman Slavery.* Baltimore: Johns Hopkins University Press, 1981.

Williams, Gertrude. *Women and Work.* New York: Essential Books, 1945.

Wiston-Glynn, A. W. *John Law of Lauriston.* Edinburgh: E. Saunders, 1907.

Wyllie, Irvin G. *The Self-Made Man in America: The Myth of Rags to Riches.* New Brunswick, N.J.: Rutgers University Press, 1954.

INDEX

ABOUT THE AUTHOR

CYNTHIA CROSSEN is a senior editor at *The Wall Street Journal,* where she has been a reporter and editor since 1983. Her beats have included the financial markets, publishing, education, and social trends. Her previous book, *Tainted Truth: The Manipulation of Fact in America,* was one of *Business Week*'s top ten business books of 1994. She lives in Garrison, New York, with her husband.